Mohammad Reza Shajarian's Avaz in Iran and Beyond, 1979–2010

Mohammad Reza Shajarian's Avaz in Iran and Beyond, 1979–2010

Rob Simms and Amir Koushkani

LEXINGTON BOOKS
Lanham • Boulder • New York • Toronto • Plymouth, UK

Published by Lexington Books
A wholly owned subsidiary of The Rowman & Littlefield Publishing Group, Inc.
4501 Forbes Boulevard, Suite 200, Lanham, Maryland 20706
http://www.lexingtonbooks.com

Estover Road, Plymouth PL6 7PY, United Kingdom

British Library Cataloguing in Publication Information Available

Library of Congress Cataloging-in-Publication Data

Simms, Rob, 1962–
  Mohammad Reza Shajarian's avaz in Iran and beyond, 1979–2010 / Rob Simms and
Amir Koushkani.
    p. cm.
  Includes bibliographical references and index.
  ISBN 978-0-7391-7209-4 (cloth : alk. paper) — ISBN 978-0-7391-7210-0 (electronic)
  1. Shadjariân, Mohammad Rezâ. 2. Singers—Iran—Biography. I. Koushkani, Amir,
1968- II. Title.
  ML420.S52415S56 2012
  782.42169092—dc23
  [B]

                                                                          2011046466

♾™ The paper used in this publication meets the minimum requirements of American
National Standard for Information Sciences—Permanence of Paper for Printed Library
Materials, ANSI/NISO Z39.48-1992.

Printed in the United States of America

*Dedicated to
the spirit and freedom
of the people of Iran*

Contents

Preface

This book is the second volume of a three-part study that examines the music and public profile of Mohammad Reza Shajarian as a major artist and figure through the late-twentieth/early-twenty-first century. The first volume, *The Art of Avaz and Mohammad Reza Shajarian: Foundations and Contexts* (Simms and Koushkani 2012) examines Shajarian's musical biography up to the Islamic Revolution of 1979 while sketching out the broader context of the tradition of avaz that he inherited. The latter domain includes the following topics and issues: the aesthetic of *iham* or the polysemous quality exploited in poetry and other areas of Iranian culture; the history of avaz; tradition, modernity, and the role of the individual in Iranian culture; Iranian traditions of narrative performance, along with the concomitant activities of rhetoric and "truth-telling." The first volume also contains a detailed examination of Shajarian's creative "toolkit," the materials and processes he engages while weaving together poetry and music into a performance of avaz. The present volume focuses on Shajarian's activities, oeuvre of recordings, and sociopolitical significance in the postrevolutionary period—his ascendency to national superstar status and an increasingly global presence—while sketching out and placing him within the larger context of Iranian musical culture. The third component of the study is a collection of transcriptions of the complete performances of Shajarian's avaz from his most important albums (Simms 2012), which are discussed in detail in the present volume.

This book picks up the historical-biographical trajectory of the first volume and continues in the "trialogue" format of the latter. Each of the topics and headings that form the narrative flow of the book are directly expounded upon from the very different perspectives and subjective experiences of the artist, the cultural insider, and the ethnomusicologist. Our voices are clearly differentiated and identified through the use of contrasting fonts and the inclusion of our respective initials at the opening of individual statements:

OS: Ostad Shajarian
AK: Amir Koushkani
RS: Rob Simms

Details and the rationale for employing this style of presentation, along with conventions of transliteration and italicization in the text are given in the Preface of the first volume. Likewise, the specific multidisciplinary approach described in the latter carries over to the present volume. All translations of poetry in this book are by Camran Chaichian, Amir Koushkani, and Rob Simms, unless otherwise specified. As noted in the previous volume, Amir Koushkani's personal word-painting glosses, which figure prominently in this book, retranslate selected lines in explicating a particular layer of *iham*. Translations of Ostad Shajarian's interviews were again primarily crafted by Mahmood Schricker, with occasional contributions by Amir Koushkani and Rob Simms. Due to restrictions of space, this book only includes short excerpts of transcription from the Performance Examples of Chapters 2 and 3. Complete transcriptions of the excerpts discussed in the text, along with the complete comparative transcription of the two alternate performances of *Dastan* discussed in Chapter 3, are posted online at www.yorku.ca/robsimms/shajarian.

The authors again extend their sincere thanks to Camran Chaichian, Jean During, Christy de Felice, Teymour Dowlatshahi, Jim Kippen, Irene Markoff, Pari Azarm Motamedi, Mansour Motamedi, Bruno Nettl, Hossein Omoumi, Ehsan Ovisi, Valorie Salimpoor, Homayoun Shajarian, Vladimir Simosko, Mahmood Schricker, Urszula Starzec, and Shahrokh Tuisrkani and his family, with special thanks to Shabnam Ataei. Our ultimate and deepest thanks go to Ostad Shajarian.

Chapter 1
Revolution, War, and Music

RS
Centering on 1979 and the decade of the 1980s this chapter deals with phase transitions[1] and chaos on multiple levels: Iranian politics (both domestic and international), culture, musical life and mediation, as well as Shajarian's consciousness through his meetings with Ostad Dadbeh, and how this changed his music. Shajarian's reaction to the Islamic Revolution, the huge adjustments he had to make in the chaotic and dangerous new order combined with a heightened spiritual and social awareness, the accumulative musical knowledge he had acquired, and the optimum balance of strength and maturity in his vocal mechanism all contributed to establishing his mature, "trademark" style and resulted in a remarkable series of albums (discussed in chapter 2) that were to become landmark recordings in the history of avaz in the late twentieth century, as well as issuing major sociopolitical statements.

The chapter begins with a brief overview of the political and historical events of the revolution itself before describing the radically different musical culture that followed from its ideology and bureaucracy. Shajarian's musical activities are outlined against this background of repressive measures, the new medium of cassettes, important innovations in musical style of the 1980s, modes of musical resistance, shifts in scholarly discourse, and the ways in which Persian music actually benefitted from this otherwise hostile environment.

The Islamic Revolution and the Iran-Iraq War

Shajarian's most significant musical statements were made in the 1980s, a tumultuous decade in Iran forged by the Islamic Revolution and the Iran-Iraq War. The following brief historical discussion of these monumental events is provided for

1

the benefit of those readers unfamiliar with the history, especially in view of the systemic lack of attention and transparency symptomatic of Western media and public education.

In a century full of revolutions occurring around the globe, the 1979 Islamic Revolution stands out for the prominent function that music played in both reflecting and activating ideology, resistance, and values both collective and individual. In a revolution full of intrinsic contradictions and paradoxes[2]—suspended between the polar dynamics of pre-Islamic and Islamic national identity, democracy and authoritarian theocracy, revolutionary and reactionary values, multiple political factions with opposing agendas, and a constitution riddled with deep structural contradictions—the historically ambiguous position and conception of music was an apt microcosmic attractor in the chaotic period that followed. As with much of the vast historical and conceptual baggage attached to the *samā'* polemic,[3] this is largely due to "music's semiotic complexity and semantic richness, its capacity to simultaneously symbolize many things and to embody different meanings. This mercurial quality clearly enables musicians and others to choose between a wide range of possible meanings: by the same token, the fluidity of those meanings militates against any attempt to fix and thereby control them" (Nooshin 2005: 262). In a word, music's intrinsic *iham*.[4] Twentieth-century revolutions for the most part bear witness to the futility, if not outright disaster, of rigid authoritarian cultural engineering, the synthetic ramparts of which eventually collapse under the spontaneous flow of human activity and needs for expression. While the Islamic Revolution has been sagging under its own weight for decades, the unmistakable boost given to Persian music in its wake stands in stark contrast to these doomed case histories. Spontaneous cultural responses combined with official state policies employing both carrot and stick to revalue and reinvigorate Persian music, particularly among young people, who became engaged as listeners, students, and inspired performers in their own right. By now other signs of creative stifling, fatigue, and vacuity are apparent but in the 1980s the scene was very dynamic and vital.

The general contours of the revolution are well known.[5] The longstanding, sustained imperialist interventions of France, Britain, Russia, and the United States interspersed with brief fits of national consolidation and democratization play key defining roles throughout the modern history of Iran. The 1925 implosion of the dysfunctional Qajar dynasty (the culture from which contemporary Persian music emerged) dovetails with the increased intervention of Western oil interests, political manouevering and intrigue, resulting in the authoritarian modernization of Reza Shah. A brief period of democratic advance is stymied by an American-British sponsored coup in 1953 against Mohammad Mossadegh, who was intent on nationalizing Iranian oil concessions, resulting in the reinstallation of the exiled Shah, Mohammad Reza Pahlavi, who henceforth functioned as Washington's policeman in West Asia and its most reliable supplier of oil.

The Shah increasingly created popular discontent through his policies of modernization, Westernization (locally referred to as "Westoxification"), ruthless authoritarianism, the widening of the income gap, along with his personal conspicuous consumption, and delusional self-aggrandizement. His land policies in dealing with the massive influx of migrant workers from rural areas to Teheran were disastrous (Saunders 2010). He specifically targeted the popular Shi'a clergy with repressive measures, systematically eroding their power. These fatal miscalculations and the general dissent they created culminated in the revolution of early 1979, the Shah's eventual exile, and the subsequent assumption of power by the charismatic Aytollah Ruhollah Khomeini. The driving force of the revolution was social—it united diverse, multiclass groups across Iranian society in common opposition to the Shah—but quickly veered into being conceived as Islamic (Khiabany 2008: 28; Abazari 2008: 239). The United States experienced serious "blowback" from their sustained covert manipulation of Iranian politics in the form of the hostage crisis that began in November 1979, whereby American embassy staff were held hostage for 444 days, while files were opened to the Iranian public revealing the vast scale of America's machinations.

Early revolutionary democratization was cut short by the onset of the Iraqi invasion of Iran in September 1980, which critics such as Dabashi consider a "U.S. invasion of Iran camouflaged in the form of the Iraqi army" (2005: 299n21). The ruthless policy of euphemistic "Dual Containment" during this war—in which the U.S., France, and Israel supplied both sides with illegal arms sales to prolong a brutal stalemate in the trenches reminiscent of World War I, killing over one million people—unwittingly helped consolidate the revolution and unify the country through a natural reflex of closing ranks. While the revolution brought massive changes to Iranian society, the war with Iraq was an equally powerful and strategically related shaping force throughout the 1980s. Throughout the decade the tenor (and terror) of daily life ebbed and flowed with the vicissitudes of the war, effecting a rollercoaster ride of emotional madness and material deprivation. Tehran was regularly targeted with devastating Scud missile attacks. Successes and failures on the front translated into parallel civilian spheres, resulting in an overall instability and psychologically ravaged home front throughout the marathon struggle, which was further compounded by the ever shifting revolutionary political ground. This deep duress and instability is the most essential "social context" to be kept in the forefront of any view of the recordings of Shajarian examined in this book.

> Still, giants of Iranian music, like Hossein Alizadeh and . . . Mohammad Reza Lotfi, went to the front to perform their own music for the troops. As the war ground on, many young talents died, among them technicians, poets and musicians who might have continued the Chavosh movement [discussed below] or changed the direction of musical production. Instead, the normal development of this movement was arrested. Together with the international isolation of Islamic Republic (answered in kind by the regime), revolution and war put Iranian music into a state of hibernation. (Sadighi and Mahdavi 2009).

The revolution and war provided the motivation, leverage and scripting for the performance of mass public drama on many levels: performing patriotism, anti-Americanism, Islamic piety, martyrdom, and for the new regime, a ruthless and self-righteous despotism.

Music in the New Islamic Republic

The first eight years of the revolution, in which the recordings examined in this chapter were produced, were characterized by revolutionary fervor, authoritarian governance, and mass mobilization. All cultural activities were now cast in an Islamic framework, with religious governance imposing itself in social and (paradoxically) religious areas that were previously private (Abazari 2008: 245). "The profound contradictions in cultural policy during the 1980s were partly a result of a government trying to impose a hegemonic Islamic identity on a people intensely aware of, and unwilling to forfeit, their pre-Islamic heritage" (Nooshin 2005: 236). In a serious miscalculation, the revolutionary government made a concerted but futile attempt to wallpaper over the deeply embedded identity marker of the ancient Iranian/Zoroastrian past with an exclusively Islamic facade. Decades later, many Iranians eventually came to refer to the revolution as the "second Arab invasion," a fundamentalist ploy that "appears to have strengthened the very ties to antiquity it tried to sever" (Del Guidice 2008: 67). Not surprisingly, the very attempt to enforce the rejection of these deep cultural roots brought about and increased interest among many Iranians regarding their pre-Islamic, imperial identity. This dynamic was given a considerable boost following the discovery of the site of Konar Sandal in 2000 (near Jiroft in the south central province of Kerman), a sophisticated bronze culture currently being excavated that dates from 3000 BC, and thus contemporary with ancient Mesoptamia (ibid: 46).

The pervasive Islamization of culture also immediately led to contradictions and controversy with regard to music, especially given its longstanding heritage of the *samā'* polemic. As documented by During (1984, 1992) and Youssefzadeh (2000), Iranian musical culture went through a sea change from that of the Shah's era. Light (*motrebi*) and popular music (both Western and Iranian) were proscribed, while religious, national folk music, and especially *asif*[6] genres gradually rose to levels of public prominence never seen before, despite myriad constraints. This veritable renaissance succeeded in both attracting many young people to study and/or listen to Persian music as well as reconnecting the fading transmission lines with the old guard of Ostads (masters), many of whom had been sidelined into obscurity during the Pahlavi period.

Public concerts were severely restricted and when they occurred, the lyrics and musical style were subject to rigorous censorship, measures that are still in effect today. In the zeal of the early postrevolutionary period, virtuosic stylistic features that provoked auditory excitement—*chaharmezrabs, rengs,* even vocal *tahrirs*—

were considered illicit (During 1984: 12). The mad terror of institutional purging that swept through all walks of Iranian society in this early period saw many performers blacklisted from engaging in public activity due to possible affiliations with the previous regime (ibid: 14). Along with untold others, many musicians were killed. During the worst years of lawless excess immediately following the revolution, raids on private musical soirees resulted in the destruction of instruments and recordings. Special licenses were required for owning instruments and steep "deposits" placed on instruments leaving the country, to be returned on reentry with the instrument. Expatriate Iranian musicians in Toronto claimed that contraband instruments (especially *setars*) were smuggled like drugs out of the country to Dubai on small boats. Coldly clarifying any lingering doubts as to where music stood in the new order of things, several prominent musicians—Vaziri, Davami, Taj Esfahan, and Adib Khansari—died in the early days of the revolution with no public acknowledgement of their contribution to musical life in Iran (Miller 1999: 50).

Television and radio broadcast of music was suspended, except for revolutionary propaganda songs (*sorudha-ye enqelabi*), the composition and dissemination of which flourished. While 'Aref Ghazvini had harnessed the tasnif to support nationalist causes in the aftermath of the Constitutional Revolution of the early-twentieth century, the modern *sorud* (the word has pre-Islamic origins to refer to songs) emerged directly from the Western influence of the march and martial songs of the brass band. This military context was the initial entry point of Western music to mass Iranian society, as indeed it was around the world (Flaes 2000). *Soruds* were upbeat, set in Western tonality (usually major) with Western-style melodies (though occasional local nuances could slip in), with lyrics extolling the virtues of one's country, province, school, the Shah (i.e., a pride and solidarity of the in-group, of "us"), and sung in a choral unison. *Soruds* were particularly cultivated under the reforms of Reza Shah in the 1920s and 1930s (Chehabi 1999:147). In short, the *sorud* was typical of other non-Western appropriations of military marches for propaganda purposes, such as the "Songs for the Masses" during the Chinese Cultural Revolution.

> Throughout the monarchy, surud singing was the mainstay of Iranian school children's musical education. Young Iranians learned neither to distinguish the various dastgahs, nor to read music properly nor play an instrument: they sang in unison martial songs that taught them to love their country, exhorted them to be ready to sacrifice their lives for it, and suggested that they were superior to their neighbours. The nationalism for which this type of music was a vehicle was organic nationalism of the Blut und Boden (*khak u khun*) variety, not a civic nationalism stressing the rights, duties, and equality of citizens. The romantic preoccupation with a mythical past, the intolerance for ethnic and linguistic diversity, and the disdain and disinterest for neighbouring peoples that, alas, still characterise much of the Iranian intelligentsia are the legacy of an educational system that inculcated these values into the mind of the young, but that did not teach them to value freedom, tolerance, and the rule of the law. And so the transition from the libertarian and patriotic tasnif to

the nationalistic and monarchist surud illustrates the authoritarian turn that Iranian politics took after World War I. The transformations of tasnif and surud are telling indicators of the evolution of Iranian nationalism, and of the political culture of which it has been a part. (Chehabi 1999: 151)

Cassettes continued to be produced throughout the 1980s but were subject to strict censorship, their proliferation playing a major catylytic role in accelerating stylistic change establishing standards; the restrictions on concerts necessitated that these were largely studio recordings (During 1992: 152, 154). Continuing the longstanding heritage of the samā' polemic, government decrees regarding music were appropriately vague and unsystematic (During 1984: 13, 1992: 137). Throughout the following decades, musicians got good at finding and exploiting loopholes in making their music, "subtly pushing at boundaries without appearing to contest them openly and thus averting a reaction from the authorities. In large part, this is made possible by the cleavages opened up by contradictions in cultural policy, which are in turn symptomatic of deep divisions within the government itself" (Nooshin 2005: 246).

    In a seemingly strange paradox for a revolution vilifying Westoxification, Western music was viewed as a relatively innocuous genre wherein even female vocal soloists were considered acceptable, in stark contrast to the strict proscriptions against female vocalists of Iranian genres (During 1984: 14, 1992: 141; Nooshin 2005: 256 and note 74). It was, and still is, illegal for women to sing solo for "mixed" audiences of men and women. DeBano argues, however, that the strictly segregated state-sponsored public musical events such as the Jasmine Festival, established in 1999 in the wake of President Khatami's reforms, have counterintuitively strengthened the role of women in public (albeit an exclusively female public) musicking (2009). Various educational institutions were engaged in propagating the transmission of Persian music at an unprecedented level, along with new compositions in the traditional idiom. This high public profile of Persian music in the fresh wake of the revolution was buttressed by a concomitant surge in private musicking (During 1992: 150), which, lying outside the enforceable reach of the authorities, has always been its refuge and venue for resistance in periods of political turbulence throughout history. While public and private domains rose in synergy, there are always sharp qualitative differences between them in Iranian culture. Modes of public and private behavior are always differentiated in any culture, but Iranians (along with many millions of people around the world subjected to authoritarian regimes) have to maintain double, quasischizophrenic lives in this respect simply in order to stay safe and sane.[7] Under such conditions public space becomes a stage for performing obedience to the dictates of a revolutionary ideology that increasingly loses any true basis or legitimacy among the majority of people. By rigidly separating public and private worlds, many Iranians feel that the authorities "don't really control us, because they can't control what's inside us" (Del Giudice 2008: 64).

With the competition of *motrebi* and popular music kept at official bay, the number of people participating in Persian music as both listeners and performers soared. The wonderful paradox here is that playing Persian music was both an expression of nationalistic and "traditional" identity as espoused by the revolution, salvaged from the losses of the Shah's era, and at the same time an open defiance against the regulation of culture by revolutionary authorities. The sheer activity of playing music in an Islamic Republic, with its attendant baggage of the *samā'* polemic, was a platform for personal resistance (ibid.; Nooshin 2005: 241). Despite the government's attempts at constructing a unifying ideology of music, a diversity of forms and lack of stylistic and aesthetic consensus among musicians prevailed (During 1992: 156).

While most musicians were either fleeing in exile or reduced to "silence and despondency" (Wright 2009: 18), Shajarian remained in Iran and took center stage, both figuratively and, whenever it was possible, literally: his voice very much heard. At the peak of his powers, he remained active and prolific, producing a remarkable series of recordings that are regarded by the general public, connoisseurs and musicians alike as masterpieces of the art of avaz. His meeting and continued study with Ostad Gholam Reza *Jahān Suz* ("World Burnt") Dadbeh would play a significant role in everything he did thereafter.

Shajarian's Activities in the Postrevolutionary Period

Ostad Dadbeh

OS
In terms of cognition and consciousness, no one has influenced me the way Ostad Dadbeh did (2009).
Dadbeh is one of the Ostads of thought and mystical people who also had musical skills. I got acquainted with him through meetings that concerned discussion and debates about art, the foundations of art, sociology, the historical periods of art. . . . We didn't work on radif and tasnifs but I learned some parts of the Dashtestani style of singing from him. Meeting him was possibly the most important contribution to my artistic life (ibid.:138).
Question: You have mentioned previously that when you pick poetry from Hafez, Sa'di or Attar the poems are no longer theirs but rather their poetry becomes yours.
Yes, that poetry becomes mine. You see, in the process of life one gains experience, and when you are young you are only concerned with your dreams and ambitions. Some of these ambitions and goals become a reality and others don't, and you realize that you should probably think differently and look at life from a different perspective. I personally reached that point when I met someone very special who was very important to me and he gave me many crucial keys that

enabled me to open many doors and many things became clear to me. This person was Ostad Dadbeh, who was a philosopher and a great thinker. I have never seen anyone like him, despite the fact that I have met many people, including scientists, ayatollahs, and poets and I have read many books. But this man could actually move into the world of any subject and analyze it. He taught me many things, including the fact that man is God, that he is everything, and he is an impression of God. Anyway, since 1979 I spent time with Dadbeh, until he passed away about seven or eight years ago. (2009)

AK

To my understanding, the people who were around Ostad Dadbeh kept this as a kind of closed group. My sense was that he was a leader and teacher of only select, special people. He was working with people who had a particular kind of character. I knew people who were trying to get to know him through those who were already in his circle. His teaching was oral; I've never seen or heard of any book or writings of his but they may exist. It's certainly not well known, if that is the case. He kept a very discreet, low profile.

Ostad Dadbeh was a teacher of a spiritual idea of how a person should be as a human being, and this has affected Shajarian's character and later work. As I understand it through my teacher Mr. Pirniakan, who was a student of Dadbeh's, his teaching included some pre-Islamic ideas, and I later realized that it had a direct connection to *ā'in-e mehr*, "the path of *mehr*." Through Dadbeh it seems that my teacher and Ostad Shajarian believe in this specific path of living. *Mehr* means "kindness" and we see this word a lot in Persian culture: the month of Mehr, night of Mehr, festival of Mehr, and so on. A key idea in the path of *Mehr* is *farhang-e pulmani*—"the culture for being a bridge for others"—being a bridge, helping other people to get what they seek, providing a service that people can pass from and through you to their goal. This corresponds to teachings that were later central to Sufism wherein you have to be selfless.

There is another element that Ostad Dadbeh helped instill in Ostad Shajarian that is very important: confidence. Because when you are a student and you don't have a lot of concerts and exposure you cannot claim lofty changes in avaz. You cannot change direction very well, especially with Ostad Shajarian's humble behaviour and attitude. So the confidence gained from presenting a lot of music and getting the approval of so many people gave Shajarian freedom and confidence. I think this is a very important concept here because when he went to regular classes with Ostad Dadbeh the main thing he learned was the philosophical aspect of his art, and not so much the technical side, as Shajarian was able to master the musical techniques he was taught very rapidly. On the other hand, a very important musical point regarding their relationship that is not often noted is that Shajarian studied how to sing Baba Taher with Ostad Dadbeh, who was a master of that. You really hear this influence in the album *Astan e Janan* (see chapter 2). Shajarian mastered this Dashstestani style even though Dadbeh sang with a lower voice and a slower tempo.

Furthermore, as Shajarian's confidence continued to build, he found himself going further, and speaking *for* people. This could be regarded as a shift to a higher, more noble level in art: from being an entertainer or singer of Persian classical music on radio and television to becoming a voice of sixty million people or at least those people who are listening, maybe ten million people. That's powerful, he has a lot of power. These are new goals. In other words, Shajarian's art progressed from art as entertainment to art as a meaningful expression of humanity.

RS

Shajarian first met Ostad Dadbeh at the home of master calligrapher Morteza Abdolrasuli (see photo 1). We will look at Shajarian's activity as a calligrapher in chapter 3 but note that the circle of master calligraphers in Iran is very exclusive, one of the most difficult social cliques to gain access to in Iranian culture. Shajarian mentions regular "classes" with Dadbeh between 1979 and the Ostad's death in 2002, implying a study group. Photo 2 shows Dadbeh and Shajarian together with the musicians Kasa'i, Taj Esfahan, Manouchehr Ghaouri, and Sa'idi; Dariush Pirniakan was also in this circle, as was ney-player Mohammad Musavi (see photo in *Daftar-e-Honar* 2003: 2182).

Abdollahi's timeline describes Dadbeh as being a master of unity (*yegāne*) philosophy, followed by some further qualifications that are rather obscure (2003: 2070). From his own accounts quoted above, Shajarian clearly received the transmission of esoteric teachings from Ostad Dadbeh over a period of twenty-two years. Two aspects of Dadbeh's "unity philosophy" recur in Shajarian's allusions to the teachings in interviews: the intrinsic divinity of humans and the importance of practicing and living loving-kindness. Both principles are of course central to many esoteric traditions. In the Sufi tradition the former is emblematic of al-Hallaj's archetypal statement of enlightened blasphemy (according to orthodox Islam) "I am the Truth," echoing the older Vedantic formulation "Thou art That." Shajarian even includes aspects of this principle on his Delawaz Persian homepage mission statement (termed *mardomkhodāsāz*, www.delawaz.com). The second principle is even more universal, included as it is in exoteric religious teachings (particularly emphasized in Buddhism and Christianity) and indeed, secular ethical values found in all cultures. Amir Koushkani pointed out that in the photos of Dadbeh attending the wedding of Shajarian's daughter Asfane Shajarian and Parviz Meshkatian in 1984 (published in *Daftar-e Honar* 2003: 2181), he is wearing a hat associated with Zoroastrian priests, along with what appears to be a white suit in the black and white photos. Amir also noted that Dadbeh's philosophy highlighted the Zoroastrian concept of *mehr*, which was taken up as a central tenet by a lineage of Iranian Sufis.

Mehr refers to a range of related meanings in modern Persian, including love, affection, friendship, kindness, reconciliation, mercy, compassion, and promise. It was synonymous with Mithra (Avestan; Mitra in Sanskrit), one of the five Zoroastrian divinities (*Yazata*), associated with the sun and petitioned for kindness and mercy. In addition to "the sun," *mehr* literally meant "covenant" or "contract" and had a strong association with relationship, responsibility, and faithfully keeping promises. The new Islamic Republic of Iran as it was forged after the revolution conspicuously lacked *mehr* in its various senses. Khomeini's vision of Islam likewise paid little heed to Qur'anic verses such as "There is no compulsion in religion" (2:256) or the famous *hadith* (tradition of the Prophet) that above Allah's throne is written: *"Verily, My Mercy prevails over My Wrath."* Shajarian—whose birthday on the autumnal equinox is coincidentally the first day of the month of Mehr, according to the Iranian calendar—released two albums that include *mehr* in their titles: *Peyvand e Mehr* ("Relationship of *Mehr*," though translated as *Bond of Affection* on the album) in 2000, and *Sorud e Mehr* ("Anthem of *Mehr*") in 2007. The former title explicates the quintessential notion of relationship, while the latter associates *mehr* with a pre-Islamic word for music or song (despite its early twentiethth-century denotation of martial songs, discussed above).

Shajarian's study with Dadbeh also included mystical musics (*musiqihāyi 'erfāni*) and Dashtestani, a style of folk singing from the southern province of Bushehr (Shajarian et al. 2004: 101). It is interesting to note that Shajarian's first Delawaz release in 1978, *Golbang (vol.2)*, includes a recording from the previous year made with Ebadi in dastgah Mahur, wherein his singing in Delkash copies almost exactly Ostad Dadbeh's rendition of the Baba Taher *robaiyyat "Dele diram kharidare mohabbat" ("My heavy heart, the buyer of affection")* from his *Barge Sabz* 115 performance that Shajarian so admires. According to the recording date (1977) of this obvious salute, Shajarian knew of Dadbeh before they met. A translation of the quatrain follows:

> My heavy heart, the buyer of affection
> Bought from you, if drunken with bitter affection
> I've sewn clothes to the size of my heart
> From the loom of suffering and the string of my affection

Shajarian performed a beautifully moving commemoration to his spiritual mentor on the album *Saz e Khamush* ("The Silent Instrument" or "Instrument of Silence"), a short Dashtestani on two dobeytis of Baba Taher performed in his lower register with a relaxed vocal tone reminiscent of the Ostad entitled *"Be Yāde Dadbeh"* ("In Memory of Dadbeh"). Here is a translation of this short but intense tribute:

> At the time of joy, I have the desire for your dwelling
> I have a replica of the signet of your moon-aspect
> Oh my idol, my Ka'aba, my altar
> Oh you who are every direction, I gaze towards your direction
>
> There is no one who finds his way to my cry,
> There is no one who would take news to my freedom tree,

Should all the good of creation gather together
There is not one who can erase your memory from my memory

We noted in our companion volume (chapter 4 of Simms and Koushkani 2012) that the gushe Dashtestani has a wide distribution in Shajarian's oeuvre of recordings. It seems reasonable to posit that Shajarian's admiration of Dabeh's vocal tone contributed to his somewhat surprising preference for the bass register (ibid.), given his trademark tenor and remarkable abilities in his upper register, along with his exploration of his lower range beginning with the album *Nava (Morakab khani)* in 1982 (discussed in chapter 2) and especially characterizing his work of the early 1990s.

Shajarian intimates some general features of his time spent with Ostad Dadbeh but given the profound impact this experience had upon him and the ultimately personal and inexplicable nature of such things, we will leave the matter with this brief but emphatic notice of its transformative significance.

Professional Activities

Despite the huge disruption and redefinition of public musicking brought about by the revolution, Shajarian forged ahead with both live and studio work. The latter was more easily accomplished, as cassette sales continued throughout the uncertainties of the early revolution. Following the initial euphoria of the Shah's exile, amidst the fogginess of what would happen next, Shajarian recorded and released a total of five nationalistic *soruds*—the only music allowable in the legal cassette market at the time—between February and July of 1979. These were later collected and published by Lotfi's Chavosh Institute as the B-side of *Chavosh 7: Be Monāsebat-e Salgard-e Enqelab* ("On the Occasion of the Anniversary of the Revolution"), the A-side containing seven *soruds* sung by Shahram Nazeri. But as the hopes of post-revolutionary Iran transformed decisively into an ostensibly theocratic Islamic republic through the machinations of Khomeini, Shajarian abruptly changed course and henceforth "discontinued further collaborations with government organizations. On his own, in the privacy of his home, he continued his research of the collection and reorganization of the vocal radif and sometimes also taught former students. He hated (*motanafer*) all political parties and shunned all political activities" (Nasirfar 1990: 402).

In general, Shajarian seems to have a good intuitive sense of how political winds are blowing and how to best adjust his sails to maintain course or weather a storm. As with his previous experiences in the 1970s with the national radio and the *Center for the Propagation and Preservation of Iranian Music* (detailed in chapter 3 of Simms and Koushkani 2012), he carefully distanced himself from the new government and official political affiliations. Despite Shajarian's quite understandable decision to record the *soruds* given the circumstances of the time, it left a bad impression for some Iranians during this hyperpoliticized, polarized, and dangerous period. I met one expatriate Iranian intellectual in Toronto in the mid-1990s who was a great fan of Shajarian but regarding the *soruds*, gravely declared "I'll never forgive him for that." Perhaps by now people like this view the episode in its larger context and see Shajarian's unquestionable integrity over the past three decades.

Concerts were severely restricted—if nothing else because a large gathering of people in public under any pretext was highly volatile during these uncertain times—but Shajarian managed to appear in the few concerts that were permitted. The first such concert was in October 1979 with the Payvar Ensemble in Rudaki Hall, performing poems by Hushang Ebtehaj in Dashti; the concert was recorded and later released several times at different dates, usually under the title *Raz e Del*.[8] He also performed with Lotfi's *Sheyda* Ensemble in Rudaki Hall the same month, singing different poetry by Ebtehaj in dastgah Mahur; the same program was performed in November[9] at the *Dāneshgāh Beheshti (Melli)* [National University]. The latter was recorded and quickly released under the title *Sepideh* ("Dawn"). It was wildly successful, largely due to the concluding tasnif *Iran ey sarāye omid* ("Iran, a House of Hope"; alternately entitled *Sepideh*) composed by Lotfi to the text of Ebtehaj. The defiant nationalistic pride of the lyrics and the uplifting, triumphant setting in Mahur perfectly captured public sentiments at this turbulent juncture, transforming the piece into an "unofficial national anthem" (Nooshin 2005: 241). The lyrics are translated below:

Iran, a house for hope
The first light of day illuminates your crown
Witness that through this blood-filled road
A blessed sun has arisen
Although the heart is filled with blood
The splendor of happiness has risen
Our dawn is rosy red, it is rosy red
That the hand of the enemy is in blood
Oh Iran, have no sorrow
Long live your eternal glory
Our path is the way to truth, the way to prosperity
Unity, Unity is the secret to victory
Long live peace and eternal freedom in all the world,
Oh, Long live the fresh spring of generosity in this blooming grass

Despite its huge success, reports emerged within Tehran's musical community that the concert did not sit well with Shajarian. Both Lotfi and Ebtehaj were involved with the leftwing Tudeh Party, and unbeknownst to Shajarian, there was a decidedly Tudeh atmosphere prevailing at this public event. Given his experience earlier in the year with having his artistic intentions hijacked by politics that he did not necessarily agree with, and his concomitant stance of neutrality with regard to political organizations, the concert presented a familiar danger. His political intuition was quite correct here, as the Tudeh party would soon become the target of a severe crackdown by the government, whereby Ebtehaj was imprisoned and Lotfi had to leave the country. An untold number of Tudeh affiliates, both real and perceived, were executed in the early 1980s.

Public concerts were completely forbidden in Iran shortly thereafter. The Iran-Iraq War settled into the deadly and draining holding pattern it would maintain throughout its eight-year duration, and some of the worst chaos of police and judicial excesses were perpetrated on the dazed, terrorized public during the early years of the 1980s. The image of blood in the lyrics to *Sepideh* began to take on a chilling prescience. Shajarian had little choice but to retreat to the privacy of the recording studio, often the one he set up in his home. In the latter part of 1979 (or perhaps early 1980, the month is unclear) he recorded a Hafez ghazal in Segah with Payvar and his ensemble with a large string section that was released on two different albums: an abbreviated version as one side of the cassette *Entezar e Del*, a longer unedited one as the first side of *Sazeghesehgu*. Another session with Payvar around the same time but with a smaller ensemble, featuring a Hafez ghazal in Afshari, supplied the B-side of the album *Entezar e Del*, which was packaged together with *Raz e Del* (the Rudaki Hall concert of October 1979) for a double-cassette entitled *Peygham-e Ahl–e Rāz* ("Message of the Secret People") released in 1980, the sole Delawaz release until 1983. In 1980 he recorded again with Payvar (and Musavi), a Hafez Ghazel in Shur that was released over a decade later as the A-side of *Khalvat Gozide* ("Voluntary Seclusion"). Shajarian keeps an extensive archive of his performances and often releases recordings on Delawaz even decades after they were recorded. Just as often, he will release recordings immediately after the performance or with a delay of a year or two. One assumes that this is the case when he is particularly pleased with the performance.

After a two-year enforced hiatus from the concert stage, Shajarian hit upon the loophole of performing at foreign embassies and cultural institutes in Tehran, a strategic move that signaled his readiness to seek global outlets for his art, here in the microcosm of Tehran's diplomatic community (decimated though it was following the revolution and American hostage crisis). Among the first (if not the first) of these "internal international" concerts was a duet performance with Lotfi in the German Cultural Center on March 4, 1981. Lotfi was the head of the besieged, soon-to-be closed Music Department at the University of Tehran at the time and was caught up in a large student and faculty demonstration just prior to the performance, one that erupted into a violent clash with revolutionary factions. Many students and faculty were arrested or detained by police, including an enraged Lotfi, who arrived to the Center an hour after the scheduled performance time and took another half hour to gain his composure before heading to the stage.[10] The concert was recorded and released by Delawaz as *Eshq Danad* in 1997 and in the same year by the California-based Kereshmeh Records. Shajarian sets a ghazal by Hafez redolent in thinly veiled criticism, debuting what would become his trademark technique of mining classical poetry for atavistic messages that he would marshal to devastating effect under the strict censorship musicians were subjected to. Set in Abu Ata, he takes considerable liberties with reordering and omitting some of the beyts in the

original ghazal (#188) in order to have it say what we wanted to say. Below are a
few select lines:[11]

> Those without awareness are bewildered by our eye-play.
> I am that which I seem. The rest, they know.
>
> The rational are a compass point of existence, but
> Love knows that in this circle their heads are spinning.
>
> Boasting of love and complaining of the friend? Splendid the
>   lying boast!
> Such players at love as this merit desertion.
>
> Perhaps your dark eye will teach me how to act.
> But otherwise, not everyone is capable of temperance
>   And drunkenness.
>
> If the Magian children become aware of our meditations,
> After that will they not take as a pledge the Sufi gown?

The opening two beyts are set to the daramad and introduce a theme (at least
on the most immediate layer of *iham*) that Shajarian emphasized throughout the
decade: that in the current polarization of society amidst great chaos, one must hold
strong to inner knowledge, perception of the real nature of things, of interior values.
There are those who know this and others who don't. The title of the album is taken
from the second beyt: "Love knows." The third beyt given here, deriding hypocrisy
and again, advising that one only keep company with those "who know," is set to the
gushe Hejaz and therefore an emphatic moment in the performance. One layer of
interpretation of the following excerpted beyt offers further advice that Shajarian
will repeat throughout the decade: to be shrewd and intelligent in negotiating the
dangers at hand laid by those who "don't know." The final line is, among other
things, a cautious nod at pre-Islamic currents in Iran—"Magian children"—and the
Sufis of esoteric Islam, the deeper, esoteric spiritual currents that the fundamentalists
also revile, at least in part alluding to the possibility of a deeper continuity of living
based on the truth that overrides denominational affiliation and dictates. Of course,
other meanings abound. It is curious that Shajarian chose to not recite the seventh
beyt of the ghazal:

> The description of the sun is quite beyond the scope
>   of the blind bat,
> When those possessed of vision are amazed at this mirror.

Perhaps he felt it best to ease in gradually with this, his initial deployment of veiled
critique; the situation outside the porous walls of the German Cultural Center was
indeed dangerous. Omitting the final beyt is more understandable, for the same

reason as the latter and the fact that its second *misra* can be spun to turn his argument on its head:

> If the devout one doesn't understand Hafez's *rend* behaviour,
>   what of it?
> The devil flees those folk who recite the Qur'an.

These were incredibly difficult years for Iranians on various fronts, where life-and-death issues were a daily concern. Continuing professional musical activities was practically out of the question. And yet, as is often the case in such conditions, artists dig in deep and operate on a level wherein continuing to work becomes a matter of survival, remaining human, and flying free. Like a profound form of judo or miraculous alchemy, they flip the pervasive negative energy into positive energy through inspired art. Shajarian thus set to work.

Amidst the bleakness of 1982, he recorded landmark recordings, masterpieces that are discussed in detail in chapter 2. He also continued recording his Qur'an recitation, a project begun in 1978 that he would work on through to 1982, although the recordings were not released until 1999, dedicated to his father (*Be Yad e Pedar*). While this project was initiated shortly before the revolution, possessing and documenting his great skill as a reciter at this time also provided credibility and respect from the new fundamentalist regime, perhaps even a limited amount of insurance against harassment. Nineteen eighty-three initiated a brief period wherein he stripped down to essentials, recording a series of duets (with and without tombak accompaniment). The first two of these were with his long-time colleague, tarist Farhang Sharif. According to Gudarzi et al. (2000: 222) this session was released in 1983 as *Chahargah* but there is no trace of the recording otherwise; perhaps it was a very limited printing and distribution, which is understandable given the date. In April/May of 1984 he recorded again with Sharif and veteran tombak-player Jahangir Malik, a performance of ghazals by Sa'di in Shur that was released as *Peyvande Mehr* (literally "Relation/Union of *Mehr*," translated on the Delawaz release as "Bond of Affection") considerably later, probably the late 1990s. Near the end of 1984 his duetting partner was santurist Mansur Sārami, a performance that was released as *Homayoun Masnavie* in 1995. Amir Koushkani considers this underappreciated album to be one of Shajarian's greatest masterpieces; Ostad Shajarian also holds it in high regard among his oeuvre.

While Shajarian had been busy recording and performing in private contexts, the revolution had severely impeded the productivity of Delawaz releases. Nineteen eighty-five proved to be a pivotal year, for the release of the seminal, spectacularly successful *Bidad (Homayoun)* auspiciously marked the beginning of a prolific string of regular Delawaz releases that continues to this day, paving the road to his national superstardom and subsequent international renown. In the following year he mounted a veritable blitzkrieg offensive of masterpiece releases recorded in 1982 that decisively breached the Islamic

Republic's heavily fortified walls of icy silence: *Astan e Janan, Serr e Eshgh*, and *Nava (Morakab khani)* (discussed in detail in chapter 2). It was a daring plan and it worked brilliantly. Having found his footing in the harsh postrevolutionary environment, he meanwhile shifted from the minimalist duet performances that marked 1983–84 to work on full orchestral productions in 1985 through 1987. Composer and santur virtuoso Parviz Meshkatian (1955–2009) was his gifted collaborator throughout the critical, triumphant period of 1982 to 1989 that most connoisseurs agree mark Shajarian's greatest musical achievements. Of course, Shajarian had worked frequently with large ensembles on the radio—through the 1970s this was often under the supervision of composer Hassan Yousefzamani, who indeed composed and arranged large ensemble material for his first Delawaz release, *Golbang*. Attempting such a production in 1985 under the new order of the Islamic Republic was quite another matter and in some ways can be read as a defiant gesture to return to the musical environment of the Pahlavi era, even if the recordings were not released for another decade.

These new works, entitled *Jan e Oshagh* and *Gonbad e Mina*, were composed by Meshkatian and very finely arranged by the composer, conductor, and musicologist Reza Darvishi (b. 1955). For my taste the ensemble writing and arrangement of *Gonbad e Mina* is a particularly effective and successful blend of Iranian and Western musical languages. While there was some interesting experimentation integrating avaz into an orchestral accompaniment in occasional radio programs of the 1950s to 1970s, the convention more often followed was to juxtapose sections of polyphonic, large ensemble writing with avaz accompanied by a solo instrument, with the large ensemble rendering the tasnif. In these cases the production of the avaz and the orchestral music were of entirely separate projects edited together later; the singer could simply overdub the tasnif to the completed orchestral tracks. Shajarian's avaz can be removed from these framing orchestral contexts and sound perfectly consistent with his other traditional work (though the piano accompaniment on *Jane Oshagh* may seem incongruous to many listeners, it was common at the time, having been introduced in the 1940s and the mainstay of singers such as Zelli and Banan); the experimental elements of these recordings was contained in the framing instrumental arrangements.

This is indeed the format featured in Shajarian's work under discussion, the avaz of *Jan e Oshagh* (a Hafez ghazal in Bayate Esfahan) is accompanied by Javad Mar'ufi on piano, *Gonbad e Mina* (Hafez in Dashti) by Meshkatian's santur. The two pieces were released together in 1995, as well as separately under their respective titles with B-sides featuring traditional ensembles of more recently recorded performances. A similar orchestral project followed in 1987, again with Meshkatian's compositions but this time arranged by Kāmbiz Roshanravan and performed by the strings of the Tehran Symphony Orchestra and a "concertino" of traditional Persian instruments, the juxtaposed avaz section accompanied by Bahari on kamanche and then Tala'i on setar. In contrast to the 1985 project, this work was released in 1988 under the title *Dud-e 'Ud* ("The

Smoke of the 'Oud"). The reasons are unclear why this recording was released so quickly compared to the earlier orchestral productions. Perhaps the participation of the TSO included some institutional support (or at least solidarity and prestige) that was lacking in the latter or Shajarian simply preferred the performance. It is interesting to note that the public had warmly embraced Alizadeh's instrumental work in Nava for ney and string orchestra, *Ney Nava* in 1983, and might regard Shajarian's release in the same dastgah as being a desirable follow up.

Shajarian performed at a private gathering in 1988 dedicated to Banan and recorded live, three years after the great singer's death, which was subsequently released[12] as *Dar Soug e Banan* ("In Mourning Banan"). Shajarian sings Shushtari for his hero on one side, while Ostad Dabeh renders Dashtestani on the other, both singers accompanied by the ney of Musavi.

AK

Many musicians viewed Persian music as entertainment, and they would sing anywhere. Shajarian's vocal colleague Iraj (stage name of Hossein Khaje Amiri, b. 1932) never had a chance to present his voice after the revolution because people with this kind of background weren't appreciated or welcome. And in Iraj's case, he was also quite involved with the Pahlavi regime and often singing for them. This was now quite dangerous. One of the first people they killed after the revolution was Javad Zabihi who was singing religious music on the radio for a long time and was similarly associated with the Pahlavis.

The timing and rise of Ostad Shajarian's career was very fortunate, because if he had been among the elite singers of the Shah's time—he was well-known but not a superstar like he is now—they wouldn't have allowed him to perform after the revolution and become who he is now. Shajarian really rose after the revolution and at the beginning of it he was actually known as a "revolutionary singer," with those early *soruds* and especially *Sepideh*. This was great propaganda for the new regime and some people outside of Iran regarded him as a traitor in those early days of the revolution. But many artists were shut down after the revolution, especially the female singers. They became "indoor," private performers, singing at the homes of rich people for small gatherings. This kind of singing will actually damage your voice because you're not practicing and the ambience is not very serious. Shajarian managed to move forward both artistically and professionally while others were sidelined.

Musical Developments in the Postrevolutionary Period

Cassette Culture

RS
While there was a fairly wide selection of twelve-inch LPs of Western art music available in Iran in the 1960s and 1970s (presumably imported), by the mid 1970s only about fifty LPs of Persian music—less than half of which were produced in Iran—were on the market and then only beginning in 1969 (Nettl 1978: 155). Their impact was thus quite minimal. These LP recordings presented short performances featuring a variety of dastgahs, i.e., Persian music "not as it would be heard in a live traditional performance, but as non-Western music is typically presented on recordings to the Westerner" (ibid.: 156). Radio and television were much more important media for the dissemination of Persian music to the public at large. This was to change with the introduction of the cassette, which rose to become the predominant medium of music dissemination in the 1980s, as it did (and remains) in many Asian countries. Thanks to their use in car stereos and the revolutionary Walkman in the West and its relative affordability for playback, recording, and duplication in developing countries, cassette sales peaked worldwide in mid 1980s: 900 million units per year, constituting 54 percent of total global music sales (BBC 2005). "Turkey still sells 88 million cassettes a year, India 80 million, and that cassettes account for 50% of sales in these countries. In Saudi Arabia, it is 70%" (ibid.). While I was unable to find similar statistics for present day Iran, it is surely in the same category.

Cassette culture in Iran got its earliest boost not in the domain of music but rather through recordings of the agitating discourses of the exiled Ayatollah Khomeini, who distributed a "massive and systematic body" of cassettes from 1960s, when the format was in its infancy, through to the eve of the revolution. Particularly during his exile in France, Khomeini's followers would smuggle a single copy into Iran (or simply play it over a long-distance phone call to a receiving recorder), arranging for mass distribution through mosques and making them available in the bazaars of Tehran, Tabriz, Qom, and Mashhad (Dabashi 2005: 140–41; Sreberny-Mohammadi 1990). The medium constituted an "electronic pulpit" (Sreberny-Mohammadi 1990: 358) that was absolutely crucial for establishing his pre-revolutionary positioning and subsequent assumption of power. "Cassette tapes were a suitable form for Khomeini's lengthy diatribes against the Pahlavis, suited the cleric's elaborate oratorical style and allowed full play to be made of the emotional and dramatic power of *rowze* mourning symbols as well as recitative repetition of the failures of the shah's regime and the need for action" (ibid.). Music cassettes followed suit with widespread popularity. Music broadcast on the radio became severely restricted and while cassettes were subject to censorship, they quickly replaced the radio as the main medium for the public dissemination of music. During describes a "veritable invasion" of cassettes of all genres of Iranian music between 1975 and 1979, placing sales figure in 1983 to be in the hundreds of thousands (1984: 17–18), though precise figures are impossible to ascertain. Between cultural habits with the introduction of the copy-friendly format of the cassette and the fact that Iran never signed international copyright agreements, piracy is rife and socially acceptable in Iran.[13]

Shajarian had a substantial share of this large market and while he was already quite well-known through his radio performances throughout the 1970s, he consolidated his fame in the 1980s through the medium of the cassette. Like most of his fans, both authors of this study discovered and grew to love Shajarian's music through the mediation of his cassettes in the 1980s—Amir Koushkani in Iran and me in Canada. When most musical activities stopped after the revolution, the production of cassettes continued throughout the postrevolutionary period, albeit under strict censorship with regard to content. Most musicians also experienced great difficulties in obtaining the licenses required to record and release their productions (e.g., Meshkatian quoted in During 1992: 159n8). These policies kept an effective lid on the decentralizing, demonopolizing dynamic that often characterized the spread of the liberating micromedia in other countries (Manuel 1993: 2). Internet blogs offered the requisite freedom from controlled distribution to fufill this function for Iranians two decades later (Alavi 2005). As live performances were severely restricted throughout most of the 1980s, the vast majority of cassette releases were studio recordings (ibid.: 154). Shajarian proved to be an exception to these general trends by releasing several important live recordings;[14] *Raz e Del* (recorded October 1979), *Sepideh* (November 1979), and *Astan-e Janan* (1984). The latter cassette was recorded in the political and cultural neutrality of the Italian embassy. Given his preferences, it is not surprising that Shajarian's first two releases on Western labels were also live recordings (CDs on Ocora and World Network), which quickly made their way back to Iran as bootleg cassettes. As noted above, he also recorded a great deal of material in the privacy of his home that led to cassette releases that are examined in the next chapter.

The unprecedented boom of cassette consumption brought Persian music into more homes and private lives than ever, and exponentially accelerated the changes in musical culture that were introduced throughout the twentieth century with the earlier recording formats. In addition to exacerbating the ongoing polemic of banalizing Persian music by casting it to such a wide and undiscriminating audience, the flood of cassettes affected transmission and acquisition among musicians, business practices (particularly the growth of piracy noted above), increased canonization of repertoire and standardization of style, and altered musical forms and their pacing to suit the new frame of its format. While each of these components was significant itself, their sudden confluence had a marked impact on the overall aesthetic basis of Persian music.

Recordings combine oral-aural transmission with a degree of fixity that results in an interesting hybrid of "old" and "new" dynamics. The rewind button proved to be an efficacious, precise, and patient instructor. Recording lessons of radif or any other material transmitted on the highly portable cassette recorder sped up the rate of acquisition. Learning through lifting from recordings of master musicians became a vital activity in the *Markaz* (as the Center for the Propagation and Preservation of Iranian Music is conventionally abbreviated) for younger musicians in retrieving and cultivating older, "purer" styles of Persian music to combat the massive changes occurring in the 1960s. The accessibility of recordings by these masters also marked the initiation of an archiving dynamic, a precise awareness of what had been played in previous decades that was hitherto unknown in Iran (which During calls "magnetic memory" [1988: 105]). While highly informative and valuable, these changes of media inevitably impacted the consciousness of musicians, corroborating McLuhan and subsequent studies in orality-literacy theory. As the recordings accumulated there was a new danger of over self-consciousness regarding the tradition that had a potentially constipating effect, impeding the natural flow, just as the establishment and accumulation of the Western musical canon had in nineteenth-century Europe of fixing our "classical" musicking in the past, to which almost any contemporary concert program testifies.[15] Cassettes plugged up natural change by imposing "new old standards." While this archiving effect went even further in the CD era, in which the first attempt at a systematic retrieval of pre-1940s recordings appeared (though still only a small portion of these have been restored and published [Tabar 2005: 121]), its forward motion was reaching critical mass in the cassette era of the 1980s.

> In the past, traditions were relying not so much on memory as on oblivion. . . .
> Few people could say: "100 years ago they were playing like that and not like
> this" . . . (S)ince the tradition is fixed by recordings and notations, young
> musicians have no other choice than to assume it by learning all that they can,
> in order to reach the artistic and technical level prescribed by the tradition. But
> on the other hand, as these sources are well-known, they are blamed to satisfy
> themselves by imitating the Ancients, and in almost all the cases, to be not as
> good as the Ancient ones. (During 2009: 124–25)

At the same time, due to the wide range of styles—both Iranian and foreign—suddenly made available and routine, cassettes accelerated stylistic change, usually in the direction of hybridization with Iranian folk traditions (During 1988: 107; 1992: 152ff.), especially Kurdish, during the 1980s and 1990s. While Iranian culture (indeed all human culture) is markedly hybrid, this injection of diversity was particularly rapid and resulted in many artificial, ungrounded mutations that made no lasting impact beyond the fleeting exuberance of experimenting with something new.

The cassette explosion further complicated ideas surrounding an artist's creative output and the conception of performance that were percolating since the advent of recording and radio. The occasion[16] of recording or radio broadcast is by definition abstract, an impersonal communication with a mass, anonymous audience. As in the West, radio programs and earlier recording formats were in the form of "singles," and released as such; even when collected on LPs, they were an aggregate of relatively short, unrelated pieces. But cassettes in Iran paralleled the Western notion of the "concept album" that emerged in the late 1960s: a large-scale musical work (usually one hour) presenting an integrated conceptual whole, along with appropriate artwork on the cover and often notes and photos (occasionally with multiple folds) on the liner. A cassette "album" would usually be conceived with a strategic formal division between the two sides of the cassette. The cassette was thus a larger musical canvas in the form of a diptych of two thirty-minute units (each usually one continuous piece) or, less frequently, one sixty-minute unit necessarily interrupted halfway through.

Furthermore, the goal now emerged of making polished recordings and the accumulation of a personal oeuvre of cassette albums that would stand the test of time (Nooshin 1996: 160–61). In stark contrast to the traditional function of serving the immediate occasion, musicians were now making abstract, detached artistic statements addressing both the present and the future. While this also occurred in early recordings, the short duration of the format mitigated against this more ambitious vision of creating an opus and, over time, a recording legacy parallel to large-scale Western compositional ouevres. A new selfconsciousness thus arose as to the concept of the music itself and its reification as a cassette album. Another profound shift was the total lack of immediate audience feedback integral to good performance of Persian music. This would now emerge in the form of counting cassette sales—delayed, alienated, and mediated by money—or perhaps a newspaper or journal review.[17]

Still further changes involved the manipulation of sound in the studio. One particularly characteristic development in this regard is the use of reverb and echo, often quite excessive by contemporary Western standards (though commonplace in American popular music in the 1950s). The use of "slapback" echo first arose with Iranian radio recordings in the 1960s, as is evident in many of the *Golhā* programs, and was frequently used on solo ney recordings through the 1960s and 1970s. It was particularly associated with the setar recordings of Ahmad Ebadi and became somewhat of a trademark of his style—a *de facto* electric setar.[18] Reverb/echo effects are an artificial means of creating a sense physical open space, grandeur, solemnity, and meditative ambience, and indeed a touch of otherworldly psychedelia conducive to mystical states. Shajarian's recordings often feature a warm reverb and occasionally the more distorting echo (see performance example 4 in chapter 2 below). Such technical innovations naturally led to further experimentation and exploitation:

> More recently, cassette recordings have led to new forms of performance that break completely with traditional performance conditions, which had already been modified by the demands of concert halls. Studio musicians see the music as a layering of sounds (using multiple tracks) and a montage

of various discrete sequences. Thus they radically change all the techniques of musical notation and definitively break with the rules of orality, creating works "in vitro" (as it were) that are impossible to reproduce "in vivo." (During 2002: 863)

None of these developments are unique to Iran but the point here is that they became part of Iranian music culture largely by means of the cassette. The dynamics of cassette culture in Iran were effectively transferred to the CD, though cassettes still enjoy considerable popularity alongside the latter, and the same album is often available in both formats (see Shajarian's website: www.delawaz.com/en). Even in the early 2000s some albums were only available on cassette. The change involved when considering the two formats is quantitative—"more and faster"—rather than qualitative. Some differentiating factors of the CD include the fact that format promotes a more continuous rather than bifurcated format characteristic of the cassette. Also, most of the voluminous releases of restored historical archive materials over the past fifteen years are released on CD, notably through the Mahoor Institute of Culture and Art (www.mahoor.ir). Of course, Iranians are generally digital-savvy and many have long since moved on to MP3 files like the rest of the world, dispensing altogether with hard copies of recordings.

Shajarian's initial rise to fame came through the radio and was consolidated with the television in the 1970s, but his rise to superstardom was by means of the cassette, launching him into uncharted territory of expression and public profile.

Musical Innovations in the 1980s

We noted in our companion volume (chapter 3 of Simms and Koushkani 2012) how the work of Mirza Abdollah, 'Aref, and Vaziri was revolutionary for their time. Innovation in the postrevolutionary period was more gradual and much less "revolutionary," given the massive emphasis on purging Westoxification and reasserting Iranian tradition, however the latter may have been conceived and constructed. Hossein Alizadeh's (Sarkoohi 1989: 32, 36) and particularly Shajarian's (chapter 4 of Simms and Koushkani 2012) subordination of the radif to individual artistic license, as they were eventually to maintain in the 1990s, is somewhat "counterrevolutionary" in a uniquely Iranian way, working against canonization and the lionization of tradition prevalent at the time. While reinvigorating traditional Persian values and successfully transmitting these to a large number of musicians and listeners of the younger generation, the revolutionary ideology attached to this rebirth was authoritarian and moved Persian music increasingly away from living art to ossified craft. The society and context of the music had changed significantly since the glory days of Mirza Abdollah and the early-twentieth century masters who were held as the primary models to emulate.

A tendency with roots in the early twentieth-century that particularly coalesced in the 1960s and became increasingly prominent in the early postrevolutionary period was the rise of instrumental music. Possible reasons for this include influence from the prestige and preoccupation attached to instrumental music in the West along with importation of the Western notion of virtuosity—factors that assisted in raising the social standing of instrumentalists throughout the century. Internally, the Farahani lineage of the radif was clearly an idiom of the lutes tar and setar. Manifestations of this shift of focus away from vocal music—a rather revolutionary departure from tradition, considering the central tenets of the *samā'* polemic were aimed at instrumental music—include the commonplace acceptance of instrumental music without vocals; the prevalence of Western-style virtuosity (particularly for the santur and violin); the rise of the virtuoso percussionist (tombek and later daff) from its previous role in providing simple accompaniment; an increase in the number of virtuoso solo instrumental compositions, such as *chaharmezrabs*, both written and memorized; and increasingly "democratized" balance of instrumental and vocal prominence in ensemble performances (Nooshin 1996: 163–67).

While recordings of instrumental solos were made throughout the recording history of Iran, their position relative to mainstream music could not compare to the role of instrumental music in later radio programming, particularly the *Golhā* series that did much to raise its profile. The series of cassettes *Taknavāzān* featuring these exclusively instrumental radio recordings were popular throughout the 1970s and continue to be so through their reissue on CD. These recordings included solos for various instruments, duets where two instruments alternate in *jawab*-avaz fashion (those of Ahmad Ebadi and violinist Asadollah Malik are particularly noteworthy), as well as the incorporation of Persian instruments in the hybridized Western chamber or symphonic idiom common to the period. Despite this shift toward the instrumental, good singers still commanded greater popularity than their instrumental counterparts (Nooshin 1996: 165).

Alizadeh emerged as an influential musical force in the postrevolutionary period through his prolific activity as performer, composer, and recording artist. His *Ney Nava* of 1983, ostensibly a concerto for ney and string orchestra, was particularly popular; clearly related to the prerevolutionary hybrid genre, the string writing was subtly polyphonic while evoking an Iranian expression. Alizadeh was also prominent as a film composer, where he alternated or blended orchestral and solo Persian idioms in films that exposed him to a large international audience (his later work in the films *Gabbeh* and *A Time for Drunken Horses* are the best known examples for North Americans). His soundtrack for the 1991 film *Delshodegan*, discussed in chapter 3, stretched out into deeper hybrid territory juxtaposing and superimposing Western and Persian idioms with increasing sophistication. As a tar and setar soloist, he contributed many *zarbi* pieces to the repertoire, both composed and memorized. He also sought to make the idiom of Persian instrumental music autonomous in a spirit akin to Western music. "Alizadeh, in particular, has worked towards the 'emancipation' of instruments from the voice, maintaining that the '. . . sheltering of music behind words inevitably resulted in the potential of the voice and poetry affecting the music . . .' (Sarkoohi

1989: 37), particularly the rhythms of the music, which he regards as limited by the prosody of poetry. Discussing one of his pieces, he states: 'The basis of this work was the relationships between the instrumentalists . . . and the voice was just where it should be, like another instrument and not more [important] (ibid.: 38)'" (Nooshin 1996: 164). Staking his ground in a debate originating in the mid-1980s, Alizadeh consciously pressed forth in this direction at precisely the same time Shajarian was working in the opposite direction to reassert the primacy of the text of the poem in addressing the occasion—rejecting autonomy, music was entirely dependent on the context of the occasion and the word painting of the carefully chosen text.

Parviz Meshkatian (1955–2009)—Shajarian's onetime son-in-law and principal creative collaborator for the landmark recordings examined in this study—rose as another important innovator and leader of Persian music in the post-revolutionary period, one staying closer to core Iranian musical values than Alizadeh. Meshkatian wrote a number of highly successful compositions based on the radif but with subtle polyphonic features and an effective, original exploitation of the orchestral potential of a large ensemble of Persian instruments. His hybrid Persian-Western ensemble compositions *Gonbad e Mina, Jan e Oshaq* and *Dud e 'Ud* (mentioned above) were orchestrated by others but reveal a visionary facility for blending the two languages. Meshkatian also composed a large number of innovative *chaharmezrab*s for santur, many of which are not notated (see www.Meshkatian.ir).

Following the nationalistic identity politics of the revolution, elements of Iranian folk traditions, especially Kurdish, were incorporated into Persian music (During 1992: 152–53). While this approach is nothing particularly new in the tradition,[19] the intensification of this after the revolution was widely visible and strongly demarcated contemporaneous practice from the Pahlavi period. Shahram Nazeri and the Kamkars were at the forefront of this movement, shifting deftly between *asil*, traditional Kurdish, and variously hybridized styles. The *daff* frame drum became particularly ubiquitous in accompanying a wide range of Persian performers. Kurdish tanbur and Khorasani dotar techniques and stylings were incorporated into the setar by Jalal Zolfonun and Alizadeh (notably the latter's popular 1986 cassette *Torkaman*); likewise Mohammad Musavi began incorporating elements of folk music into his ney style, apparently with the blessings of his Ostad and doyen of ney in Persian music, Hassan Kasa'i. The tanbur-setar influence became mutual when tanburists such as Aliakbar Moradi incorporated modal and formal aspects of Persian music into his renditions of ostensibly Kurdish repertoire. Furthermore, in the 1980s Zolfonun began experimenting with large, "Soviet-style" ensembles featuring dozens of setars that Moradi emulated using ranks of tanburs. In chapter 3 we will examine Shajarian's substantial contribution to designing and building new instruments that expand the tonal and timbral range of Persian music.

Shahram Nazeri (b. 1951) rose to national renown as a singer of avaz in the 1980s. He had studied with Shajarian for a year (Shajarian et al. 2004: 64) but presented a different style and approach to avaz, in particular highlighting his Kurdish background and championing the incorporation of Rumi's poetry—which, curiously, was rarely used in avaz outside of the generic gushe Masnavi—and cultivating an overtly Sufistic image. While he had been singing Rumi since the 1970s, his album *Gol-e Sad Barg* ("One-hundred-petaled Rose"), released in 1984 to celebrate the great soul's eight-hundredth birthday[20] exclusively featured Rumi's lesser-known poetry[21] and was an immense success, often described as the biggest selling cassette of Persian music and "Sufi music" in history. The album was accompanied by the setars of Zolfonun and Reza Ghassemi and *daff* of Bijan Kamkar and had a decidedly folksy and upbeat feel, which was a welcome relief during these precarious times. The album is also popularly credited with inspiring a huge surge of people, especially the young, to become interested in learning to play the setar—the most iconic and Persian of instruments. Indeed, the instrumentation and poetry were strong markers of Persian identity and fed into the robust sense of nationalism that was rife at the time, in the midst of the already greatly protracted war with Iraq. In addition to leading these important developments Nazeri also experimented with singing contemporary poetry in free verse (discussed further in chapter 3), such as *Zemestan* in 1981 and *Dar Golestaneh* in 1987. Thus, Nazeri successfully positioned himself as a risk-taking innovator in the realm of avaz that was complementary to Shajarian in terms of image, style, approach, and accomplishment. Shajarian and Nazeri are two quite different voices and artistic personalities who appeal to different sensibilities and tastes; both singers were hugely popular in the 1980s and had their own (occasionally overlapping) legions of fans—a situation that still stands today.

Shajarian's innovations of bringing instrumental melodic idioms and modulatory (*morakab*) flexibility into avaz—treating the radif as a flexible resource and thus enabling new formal possibilities—date from the 1980s.[22] In addition to these important and effective developments of craft, Shajarian redefined how avaz could function in society, what it was capable of expressing, and what it could mean for Iranians at the historical crossroads at which they again found themselves.

Resistance through Persian Music

The situation in the two decades following the revolution was complex and cannot be reduced to such a monolithic formula, but in a broad outline, Persian music was hijacked by the government as a tool of nationalistic propaganda that, happily, had many positive effects during the 1980s. As noted above, simply playing Persian music in the early years of the revolution was itself a subtle form of resistance, given the marked reinvigoration of the weighty baggage of the *samā'* polemic by the new fundamentalist ideology. Through the stick and carrot of censorship and commissions, the composition and recording production of revolutionary *sorud* anthems were the most obvious engagement of Persian music (if only in the form of the tasnif) as propaganda. All aspects of society, and especially music, were strictly controlled; any expression of dissent toward the revolutionary agenda was not tolerated and, indeed, dangerous—untold numbers of political dissidents, both real and perceived, were imprisoned or executed. Explicit, freewheeling rallying calls such as 'Aref Ghazvini boldly asserted after the Constitutional Revolution in the early decades of the century were unthinkable now.

While Shajarian did release a total of five *sorud-e enqelabi* during the first months following the revolution in the hopeful wake of deposing the Shah, he quickly dissociated himself with government and political organizations, maintaining that his allegiance was solely toward Persian *adab* (literary humanism[23]), Persian music and a generic attachment to "his mother country" (Nasirfar 1990: 403–04). Thus began his game of cat and mouse with the revolutionary regime that has continued for three decades to the present. With great intelligence and strategic savvy, using *adab* and Persian music itself as his "cover," Shajarian forged a path of oblique but profound resistance in the face of unbelievably formidable constraints. He attacked the heart of the revolutionary matter by targeting the hearts of the people, deftly threading through loopholes in the censorship while underscoring core Iranian values that highlighted the hypocrisy of the regime. His 1985 release of the cassette *Bidad* (discussed in the following chapter) was an unprecedentedly shrewd masterstroke in this regard, a poignant coup that remains unequalled in the postrevolutionary period. Of course, the practice of oblique, veiled criticism is nothing new in Iran and is a standard practice of poets and musicians of other cultures working under repressive regimes in recent times (e.g., many works of Shostakovich in Soviet Russia, the Ethiopian "wax and gold" idiom of the Mengistu era [1974–1992], among others). Speaking of Rumi's milieu in medieval Konya, Lewis notes: "Even in the Friday sermon at the mosque a preacher (*khatib*) would have to choose his words carefully so as to admonish the ruler without blatantly insulting him" (2008: 328).

Throughout these trying times Shajarian reactivated poetry and Persian music as political critique, a function that had essentially atrophied since 'Aref's bold activism more than a half century before. While Shajarian seemed to be clearly leading the way with this reinitiative, Sadighi and Mahdavi maintain that this was in fact the mandate of the broader *Chavosh* movement:

> So it was actually the classically trained Iranian musician who sowed the seeds of resistance to Western-inspired pop that sprouted in the days of revolution. Composer-instrumentalist Hossein Alizadeh dubbed his music *razmi* (militant) in contradistinction to the *bazmi* (banquet) style heard at the *fêtes* of the elite. The same was true of the well-known Mohammad Reza Lotfi and Mohammad Reza Shajarian. They never challenged the political system directly, participating in state-organized events like the landmark Shiraz Art Festival in 1977, but they practiced a brand of music of which orthodox musicians disapproved. They argued that classical Iranian music was less a means

of entertainment than a vehicle by which the musician could speak the truth about the issues of the day. At the Shiraz Art Festival, Shajarian sang the constitutional revolution *tasnif* (art song), "All night sleep doesn't come to my eyes / Oh, you who are asleep / In the desert those who are thirsty die / While water is being carried to ostentatious palaces." Music, by the lights of the classically trained, was to be political in orientation and iconoclastic in structure. (Sadighi and Mahdavi 2009)

The following chapters will detail how Shajarian's vocal style brilliantly consolidated and renovated the tradition of avaz he inherited and became hugely influential in the decades following the revolution. Indeed, it was so widely copied and regarded as *the* standard of avaz for those who followed that it flattened out the variety of individual stylings that characterized previous periods of avaz, presenting a stasis, homogenization, and for many a crisis akin to Charlie Parker's overbearing influence among jazz saxophonists in the 1940s and 50s (cf., Bloom 1973). Shajarian's music was an artistic creation that was relatively quickly appropriated as a craft among other singers, especially younger ones. This tendency was exacerbated by, or entrained with, the strong overall authoritarian dynamic of postrevolutionary Persian music in conforming to traditional models. Shajarian's avaz was a perfect blend of the old and new, a freshly reinvigorated tradition that powerfully embodied, captured, and reflected the spirit of the time. Contemporary musical resistance has since shifted to the idioms of rock and rap music, a potent force among young Iranians (Nooshin 2005), though Sadighi and Mahdavi (2009) believe its significance and impact is often overstated, particularly when reported by the Western media.

AK

In the time of Mohammad Reza Shah, Persian classical musicians were just trying to cultivate art, like in most countries. But when you think about countries like Jamaica at the time and the music of Bob Marley, this music has its own occasion and his words are really meaningful and important for people—but it wasn't like that in Iran at that time before the revolution. In Iran in the 1970s some pop musicians increasingly wanted to imitate the kind of function and style of music from countries like Jamaica, Chile, and other South American nations. Musicians were trying to protest and they started to use this approach. Musicians such as Farhad, Faraydin Faruqi, and Dariush started to sing about issues that reflected the sentiments of people in our society. They were arrested by the government several times and that, of course, made them even more famous. I remember they were coerced by the government to release songs that retracted what they had previously said. I remember Dariush sang two songs that were critical of the government and then they arrested him and forced him to sing something about the "superman from East," which was a not-so subtle reference to the Shah. Everyone knew it was supposed to be about the Shah.

But Persian classical music of the time—if you listen to Banan, Marzieh, Delkash, Shahidi, Khānsari—generally featured safe, innocuous poetry. They didn't preserve or revive 'Aref's music, which was protest music—he was a *Mashrute* warrior. But singers didn't really put themselves in that situation, even singing things like *Morghe Sahar*.[24] So the period after the 1920s through the 1970s was vibrant and creative musically, people were composing new poetry, setting it to music and performing with great talent but it was politically evasive, sticking to safe themes like unrequited love. They sometimes would set really old poetry like Rudaki. The mood was not very joyful or happy, which may have reflected the real feelings of listeners in general. Avaz was very important during that time and was especially featured on the *Golhā* programs of the 1960s and 1970s produced for the radio by Davud Pirnia. Many great singers and instrumentalists appeared on the program, which consisted of instrumental solos, two tasnifs with string orchestra and highlighted avaz in the middle. But the occasion, the *monāsebat* of this music was personal. The singers had their own lives and they were enjoying their lives, but the occasion was their personal life and probably other persons' personal lives. Then the revolution happened and it suddenly changed everything and brought people together.

But then Sayeh (Hushang Ebtehaj) started to write political poetry and Meshkatian, Lotfi and Alizadeh started to compose for this and Shajarian and Nazeri sang for them. But Shajarian started to develop something new in avaz: choosing the poem to reflect and comment upon what was going on in society. He had close relationships to Dadbeh and other people who enlightened him as to what was going on and what he might do in response. Shajarian was one of the first to get politically engaged through the music, through avaz in the period following the revolution.

Nazeri did too but in a very different way, less explicit or confrontational. His character is not like Shajarian: to be a student, constantly learning and exploring. He started to become famous at that time for choosing to sing the poetry of Rumi, Mowlana. Why? A year or two after the revolution, people realized they made a mistake, that the mollahs had hijacked the country and turned it into the Islamic Republic. As a result people were emotionally looking for something else to substitute and "subsidize" their beliefs. They can't just say there is no god and become atheists. So they realized words of Rumi's Sufism were very suitable and many people engaged themselves with this kind of belief. Nazeri was presenting those poems and became so famous. Meanwhile, Shajarian was staying with Hafez, Sa'di, Attar and gradually to 'Eraqi and other people like Fayz-e Kashani: this is Sufi poetry. But he actually was looking for a different kind of audience. He had his own boundary and didn't want to present a kind of folk music. He wanted to stay in classical music. Nazeri did not have that border. He could sing folk music, *Masnavi khāni* and *Khānegahi* music—anything—which is why he sometimes calls himself avant garde. But that's not true, he's not avant garde: he's eclectic. The character of his singing will change depending on what group he works with. So when he works with Alizadeh, he's different than when he works with Zolfonun—the composer is very important for Nazeri's productions. But with Shajarian, you always hear him consistently in any kind of work.

Scholarly Discourse

RS
Movahed (2003) provides a highly illuminating review of "emic Iranian" musical scholarship that emerged in the two decades following the revolution—a period of robust, ideologically driven discourse—which she divides into three categories:

> 1) scholasticism, represented through the continuing quest for an older scientific music in the treatise of Persian-Islamic scholars to tacitly create a form of coexistence between religion and music and overrule the religious assimilation of Persian music to decadence, 2) anti-westernization, represented through the quest for a pure and authentic music to exemplify the richness of an indigenous culture uninfluenced by western elements and proud to make a local realization of its own traditions, and 3) easternization, represented through the quest for genuine musical idioms present in the music of folk cultures to represent the "eastern" phenomenon and mold it as an ideological construct toward the establishment of a new cultural identity. (Movahed 2003: 102–03)

She organizes her review of sources into three periods and shaped by the above categories: sources written between 1979–1989, "Policy of Isolation" and the Obliteration of Persian Music; 1990–1994: "Resistance against the Cultural Invasion of the West" and the Return to Authenticity; and 1995–2001: "Search for a National Identity" and the Endorsement of Persian Music. The prerevolutionary "identity crisis" that Nettl sensed in the 1970s (1978: 179) gives way to a clearer path of (romanticized?) nostalgia and a more proactive/reactive restoration of loss—loss of a perceived golden age of "homefulness," individuality, simplicity, authenticity, and spontaneity (Movahed 2003: 105). Authors of this substantial body of writings include both trained musicologists and musicians without musicological training, the latter offering a valuable, if often subjective and partial, perspective. While the inevitable confrontation of East-West, tradition-modernity, spiritual-material is alive and well in this literature, she finds that this results in a mutually arising awareness and confluence of the personal and the objective, an invigorating dialectic that marks a uniquely Iranian view of Persian music with great potential for global scholarship in general:

> [Iranian musicians] have used writing to ultimately recontexualize musicology and look at the medium of feeling through a scientific mirror. . . . Perhaps postrevolutionary music scholarship in Iran is the strongest testimony on the part of any group of indigenous scholars around the world that no music historiography can and should ignore the fundamental challenge in

bridging between the mind and the heart, between science and practice, between emic and etic. Objective representation can only happen when all of these have been brought together in scrutinizing, dissecting, judging and understanding any music. . . . Very rarely in the study of non-western music have scholars created images of feeling and systematically attempted to perceive the sensory and expressive properties of any music. This new dimension in the study of Persian music provides opportunities for musicians, musicologists, ethnomusicologists, self and Other to revisit the character of their field and challenge the constraints which have in the past kept expression outside the musicologist's sphere of activity. (Movahed 2003: 104, 106)

The most prominent contemporary ethno/musicologists, particularly in terms of international profile, include Mohammad Reza Darvishi (whose main research area is Iranian folk traditions) and Hooman As'adi of the University of Tehran. Under the directorship of Mohammad Musavi (not to be confused with the eminent ney player), the privately funded Mahoor Institute of Culture and Art is the most prominent publisher of recordings, transcriptions, and scholarly research that has a global outreach and distribution network. The institute also publishes the quarterly journal *Mahoor*, a primary organ for Iranian research on all aspects of Persian music.

The *Faslnameh-ye Mahur*, more than being just a review, had been for long time a forum open to all, where the best mixed with the worst. Amongst the banality and sterile polemic one found information, reflection, and interesting research, but the tone was often partisan and even aggressive, the Iranians quickly forgetting their good manners when holding a pen or a steering wheel. For lack of genuine critiques of art, one resorted to disparagement. Reclaimed by and in the hands of a few true scientists, this periodical finally became a reference that cannot be overlooked. Of another class is the arts magazine *Faslname-ye Honar,* published by the Center of Cultural Research in the Ministry of Culture. For those who are interested in Occidental music, there is the less scholarly monthly magazine, *Honar-e Musiqi.* (During 2005: 390)

From the general contextualization of Iranian musical culture and Shajarian's personal and professional positioning following the Islamic Revolution, we now turn to his work during the period that secured his standing as one of the most significant Iranian artists of the twentieth century.

Notes

1. The transformation of a complex system into a markedly different state. The glossary provides brief definitions for this and other terms from the area of chaotics used in this book.
2. The "doctrinal position of Shi'ism itself, which as a historically combative and intransigent religion of protest must always be in a position of defiance and rebellion and thus can never come to power without immediately discrediting itself" (Dabashi 2005: 190, see also 217–18; 233–35 and Reckord 1987:30).
3. The lawfulness of playing and listening to music in Islam, discussed (see chapter 2 of Simms and Koushkani 2012).
4. The aesthetic of ambiguity and uncertainty integral to Persian poetry (see chapter 1 of Simms and Koushkani 2012).
5. Amid the plethora of carefully detailed, often voluminous analyses, Tehranian (2008) offers a concise and incisive overview of the political and cultural context of the Islamic Revolution and its aftermath.
6. "Rooted" or traditional classical Persian music.
7. "Nevertheless, despite all the measures designed to combat music, it could not be eliminated from Iranian culture. Besides, even if the state has a grip on the media, there is a great difference in Iran between what is theoretically allowed and what people actually do in private" (Youseffzadeh 2000:38; see also p.40 and 2004:129, 132).
8. See the appendix for title translations and discographical information regarding all the recordings discussed in this book. Transliterations are given as they appear on album covers and the Delawaz English website (delawaz.com/en).
9. The exact date is unclear in various sources but given as Aban 1358 (Aban ended on November 21, 1979) by Abdollahi (2003:2070).
10. Liner notes to Kereshmeh KCD–107, p.2.
11. Translated by Avery (2007:248).
12. Not on Delawaz. I only have access to a digital copy and have been unable to determine which company produced the original cassette.
13. This culture of piracy travels with the Iranian diaspora, where recording retailers in Western countries routinely keep a wide stock of openly pirated units of various media despite the clear existence of local copyright laws. When Western technology is exported to other cultures its accompanying "rules of engagement" are not always accepted with the delivery.
14. As noted in our companion volume (Simms and Koushkani 2012) Shajarian prefers performing to a live audience.
15. This syndrome bears some relationship to the "centipedal effect" noted by Arthur Koestler (in his book *The Act of Creation* [1964]) in reference to the Zen story of the centipede rendered unable to walk when asked how it was able to ambulate with so many legs—the very naturalness of the act tripped up by the analytical consciousness of itself.
16. See chapter 1 of Simms and Koushkani (2012) for the integral significance of the occasion (*monāsebat*) in Persian music and other performance arts.
17. The context of the following quote is different but it speaks to how two prominent Persian musicians pitched their performances to a mass audience: "(B)oth Payvar and

Meshkatian in interview stated that whilst the mood and response of the audience were factors which affected their performances, the identity and musical knowledge of the audience were not, and indeed both musicians implied that this would be 'compromising' the music to the audience" (Nooshin 1996:161). Shajarian, however, feels that the quality and knowledge of the audience is absolutely crucial to him performing well (see chapter 1 of Simms and Koushkani 2012).

18. AK: Mr. Ebadi's echo effect was a simple reel tape recorder with very limited options for delay speed and intensity, but the machine had its own sound. He picked it up in Europe or someone brought it for him in the 1960s. There is a historical tradition of rich Iranians going to Europe and returning with pianos, electronic gadgets, phonographs, cameras, and whatnot. Iranians really like the idea of echo. The musicians have learned this style; the machine creates and affects their style of music. It doesn't mean they've lost their sense of the music or their abilities. It's a new kind of music, electronic music. They stopped using some techniques that were created for purely acoustic performance—you reduce the *riz* and the *mezrab* technique because if you play too complicated the music will get distorted. This gave them the opportunity to slow down; the speed of the music decreased from earlier playing. Of course, some people didn't like this and wanted to keep the tradition of playing densely and as fast as possible. It's a matter of personal choice and taste.

Mr. Ali Akbar Shahnazi (Ebadi's cousin) didn't know how to deal with this machine, based on his style and personality. In some of his recordings you can hear him asking the technician to turn it off or change the setting to make it more subtle. He was an extremely creative performer, never playing anything the same way. His personality channelled the music in a different way than Mr. Ebadi. We have here two gifted players from the Farahani family with entirely different approaches to this music. That tells us something important about the intrinsic flexibility of the tradition, and it's very clear coming directly from the source.

19. The radif is full of folk influences from around the country and musicians would periodically reinvigorate Persian music with further importations (During 2001:139); indeed, many musicians (including Shajarian) believe that the radif originated with folk music.

20. According to the Islamic (Hejri) calendar; the corresponding Western date was actually December 4, 1983.

21. Mahmood Schricker notes that the poems Nazeri chose contained difficult words that no one else would dare to sing (e.g., *takhteh, ghalzam, nahang, ghārun,* etc.) and that Banan criticized him for using such "ugly" poetry for avaz (personal communication, 2010).

22. Discussed in chapter 4 of Simms and Koushkani (2012).

23. For a discussion of the significance of *adab*, see chapter 1 of Simms and Koushkani (2012).

24. This important tasnif is discussed in chapter 3.

Chapter 2
Landmark Recordings

RS
This chapter presents a detailed view of four of Ostad Shajarian's most important albums recorded between 1982 and 1987. It is important to remember that the destiny of Iran immediately after the Shah's departure was up for grabs and marked by both optimism and chaos. Returning to Iran on February 1, 1979, Khomeini craftily assumed total revolutionary power, out-manoeuvred the provisional government left by the Shah, and won the support of the military. In the meantime, however, multiple, uncentralized factions of various political persuasions imposed their authority *ad hoc* throughout the country. Setting an ominous precedent for what was to follow, illegitimate "revolutionary courts" carried out executions of former regime affiliates on vague charges and without due process throughout the spring of 1979. All opposition was suppressed by brutal force. In June the Revolutionary Council instituted severe restrictions on the press and transferred private sector assets to the state at their whim. After a brief period of respite widespread executions resumed in May 1980, along with a thorough purging of government bureaucracies. A standoff between the first democratically elected President of the Islamic Republic, Abolhasan Bani Sadr, and Prime Minister Mohammad Ali Rajai culminated with the former's impeachment in late June 1981 and a decisive shift of power to the clerical faction that dominated the coalition government.

This triggered a movement calling for the overthrow of Khomeini by force, opposition that was met with ruthless, wholesale terror and repression: arrests, assassinations, and executions. Of the latter there were routinely fifty per day at the peak of the crackdown, with Amnesty International documenting 2, 946 from June 1981–1982 (Curtis and Hoogland 2008:64); in the lawless chaos an untold number went undocumented. Further bureaucratic purging, arbitrary home searches, public morality squads, incarcerations, and executions continued through the fall of 1982 through the agency of the Revolutionary Guards and revolutionary committees. The breakneck pace of bloody madness eased only when Khomeini, coldly calculating the debilitating economic consequences of the atrocities and their effect on the war effort with Iraq (in which major gains had just been made), issued an eight-point decree in December 1982 calling for relative "moderation" (Curtis and Hoogland 2008: 67).

Some of Shajarian's greatest recordings were made in 1982 in the midst of two years of public seclusion since the triumph of *Sepideh* and the subsequent deterioration of revolutionary optimism, opportunities for public musicking, and the descent into terror. To mark the onset of this transition and its implications for his professional life, he recorded the album *Khalvat Gozide* ("Deliberate Solitude") in 1980, though it remained unreleased until 1991.[1] The ghazal of Hafez (#34) chosen and sung in Shur clearly sets out Shajarian's approach and rationale for the new situation. The album cover art (photo 3) features a view of instruments lying silently on the floor of a courtyard, peeking through a slightly lifted curtain. Some selected beyts are translated below:

> What need do those who have chosen deliberate solitude have for an outing?
> Since we have the path of the friend—what's the need for a field?
>
> If it's our life you're after, there's no need for pretense,
> As you're the cover from that plunder—what's the need?
>
> Oh plaintiff, get lost! I have no quarrel with you!
> Lovers have come to the court—so what's the need for enemies?
>
> It so happened that I took from the obligations of the sailor,
> When you've got the pearl—what's the need for the sea?

Among musicians, connoisseurs and the general public the recordings that immediately followed *Khalvat Gozide* have become canonized and are now part of the larger narrative of Iranian culture in the late twentieth-century. For musicians they became the benchmark for artistic excellence. They mark the first, definitive, and most powerful expositions of Shajarian's mature style of avaz; they initiate his deployment of the cassette as a "concept album"; and they kickoff his political engagement of avaz, though necessarily on a more general level of reflecting public sentiment than in any critique of specific issues or policies. In more general terms these albums mark a huge surge of positive energy both personally for Shajarian and for Persian music in general.

With the exception of *Astan e Janan*, these landmark albums were recorded at Shajarian's home studio or in other private homes. As Persian music has repeatedly sought refuge in the privacy of homes through the centuries, this move was archetypal, with the huge new difference of having the company of recording technology behind the closed doors. Making the best of a bad situation, as musicians had in the past, these historic recordings were made in an intimate *majles* atmosphere in the comfortable surroundings of friends. Indeed, this is the most traditional milieu of Persian music, for many musicians and connoisseurs the best and most natural venue for this intimate music. According to Farmarz Payvar, no stranger to recording studios and large concert halls, "[t]he best place to play is the majles. There is more improvisation in a majles—everyone is relaxed and seated comfortably" (Nooshin 1996:158–59). Performing to an intimate gathering of other musicians and connoisseurs, the expectations and aim of the performance is high, there is no question of playing for the gallery here. It was during this time that Shajarian turned to the production process described in chapter 4 of Simms and Koushkani (2012): record lots of private performances, choose from the best of these, and later add framing compositions to them. Parviz Meshkatian was the composer for all of these landmark albums and, with the exception of *Nava (Morakab khani)*, the principal accompanist.

Performance Example 1: *Bidad*

Message of the Shrewd Bird

OS
Bidad *was a complaint that we had because of the circumstances that took place after the revolution. The whole work was basically a criticism of the situation and we wanted to ask "what happened?" All these things were said and all were nothing but lies. We wanted to show society's complaints, so all the poems and all the compositions were based on this idea. The tasnif that Meshkatian composed, "*Yād Bād,*" was also based on this idea.* (2009)

AK
Bidad literally means "cry for justice" and *Homayoun* means "king, royalty." Thus, right from the start, in his selection of the dastgah and gushe, Shajarian sets the stage for the ultimate message he intends to convey. The full title of the original cassette, *Bidad (Homayoun)*, can be interpreted as "the injustice (of the King)" or "injustice, (King)" (i.e., seeking justice from the King) or both.

The words on the cassette *Bidad (Homayoun)* become very, very, important. Some words actually became part of you and functioned like a kind of lesson; a lesson for me, anyway. I have to mention that in our neighbourhood of Tehran, I know that not so many people were listening to Shajarian. But Shajarian's words—I keep saying that, "Shajarian's words," but this is Hafez's poetry!—the way Shajarian performed these words moved me to read the book of Hafez I had and was always trying to understand. Shajarian was actually helping me to go back and read that poem the way he wanted me to read it. And I'm sure many people did that. I'm sure in Tehran and big cities, those people who were involved with literature, music, and art were listening to this tape and loved it.

They would love this music. But not with the common people, the majority of the population weren't able to understand or fully appreciate it. This is my understanding of the situation and I remember those days very well. Not so many people knew. A few years later, I went into the military; it was the end of the war and this was very bad part of the war. I realized then, after meeting people from all over the country coming from different backgrounds that not so many people knew Shajarian, even though they listened to his *Rabbana* that was broadcast during the month of Ramadan.[2] This corroborated the situation in my own neighbourhood of Tehran. His voice was always there, it was part of our culture. Everybody knew his *Rabbana* or his tasnif from *Sepideh* but they didn't know Shajarian the individual, the name. He also sang some revolutionary songs for Iranians, not for the revolution, not for the mollahs, because he was very careful. He never chose those words. He didn't like the fact that some of the words he chose were used to promote war and other propaganda and complained about it several times.

During my army service I was once assigned as the temporary chauffeur for a mollah. I had to drive him around and I was trying to learn something from him in the process, and I indeed learned a lot. I gave him a copy of *Bidad* and he never returned my tape. When you give something to a mollah, he will never return it to you; and he even told me that, explicitly. I later asked him "what do you think about the singer?" He didn't answer at first. They never answer to anything that falls outside their practice or expertise, that's one thing I've learned from them. After asking him a second time on another occasion he said something curt and brushed me off. And then the third time, when I insisted, and he knew he couldn't deflect me and that I would keep asking him, he said that "he has in fact a very good voice," because these clerics have their own vocal tradition and know something about singing, and then added "but he's a *shaytan* (Satan) and he's going to affect people." So he didn't like the tape because he knew the consequences—the mollahs know Farsi very well and knew that Shajarian was actually playing with Hafez and describing what was really going on in our society.

Throughout the performance examples of this book, italics indicate beyts (couplets) included in the following discussion and accompanied by transcriptions.[3] The order of beyts marked with an asterisk was reversed by Shajarian from the original.

Hafez ghazal #164[4]

We don't see friends among the people—what happened to friends?
How did friendship end? What happened to friends?

The water of life became clouded, where is happy-footed Khezr?[5]
Blood drips from the stem of the rose—what happened to the spring breeze?

No one says that friends know the real meaning of friendship.
But what is the state of those who know the truth? What happened to friends?

It's been years since the mine of virtue last yielded a ruby.
What happened to the warmth of the sun, and the works of the wind and the rain?

*This place was once the "city of friends" and the soil of the kind ones.
When did kindness end? What has happened to our "city of friends?"*

**Hundreds of thousands of roses bloomed but no birds called out.
What happened to the singing birds? And what happened to the hundred thousands?*

*They threw the ball of grace and generosity into the playing field of life,
But no one has come to the field—what happened to the horsemen?

Venus's *'oud* plays nothing well unless it is burnt.
Has no one tasted drunken Bliss? What happened to the drunkards?

*Hafez, no one knows the divine secrets. Silence!
From whom can you ask what has happened to this wheel of fortune?*

Interlinear translation of transcription excerpts:
Yāri   āndar   kas   namibinim   yārān rā che   shod
A friend in   person   we don't see friends   what happened
We don't see a friend among the people—what happened to friends?

Dusti   ke   ākher āmad dustdārān rā   che   shod
A friend that   end   came friends   what   happened
How did friendship end? What happened to friends?

Shahriyārān   bud o khāk mehrbānān in diyār
city of friends/monarchs was and earth kindnesses this region
This place was once the "city of friends" and the soil of the kind ones.

Mehrbāni ke   sar   āmad   shahriyārān rā   che shod
Kindness   that end   came   city of friends/monarchs what happened
When did kindness end? What has happened to our monarchs?

Sad   hezārān   gol   shekoft   o   bānge morqi bar nakhāst
Hundred thousands rose bloomed and   call   bird   up not wished
Hundreds of thousands of roses bloomed but no birds called out.

'Andelibān   ke pish amad hezārān rā   che shod
Nightingales   that before came   thousands   what happened
What happened to the singing birds? And what happened to the thousands?

Hafez   asrār e ilahi   kas   namidānad   khamush
Hafez secrets of divine person doesn't know silence
Hafez, no one knows the divine secrets. Silence!

Az   ke   miporsi   ke dawre   ruzgārān rā   che shod
From whom asking   that circle   times/fortune   what   happened
From whom can you ask what has happened to this wheel of fortune?

AK

Shajarian introduces the poem with a tahrir that begins with the almost inaudible words "*ey dād*," literally "oh cry for justice"; and ends with "*ey amān*," literally "oh sanctuary," a cry for quarter or mercy. Both expressions signify oppression and a yearning for liberation at the same time. Shajarian places the melisma between these two expressions, which sets the stage for what he proposes to convey in the singing of the text that follows. The poem sung is always capable of several obvious interpretations and an infinite number of others. Two obvious interpretations of this ghazal of Hafez are the following: the poet is an abandoned, lonely soul who has lost all those that he loved; or, alternatively, that the poet is speaking of a spiritual station where one is alone, spiritually; or both of these scenarios at once. The more skilled the artist of avaz, the greater the detail and variation with which he can express his message while using the same set of words. Here Shajarian uses the words of this poem to express a specific message of sorrow and disillusionment under the yoke of oppression. Specifically, he is using the power of the poem to express a political view. It is quite possible that Hafez himself was making a political statement; however, Shajarian is not trying so much to tell us what Hafez is saying, as he is using Hafez's words to tell us what he wants to tell us. Shajarian makes those words his own through the sound designs he uses in expressing them. This is the art of the avaz: to use a poem to express the meaning that you want. It must be noted that, throughout, Shajarian places a great deal of emphasis and care in sounding and enunciating each word in its fullness and in the correct accent. Each word is not only a tool but the sound of the meaning itself; as such, it is handled with exceptional clarity and care.

The first *misra* (line of a couplet) is repeated differently to express different feelings. The repetition of words and phrases, the enunciations of words, the tenor or mood with which the word is uttered, etc., are all tools that are used to convey the desired meaning. The first time the line is sung, Shajarian employs vocal inflections that convey regret to me. Through varying the manner in which it is sung, the word for "friend" is used as a noun to make the remorseful refrain

that the poet has no friends. The second time, the word "friend" is used differently (*yāri* can mean "a friend" or "friendship/help"). In the first rendering of the line,
the second part is repeated. This repetition does not occur in the second appearance of the line. At first, "what has happened to friends" is sung with passive
connotations. When it is repeated, it becomes more aggressive. Iranian culture is
one in which one's true desires are always bound by social artifice, politeness,
and manners. The first appearance of the line is sung so as to express the passive
aggressiveness of a man who has a burning question, which he wants to pose
politely and free from political reprisal. The second time eliminates some of the
restraint and more outwardly expresses the aggression of one demanding answers. The second singing of the entire line expresses, in its essence, more questioning rather than remorse. In this second delivery of the word *namibinim* ("we
don't see") Shajarian rests on the word for a longer period of time, expressing a
sense of the passage of time, as if to say "it has been long since we have seen a
friend." He follows this by posing the question of "what happened to friends" in a
way that suggests a more hopeful question, awaiting an answer. He also sings the
words "*che shod*" or "what happened" to also ask, perhaps, what happened to the
friendship which existed within, rather than what happened to the friends physically. The second *misra* also has two parts. In the first part of the line, where he
asks "how did friendship end?" he sings the word "friendship" in such a way that
the sound of the word resembles what he believes its meaning to be: perhaps
tenderness, soulfulness, pain, and uncertainty. The general feeling has returned
to one of remorse. He also inserts a hidden rhythm, a micrometrical section of
regular accent tying the words "friendship" and "end" together.

Turning to the fifth beyt (the gushe Oshaq in the seventh avaz section) the
word *shahriyārān* can mean either "the Kings" or "the city of the friends/helpers."
Mehrbāni can mean either "kindness" or "the guardians of the faith; the holy." Depending on which interpretation of the word is chosen, two possible translations
follow:

> 'Twas the city of friends, the soil of the kind, this land
> When did kindness end, where is the city of friends?

> or

> The land of Kings, the soil of the holy was this land
> When did holiness end, where are the Kings?

Furthermore, "holiness" can be substituted for "kindness" and "kings" for "the
city of friends/helpers" in any combination. Thus, the very words of the poem are
open to various different interpretations and are very sensitive to the manner in
which they are sung.

Bidad

2: Bidad

yā - ri ān - dar kas na-mi - bi - nim yā - rān - rā che

shod yā - rān -

rā che shod yā - ri ān - dar kas na - mi -

bi - nim

yā - rān - rā che shod

dus - ti ke ā - - kher ā - mad du - stā -

rān - rā che shod kho - da ya del

la akh da ai dust

7: Oshaq

shah - ri - yā - rān bud o khā - ke mehr - bā -

nān in di - yār mehr - bā - ni ke sar ā - mad

(n) shah - ri - yā rān - rā che shod do

(n) a yi kho - da

a yi a

9: Forud

(n) sad he - zā - - - rān gol she - koft o

sad he - zā - rān gol she - koft o

bān - ge mor - qi bar na - khāst

(n) bar na - khāst an - de - li - bān - rā che

Forud to Shushtari

pish ā - - - mad he - zā - rān - rā che

shod

che shod che shod

(The complete example is posted at www.yorku.ca/robsimms/shajarian)

Shajarian lowers the intensity of the regret and questioning here through his selection of the part of the melody of the gushe Oshaq he uses. He replaces the outright questioning with an element of reasoning, the music and the words begin to be a vehicle for giving news of something and offering an explanation or an answer. Each word is intoned in the manner of a "town crier" giving news of an event. Interestingly, he emphasizes the word *diyār* ("land, region"), which points to the political tenor of his message. The word *diyār* stems from *deir* which is the Zoroastrian circle of worship. This could be a rejection of the Islamisization of the land and a reference to the ancient religion of Iran prior to the Arab invasion.

In Hafez's poem, the two parts of this line are almost mirror images of each other: the positioning of *shahriyārān* and *mehrbāni* is reversed in the second *misra*. In the second half of the line, Shajarian returns to the original theme of regret and questioning, placinging those sentiments on the question "where are the Kings?" There is, however, no reduction of intensity in this switch. In fact he raises the level of intensity, crowning it with the most sophisticated form of tahrir which, again, contains allusion to the word *dād* but now also the interjection *ay Khoda*, "oh God." In Iranian culture the expression "oh God" is used to signify many different meanings, the most common of which is one seeking redress and justice— one of the central themes in Shajarian's message of *Bidad*.

RS

The first side of the cassette *Bidad* features polyphonic framing compositions to Shajarian's avaz in the gushe Bidad, accompanied by Meshkatian on santur, and a concluding tasnif in Homayun; the second side features Bikchekhani's tar solos and accompaniment of avaz in Homayun with *morkab khāne* modulation to Shur, and concludes with a tasnif in Bidad. Bidad was recorded in 1982, Homayun in 1984. The original release of the album was fully titled *Bidad (Homayoun)* but it subsequently became known as simply *Bidad.*

Bidad is unquestionably Shajarian's most popular and renowned recording. In fact, it would be difficult to challenge the assertion that *Bidad* is the most emblematic Iranian recording of the twentieth century. Nothing comes close to it in symbolic resonance, supreme artistry, and fame throughout Iran and the diaspora. In During's review of postrevolutionary musical culture, he describes the reopening of Rudaki Hall, renamed *Vahdat* ("unity, solidarity") Hall, to concerts since the first year following the revolution:

> Concert activities only really recommenced during the year 1988. The most notable concerts were probably those given by Mohammad Shajarian in December 1988. Six evenings were planned, but after the third, the security services were completely overwhelmed by the crowd of fans, whose numbers were several times larger than the capacity of the space. The entire area of the Talar-e Vahdat was invaded and tickets resold at astronomical prices. During a concert the audience began calling for a piece entitled Bidad (lit.

"injustice," "misfortune"), previously published on cassette; two thousand
people chanted this word with an enthusiasm rarely seen before. The artists
were covered with flowers to the neck and the cheering did not stop. One
wouldn't anticipate that a singer, accompanied by two or three instrumentalists, could so mobilize the masses and provoke such a passionate reaction. It
is true that this event occurred after years of war, deprivation and suffering.
(During, 1992:142–43)[6]

The album became an attractor that powerfully embodied public sentiment. By
the early 1990s, it was totally understandable that, when Shajarian was asked to list
what he personally felt to be his best recordings, the interviewer added "excluding
Bidad" in order to make the question more meaningful (Shajarian 1993:44). By the
2000s the album had become truly legendary. It has been reprinted and repackaged
by Delawaz continuously since 1985 and has two separate releases on Western labels (al Sur and World Village [the latter only the A side]), an extremely rare, if not
unprecedented occurrence for a recording of "nondidactic" Persian music in the
West. Aside from the specific contextual and technical points discussed, the performance is extremely passionate and moving, possessing an inspired energy that
makes it stand out as one of Shajarian's greatest performances.

The poem Shajarian chose poignantly expresses deep disillusionment, hope-
lessness, loss, and resentment. Hafez lived through lean and unstable times following the brutally chaotic Mongol invasions, which would have been fresh in the collective memory. Though written six hundred years ago, the ghazal powerfully resonated with the sentiments of many Iranians in the 1980s—the two periods occupied a
common position in the cycle of stability and extreme strife so characteristic of Iranian history. While this historical resonance is dark, "misery loves company," and
some may also have found a comforting element of solidarity in being reminded
of the strife and dysfunction of Hafez's time that inspired him to write this ghazal
six hundred years ago.

Bidad, the mode to which Shajarian chose to set the poem, is a *shahgushe*
from dastgah Homayun which translates as "injustice, oppression, cruelty." That
Shajarian centers his performance on this gushe outside of its usual context in
dastgah Homayun is exceptional in terms of conventional practice. While it is
theoretically possible, even aesthetically desirable, to single out any gushe in the
radif for exclusive performance, this is rarely done. Exceptions to this are certain
modes that are on the verge of rising to primary modal status. Gushes such as
Mokhalef of Segah, Bayate Kurd of Shur, and Shushtari of Homayun have a certain
independence that is analogous to the derivative avazes (*mote'alleqat*) of Bayate
Esfahan (from Homayun) and the Shur derivatives Abu Ata, Afshari, Bayate Tork,
and Dashti, which probably underwent similar gradual separation. Although an
extensive gushe with generous scope for development, Bidad is not usually treated
independently. As Shajarian includes other gushes that function as satellites of Bidad
(i.e., Bayate Raje and Oshaq) and others that follow Bidad in the radif (i.e.,
Shushtari), one could also view his rendition as a performance of Homayun starting

half-way through the dastgah, omitting the daramad and Chakavak. While this is interesting from a purely musical perspective, Shajarian's intentions extended quite beyond this to a deeper symbolic deployment of the gushe when combined with Hafez's poem.

Shajarian devised here a most ingenious means of publicly criticizing the revolutionary regime with personal impunity, alluding to its hypocrisy by using the limited resources legitimized by its own ideology. The regime exercised strict and repressive censorship of all nonrevolutionary and nonnationalistic expression, and it extolled all cultural values that were "purely Iranian." As we noted earlier, Persian music actually benefitted from this policy in many ways. While Shajarian's message was glaringly obvious, he was doing nothing but coupling a ghazal of Hafez—Iran's prized cultural icon—and an important gushe from the traditional modal canon that "just happened" to have an unsettling name; the nomenclature of the radif contains a fair number of gushes with such semantic allusions.[7] The alibi was indeed sound: he was simply doing his job, nothing outside the traditional aesthetic and practical boundaries of the art of avaz. As a teller,[8] he was also doing the archetypal job of oblique criticism.The album cover seemed innocuous enough and typical of the period—a bird standing beside a tree branch. But the branch is thin, naked, pointing downward and wintering, the bird is grounded and bowing down, and the rich panoply of colours (reminiscent of classical miniature paintings) that were the norm for cassette covers, are here reduced to a narrow, sombre range of browns, beiges and creams, furthering the impression of cold austerity, evoking the bareness of late fall (photo 4). The original edition of *Bidad* was published with a cassette-sized mini-pamphlet written by radio broadcaster Bahman Bustan advocating that music should be serving music, thereby initiating an extensive public debate on the relationship of music and poetry among musicians over the following years. Shajarian's position on the matter couldn't be clearer.

The theme of Shajarian's brilliantly selected ghazal, cogently encapsulated by the gushe name so loudly announced on the album cover, pushed buttons that cut deep into Iranian collective consciousness.[9] The revolution brought forth a perversely ironic reversal of archetypal sacred-secular roles with regard to justice, in which secular power traditionally cast a yoke of oppression over religious righteousness:

> The Iranian Shia, however, must go beyond individual submission [to the will of the Imams]; there must be a feeling of retribution and justice. . . . These two opposing forces of justice and oppression are constantly being contrasted in religious texts and sermons and in the daily thoughts of Iranians, thoroughly pervading the Iranian consciousness. They are also a major tool for expressing the conflicts between secular and sacred institutions which result from the dominant Shi'a opinon that a government not ruled by an Imam is illegitimate. . . . The essential conflict becomes described as the dominant "unjust" in conflict with the submissive "just" through whose suffering and submission freedom comes with the promise of final justice. (Reckord 1987:21–22)

Shajarian's album thus brought into clear, massmediated public focus the breath-taking hypocrisy of the brutal theocratic regime, calling upon Hafez and the radif as his star witnesses. The call was dangerously seditious, as it is historically and archetypically, mythologically a call for redress. Shajarian delivered it with great power and compelling beauty.

Beginning in avaz section 3, the *shahed* (literally "witness"; the modal "tenor" or "dominant" pitch) shifts from the second degree (D) to the fourth (F), which becomes more established in section 4, marking the clear move to Bayate Raje. There is a clear modal shift in section 5 to Oshaq, with its chromatic alterations. While Bayate Raje and Oshaq are implied in subsections of Bidad in Boroumand's and Ma'ruffi's radifs, only Karimi presents Raje as a separate *gusheh*; Oshaq is given a separate and extensive development only in Ma'ruffi.[10] Oshaq, or depending on one's perspective, the *oj* portion of Bidad, occupies four sections (5–8). Section 8 represents the climax of the performance in terms of melodic apogee, meaning of the text (as discussed above by Amir Koushkani) and sheer emotional intensity. Further exploiting the technique of aligning gushe nomenclature and poetic text, Shajarian sets these key lines to Oshaq ("lovers"), an epithet often used synonymously for Sufis, which here functions as a semantic foil for the injustice of Bidad.

Section 9 is a structural descent (*forud*) from Oshaq (and is similar to Ma'ruffi's Oshaq *forud*), which subtly shifts by way of Karimi's Raje *forud* to Shushtari, which is clearly established in the following subsections. The *forud* divides the *misra* and highlights the text: "What happened to the (hundreds of) thousands?" While this phrase can mean a number of things,[11] I cannot help but think of the untold thousands of lives lost during the Shah's rule, the Islamic Revolution, and the war with Iraq. It is reasonable to suspect that some of Shajarian's audience might arrive at a similar association. Following this reading of the line, the musical release of tension and dramatic descent functions in a manner similarly found in Western practices of word painting. At the conclusion of this section, the ensemble plays a composed interlude, stylistically related to the opening composition and Shajarian returns with a substantial section of Shushtari, the concluding beyts featuring a denser distribution of text and a levelling off of the great intensity gathered through the Oshaq section. With the dramatic balance restored the final *takhalus* beyt of section 12 is delivered with an eerie mix of calm repose and dazed, exasperated reflection. There's nothing more to say and no one to ask. So *khamush*, silence . . .

After a short silence the substantial avaz of Bidad is followed by a wonderful tasnif composed by Meshkatian in Homayun, set to another poem by Hafez (#99) employing the refrain *yād bād* ("recall"). The poem adds to the sentiment of loss and grief established in Bidad, as illustrated by the translation of the following beyts:[12]

> That day of friendship when we met—Recall;
> Recall those days of fond regret, Recall.

As bitter poison grief my palate sours:
The sound: "Be it sweet!" at feasts of ours Recall.

And now while fettered by misfortune's chain,
All those who grateful sought my gain Recall.

And crushed by sorrow that finds no relief,
Those who brought solace to my grief Recall.

This concludes the first side of the cassette, echoing the sentiment of Bidad while establishing Homayun proper, which begins on side two of the album (but the tonic pitches of the two performances, recorded two years apart, are different: G here and D on the following side).

Performance Example 2: *Homayoun*

If the poetry of *Bidad* and the transitional tasnif expresses grief and exposes "the problem," in addition to heaping on further devastating criticism, the following side of the album offers hope and advice about how to deal with these turbulent times. Hafez's advice, powerfully seconded by Shajarian, is to forbear, be patient, and shrewd; times will change and we must hold onto knowledge and keep faith in ourselves. The beyt numbering indicates their order in the original poem.

Hafez ghazal #271

1. If the gardener must have the company of the rose for five days,
He must have the patience of the nightingale against the tyranny of the thorn of
    separation

2. *Oh heart, don't cry and be distressed because you're in the knots and bonds of his*
    locks,
When the shrewd bird falls into a trap, it must be patient.

4. *What concern does the rend have for seeing the benefit of his actions?*
You need tact and reflection for the work of that realm.

3. Flirting glances with such curls and visage as her's is forbidden,
Those people who do so need the jasmine face and hyacinth curl indeed,

5. *In the Sufi way, relying on piety and learning is infidelity,*
Though the wayfarer might have a hundred different skills, trust in God is necessary.

6. The flirtations of that bursting narcissus eye must be endured,
So long as this distraught heart needs that curl and lock of hair.

7. Oh Saqi, how long till the cup comes round again?
The cycle of continuity and sanity must fall again on lovers—when?

8. Who is Hafez that he will not drink wine without the sound of the harp?
Wretched lover, why must he have so much patience?

Hafez ghazal #285

1. My heart became disillusioned and I'm distracted—I'm a darvish
Who came forward to that bewildered victim,

2. For the head of my own faith I am trembling like a willow,
My heart is at the mercy of the bow of an infidel's eyebrow.

4. In the street of the tavern I go, my head bowed and weeping,
Because I am overwhelmed with shame for my deeds.

3. Alas, I reflect upon the vastness of the sea
And wonder what's governing this drop of absurdity,

6. I boast of that bold, salvation-slaying eyelash,
On its point flows a wave of drinking water.

7. A thousand drops flow from the sleeves of doctors,
If they place a hand on the wounded heart for an examination,

5. The time of Khezr is no more, nor the kingdom of Alexander,
Oh darvish, don't quarrel over this lowly world.

8. Friend, you are a slave. Don't complain against friends:
A condition of love is not complaining over less and more.

9. Oh Hafez, with that jewel that finds refuge in the hand of every beggar,
The treasury overflowed from the treasure trove.

Interlinear translation of the transcription:
Ey del āndar band-e zolfesh   az   parishāni manāl
Oh heart into   bond-of hairlock-her/his from distressed wailing
*Oh heart, don't cry and be distressed because you're in the knots and bonds of
        his locks,*

Morqe zirek   chun be dām oftad tahamol bāyadesh
Bird   shrewd when to trap fell   patience it should
When the shrewd bird falls into a trap, it must be patient

Rende 'alm   suz   rā bā   masalhat bini   che   kār
Rend   world burnt * with benefits   seeing what action
*What concern does the world-burning rend have for seeing the benefit of his
        actions?*

Kār-e   molk ast ān ke   tadbir o ta'mol   bāyadesh
Work-of domain is that which tact   and reflection it ought
You need tact and reflection for the work of that realm

Tekye   bar taqavā o dānesh dar tariqat kāfr   -ist
Leaning on piety   and learning in the path infidelity is
Relying on piety and learning is, in the Way, infidelity

Rāharo gar sad   honar dārad tavakol bāyadesh
wayfarer if one hundred art   had   trust   s/he ought
Even if the wayfarer has a hundred arts, s/he must trust in God

The performance contains a remarkably long development of the Daramad, taking six long sections that together occupy almost half of the time spent in Homayun. Chakavak receives a fairly lengthy treatment as well, occupying five sections, some of which are very short. Bidad receives a comparatively short exposition, perhaps to compensate for the extended treatment on the first side of the album. There is a high incidence of rhetorical repetition throughout the Homayun section in general: almost every *misra* receives at least one repetition, which Shajarian exploits for word-painting potential.

While *morakab khāni* modulations are usually executed by means of certain pivotal gushes (*pul*, "bridge") that are common to both dastgahs, Shajarian moves directly to Shur here in section 18 after cadencing on A in the previous section of Beyate Raje. He drops down to D and centers on that pitch, which immediately functions as the fourth degree of Shur (on A) with the gushe Oshaq.[13] The last two beyts of the Homayun poem overlap into the Shur modulation, beginning with the question of "Oh Saqi! How long til the cup comes round again?" The musical changes of mode (Shur, the "most Persian" of modes) and tessitura dramatically

Homayoun

5: Daramad

ey   del   ān - dar   ban - de zol   fesh   az   pa - ri - shā -

ni   ma-nāl   ya   mor - ge zi - rek   chun be dām of - tad

ta - ha - mol   bā - ya-desh

ta - ha mol   bā - ya-desh   yā-rān

jān   na   na   na

da   akh

a   man

6

ey del ān - dar ban - de zol -   -   - fesh az pa - ri - shā - ni   ma-nāl

mor - qe zi - rek   chun be dām   of - tad

ta - ha - mal   bā - ya-desh a   la

na   he   de

na   he wa

mor - qe zi - rek chun be dām   of - tad   ta - ha - mol   bā - ya -

desh   a yu   ai dust

7

ren - de 'alm suz   rā

bā ma - sla - hat bi - ni che kār

8: Chakavak

(v) rend 'al - m suz rā · · · bā mas - la - hat · · · bi - ni · · · che kār

kā - re molk ast

ān che tad - bir o ta - 'a mol bā - ya-desh

a

a

da · · · · · · · · n wo

a - man a - man · · · · · · · kho - da va la

(The complete example is posted at www.yorku.ca/robsimms/shajarian)

emphasize this beyt. The overall effect seems to be one of quiet resignation. A new poem begins at section 20, the theme of which seems to oscillate between the helplessness of the Bidad ghazal and the solution of the one just concluded in the previous sections. The first beyt speaks of a disillusioned heart and bewildered victim, but also introduces the ways of the darvish (ascetic Sufi) in dealing with this. After excursions through a series of Shur and Shur-related gushes, Shajarian uses Abu Ata to proclaim the sobering observation and advice:

> The time of Khezr is no more, nor the kingdom of Alexander,
> Oh darvish, don't quarrel over this lowly world.

This bleak conclusion is punctuated with a long, textless forud back to Oshaq (resembling an instrumental Baste Negar *tekke*[14]) that plunges gently down to the quiet perigee of A.

The final section abruptly returns back up the octave to what is nominally identified on the album index as Shushtari but has a decidedly ambiguous scale. While the shape of Shustari is evident, the descending gesture from G features an F natural before discretely slipping in the F#, thereby effecting the return to Homayun. The avaz portion of the performance concludes shortly thereafter. The modulation to Shur was sudden and deliberately contrasting. The shift back to Homayun also employed a sudden shift of register but the impact was more tentative until the decisive appearance of the F#. This section sets the *takhallus* beyt, which extolls the value of selfless clarity, and finding the jewel of our own center. The cassette ends with a tasnif in Bidad (composed by Meshkatian), thus bringing full circle Shajarian's monumental statement of collective lamentation, self acknowledgement, guidance, and wisdom—delivered with an unlikely but powerful balance of raw emotion and intellectual brilliance.

AK

The first thing that struck me about the *Bidad Homayoun* recording—before I mention anything about the avaz—was that I very much appreciated the tar playing. Listening to Ostad Gholam Hossein Bikchehkhani on that recording was a supremely exhilarating experience, far superior to what I had experienced with other great tar-performers. I had never heard that name before and I remember asking Pirniakan "Who is he?", because they come from same city; my teacher replied that Bikchehkhani was indeed great. I said "I think he plays better than anybody else I've heard," and he agreed. Bikchehkhani was playing amazingly and I don't remember how many times I kept rewinding and playing the tape, trying to imitate some portion of it and I realized he was playing Ostad Shahnazi's *pishdaramad* with different accents. His accent sounded Turkish—Azerbaijani—which is a different kind of accent. It's very different from how Shahnazi plays that piece. So, among other things this recording is significant in that Shajarian teamed up with this great master shortly before he died in 1987.

Photo 5 dates from the time of the recording and includes the other artists involved with the performance of *Homayoun*.

There is a phrase in *Homayoun* that acted as a leitmotif for me personally, it helped me through all those very, very bad years of my life after the Islamic Revolution and during the madness of war, when I was doing my military service: *morghe zirak* ("shrewd bird") from that line:

> *Morghe zirak chun bi dam oftad tahamol bayādesh*
> "When the shrewd bird falls into a trap, it must be patient"

And I told Mr. Shajarian this the first time I saw him, I couldn't resist. I had tears in my eyes. We went for a walk and I told him that "the words from your voice—not from the book of Hafez—from your voice with those tones, with those melodies, that music helped me to stand up, to stand and wait." And it was true, 100 percent true. And I was so happy that I told him because I just kept repeating that line to myself when I was guard in the army. When I was patrolling I had to stay awake the whole night. When I was abandoned, restricted from going outside, from going to the city—I have to say it was like a prison. You have to stay there wherever you were stationed on the front. Being in the military is not easy in Iran. So after all these years I wanted to tell him that. During the time that he rose to the public's attention, Shajarian's work was very important for intellectuals, for students, for those people reading literature, writing, listening, and paying attention to art. Those people were thinking about what was going on and they were looking for something, for a solution. I think his voice was heard. He was speaking to a lot of different people, each with diverse needs and in different ways.

This second beyt of *Homayoun* is very beautiful. It means that when you are in trouble, when you are placed in chains, the best thing to do is convince yourself that you can handle this pressure. There is another level of *iham* here: if you are in love with your beloved you are in chains, if you're smart you'll be patient. The first *misra* starts with *ey del*, which refers to our intuition rather than our ratiocination. The symbolism of *zolf* usually refers to some connection with the beloved. So one possible meaning here, the Sufi meaning that would likely have been uppermost in Hafez's mind, is: if you are chained to an intellectual approach to understanding the mystery of our being, be patient and perhaps try to make a more intuitive connection.

But Shajarian brings a different meaning to this by highlighting certain words. He emphasizes the *ey del* with accents and the higher notes of the melody; when he repeats the line he shifts the emphasis to *zolfesh*. But the words *morghe zirek* get really extended, almost suspended in the line. This is the real point, to be smart, shrewd. He sings the word *manāl* with a direct word painting: a short tahrir that really evokes the notion of crying, wailing, which is what *nāl* means. Shajarian will never miss the opportunity that this kind of word presents. He also repeats and underlines *tahmol* on the repetition: patience, this is another key. The long terminal tahrirs are musical glosses of the line, reinforcing the mood, not the meaning. Reviewing the "tone" of the avaz up to now, the voice or role he's playing—this is advice. There's no regret, there's no pain. For me, the tahrir also backs up this function: I'm listening to someone giving advice. With each repetition of the line he's bringing out different nuances of meaning, different emphases. This is the art of repetition and if you're a good listener you won't get bored, each time is not the same or redundant, it's digging deeper and showing multiple possibilities of meaning and feeling. He obviously feels strongly about the message of this beyt to repeat it the way he does here.

Many people feel that the most outrageously seditious line in *Bidad* is the beyt from side one referring to *shahryārān*, but the following beyt here is more important because it identifies the fundamental problem with the Islamic Republic. Hafez is saying that clerics should not be part of the government or politics, that religion should be separate from temporal power. This interpretation refers to clerics, people who are turning their back on the world and praying to God all of the time, ostensible transcendentalists. *Maslahat bini che kar* refers to people reasoning and rationalizing in the world of politics. The way Shajarian sings the second *misra*, painting the text through the placement of emphasis, is pretty unequivocal for me. *Kār-e molk* is the work, the administering of this country—which entails reasoning, logic and organizational skills regarding the secular issues of economics, security, development, management, services, public works, and welfare, etc. These are specialized skills that the clerics do not have: they are self-declared "men of God." Real men of God are transcendentalists who shouldn't associate themselves with the business of secular politics and government. He's saying they're not qualified to do the job of running a country and they shouldn't even be in this position. Their job and specialization is praying, performing rituals and (ideally) serving on a spiritual level. Shajarian's delivery of these lines shifts from the advisory voice to one that is more accusatory and sounding distinctly angry. That terminal tahrir is pretty aggressive.

The next beyt he chooses from Hafez is also very dangerous. "In our path, if you are just relying on your piety and righteous abstinence—this is infidelity." Simply avoiding sin, obeying rules, and staying clean is not enough in the deeper spiritual path. You need more, you're a pagan. This is the criticism and advice to the clerics. *Tavakol* is a difficult word to translate but it includes the notion of humility: even if you have all kinds of knowledge and a hundred different skills, you still have to consider the possibility that you may be wrong. And Shajarian is shouting this to the mollahs.

If you just read this poem to yourself from Hafez's Diwan, you may not get this meaning or feeling from it, because your perception and interpretation is connected to your own level of consciousness and, ultimately, spiritual station. We can translate the poem into the Sufi path beautifully. Among other possibilities Hafez was probably referring to himself in this beyt. "Why should I worry about tomorrow or thinking about politics? I'm the *rende 'alm suz*, I've burned this world and my connection to it. All of these political issues and crises—I don't care." But this is a situation where a skilled and inspired artist invades the poem, takes it for himself and uses the words the way he wants. Shajarian is referring to the reality of the present situation in Iran and yet at the same time you know this is Hafez's poetry.

Performance Example 3: *Astan e Janan*

Regrouping, Veiled Dissent

"A tough time. An amazing business. A world turned upside down."—Hafez

OS
Astan e Janan was also based on these ideas [first presented in Bidad] *of complaint and the poetry chosen related to that. We couldn't make it more explicit, so it was full of metaphors, symbolism, and allusions. But the experts knew what we were speaking of.* (2009)

RS
Astan e Janan was recorded in 1982 in the Italian Embassy of Tehran,[15] one of the rare "public" concerts of Persian music held in the city since late 1979. It was an early public presentation of the veiled criticism so masterfully executed in *Bidad*, which was recorded around the same time but not released until 1985. In terms of its degree of veiling and potency of barb, it stands as an intermediary statement between the initial public foray of '*Eshq Danad*, recorded in 1981 in the German Cultural Center (but not released until 1997), and the *coup de grace* of *Bidad*. The *morakab khāni* routing of Bayate Tork–Bayate Kurd–Dashtestani featured in *Astan e Janan* keeps the modal journey within the orbit of Shur, perhaps reviving old school approaches to Shur before these derivative gushes achieved independent avaz status (which applies de facto to Bayate Kurd). Shajarian goes through an elaborate reordering of beyts, presenting to ghazals by Hafez to which *dobeytis* of Baba Taher are appended. Shajarian's reordering of beyts in the two ghazals by Hafez on this album is rather complex. The first ghazal (#157) proceeds: 1 through to 5, 4, 5.2, 6.2, 3, 7 (numbers represent the original beyt order; decimal places " .1 and .2" indicate first and second *misras* respectively). Two *dobeyti* of Baba Taher intervene before the dramatic modulation to Bayate Kurd and the beginning of the next Hafez ghazal, the beyts of which are ordered: 1, 2, 3, 7, 6, 5, 9. One can't help but think of Ostad Dadbeh as Shajarian ends the performance with a lengthy series of Baba Taher *dobeytis* set to Dashtestani.

While the performance itself was quasipublic, the album was not released until 1986 (i.e., after *Bidad*). The album cover features a mildy abstract painting by the renowned folk singer Sima Bina depicting a polymorphous flower/bird (a lily/dove?) set against a bare, walled surface in the lower portion and, like the cover of *Bidad*, what can be easily construed as wintering trees on the upper. A line from the Hafez ghazal set to the tasnif on the album (before the shift to Bayate Kurd), alluding to our potential for being conduits for a higher power,[16] is written across the cover of the original in elaborate calligraphy (see photo 6):

Bar āstāne jānān gar sar tavān nahādan
Gol bānge sar bolandi bar āsemān tavān zad

If you can be selfless in the court of souls
You can exhaltedly cry out to the sky

Hafez ghazal #157[17]

When might happy verse arouse the heart that's sad?
We recited one subtlety from this notebook and this is it.

From your ruby, if I found a protective ring,
A hundered realm of Solomon would be under my signet.

Oh heart, is it not necessary to be grieved by the scoffing of the envious,
Perhaps, when you look carefully, your good may be in it.

Whoever does not fathom this imagination-stirring pen,
Even if he were a Chinese-picture maker may his images be taboo.

The bowl of wine and soreness of heart, each were given someone:
In the circle of destiny this is how things are.

In the matter of rose-water and the rose, the decree of Eternity before Time was this,
That this one should be the adored of the market place, and that one kept in the cupboard.

It is not for Hafez being a rake has departed from the mind:
What has gone before will be until the Last Day

Baba Taher dobeyti

A head have I, which rests not
A sorrow have I, which ends not
Hey, look towards me, if you believe not
See the pain, a cure which has not

Pleasant is the hour when the beloved through the door shall come
The night of separation and the day of sorrow to an end shall come
I shall expel the soul from the heart with a hundred joys
So that, in its place, the beloved shall come

Hafez ghazal #45

The breast is wracked with pain. O for a soothing unguent!
Because of loneliness the heart's at the end of its tether. For God's sake,
  a companion!

Who from the swiftly shifting sphere may look for any comfort?
O wine-boy, give me a cup, for me to know some ease a moment.

I said to a clever wit, "Regard these states." He laughed and replied,
"A tough time. An amazing business. A world turned upside down."

No real brave comes to hand in the world of dust:
Another world must be made, and an Adam anew.

In the street of licentiousness, the self-satisfied and self-indulgent has no access.
It requires a world-burning voyager, not a raw one knowing no sorrow.

In the game of the Path of love, safety and repose are a calamity.
May that heart be scarred that in pain for you wants a salve!

What price Hafez's tears before the unneedfulness of love,
When in this deluge the Seven Seas seem a drop of dew?

Baba Taher dobeyti

Oh heart, from the hands of loneliness upon my soul
I wail with the woes and cries of my self's tones
In dark nights, from the pain of separation
Screams the marrow of my bones

Beloved ones, from the pain and sadness and separation
No light remains upon my eyes
I am entangled in the trap of distance and pain
No friend or mate, no acquaintance have I

When will the sky hear my weeping and wailing
With each turning it sets fire to my soul
A lifetime I spend with sadness and pain
The sky does not turn to the wishes of my soul

I do not know for whom the heart is mad
For whose drunken aspect is in bondage clad
I do not know, this lost heart of mine
Where it searches and in whose house it is

A heart I have for which there is no cure
Speeches I make profit it none
To the wind I throw it, the wind takes it not
In the fire I cast it, no smoke arises

My sickness and cure are from the friend
My union and separation are from the friend
If a butcher separates my skin from my body
My soul shall never be separate from the friend

I am the homeless sufferer
I am the ill-fated survivor
I am the wandering tumbleweed in the desert
Which runs before any wind that blows

I look at the desert, Your desert I see
I look at the sea, Your sea I see
Wherever I look, mountain, sea or valley
Signs of your elegant stature I see

I who am in a state of sadness, how should I not moan?
Broken-feathered and broken winged, how should I not moan?
Everyone says: "So-and-so, don't moan so much"
You come into my imagination, how should I not moan?

With a sigh, Elijah's dome, I burn
The whole of the firmament, from head to toe, I burn
I burn unless you build my work
What do you command, will you build or shall I burn?

The sorrow of your love raised me in the desert
Your distance made me a featherless, wingless bird
You told me to be patient, patience
Patience poured choice earth upon my head

Interlinear translation of the transcription:
kay she're tar angizad khāter ke   hazin   bāshad
how poem excite   mood   that sadness is
When might happy verse arouse the heart that's sad?

yek nokte az   in ma'ni goftim   o   hamin bāshad
one point from this meaning we said and the same is
We recited one subtlety from this notebook and this is it.

qamnak nabāyad   bud az t'an hasod ay del
 sad   not-necessary was from taunt jealous oh heart
Oh heart, is it not necessary to be grieved by the scoffing of the envious,

shāyad ke   cho vabini kheire to dar in bāshad
perhaps that when looking good you in this is
Perhaps, when you look carefully, your good may be in it.

ān nist   ke Hāfez rā rendi beshod az   khāter
it is not that Hafez * a rend became from thought
It is not for Hafez being a rake has departed from the mind:

kin   sābeqeyeh pish in tā ruz-e pasin bāshad
that this past record before this until day last   is
What has gone before will be until the Last Day

AK
The first beyt announces to the audience right away not to expect anything joyful when Shajarian's heart is so sad. The third beyt evokes the idea of destiny. Something happens to you that seems bad at the time but later turns out to have a very positive effect on your life that you couldn't see at the time. We have a lot of expressions for this in Iranian culture. It comes down to a showdown between my authority and God's authority. Sometimes God's authority and vision doesn't match with mine in a given situation, and it feels like a great pressure on me. But in the end,

Astan e Janan

2: Daramad Bayate Tork

(n) kay she' - re - tar an - gi - zad

khā - ter ke ha - zin bā shad

yek nok - te az in (ma - ni) (n) gof - tim o ham - in bā - - - shad

ha

akh na dad a - mān a - mān hay

jan a ay

a - man - - - - - - - -

qam - nāk na - ba - yad bud az ta' - ne ha - sod

de del shā - yad ke cho va - bi - ni

(The complete example is posted at www.yorku.ca/robsimms/shajarian)

God's authority is good for me. So in the middle of what seems to be strife and nega-
tivity, Hafez encourages us to not be sad—this is going to turn out good . . . maybe
(*shāyad*)! There is a contrast here between two types of people: those with less
knowledge and potential and yet they get rewarded, and those with a lot of knowledge and skill who have to suffer. Think of all of the people who really did some
thing for the revolution but who are now sitting in jail or relegated to somewhere in
the background of society while other opportunists who know how to "play the
game" have seized power. But there is a shift of perspective when one considers that
some higher good may result in the end. So his message, in a very hidden way for
those who could perceive it, was that all of the betrayal and suffering of the revolution *may* lead to something better. Maybe.

Shajarian sets this poem to Bayate Tork—this is surely his best recorded
performance of this mode—which is interesting because Bayate Tork is a somewhat
joyful mode and yet the poem is marked by sadness. At the third beyt he shifts the
emphasis of the melody so that it evokes Dashti, Afshari or perhaps Shekaste—
instead of degrees 1–2–3 in Bayate Tork, he implies 3–4–5 of Shur. Musically, his
rendering of this beyt has the effect of a suspension; you're waiting for something
else. This sounds a lot like folk music to me, the line is static. Even the tahrir starts
and stops and has a stationary quality. I feel that this feature emphasizes the notion
of "maybe" in the line. The whole ghazal is in fact a suspension. His style of singing
for his first rendering of the beyt stands out as quite different from the rest of the
opening part of the performance. This is the only beyt that he repeats in the whole
performance, which is quite long. I think there may be some autobiography in this
line for Shajarian, who perhaps found himself in a similar situation: that nobody
understands his art. The poem is very personal to Hafez and I think it may be for
Shajarian too. It's not about Sufism, it's about Hafez and his art in relation to society.
Remember that this concert was one of the first of its kind in postrevolutionary Iran,
by invitation in an embassy, and very isolated. It was a very exclusive audience, you
couldn't just walk in to this event. There were no concerts at the time, nothing. It
was a period of the worse chaos and violence. And then Shajarian "comes out"
during a period of severe lock down and highlights this poem with the power of his
avaz, giving colour to the words. He returns to this third beyt after singing the
fourth with even more emphasis on the word "maybe." That word has less weight
when you read the line by yourself and Hafez's original intention may not have been
to emphasize it. It seems that Hafez had more hope than Shajarian. But this is the
power of avaz. Shajarian's setting of the line has a more conclusive effect on the
repetition—more conclusively uncertain! There is a lot of doubt here. *Shāyad* is
brought out with a large leap and then repeated again with less hope in it on a lower
note.

In the *takhallus* beyt of this first poem, I think the word *rend*—which means
many things in different contexts—refers to someone who has the power of *iham*,
who can present different layers of meaning, complex messages with a few words.
So the advice he channels from Hafez for himself and for society in general is: don't
be sad, this still *might* work out.

Performance Example 4: *Nava (Morakab khani)*

Looking Inward and Outward

OS
Nava (Morakab khani) *had a more mystical quality that also exists in our poetry. It was our own state of mind which was not far from that of society at large. It was recorded in a private home, I think around 1982, so it was one of those private gatherings and since it was a good performance, Parviz composed some* [framing] *pieces and it came out as an album.* (2009)

RS
Nava (Morakab khani) is significant in a number of ways. Shajarian helped to "revive" the dastgah Rast Panjgah through his famous performance with Lotfi at the Shiraz Festival in 1977, so it was logical to complement this with a performance of Nava. His title buttresses Amir Koushkani's assertion that the dastgahs Rast Panjgah and Nava are *de facto* demonstrations of *morakab khāni* (Simms and Koushkani 2012), that this is an advanced stage of mastery that frees, opening up the tight structure of the radif to personal creativity. Shajarian uses this extended approach to modulation to more effectively evoke the poem but also to display a highly refined virtuosity, which was generally not cultivated by singers before (with perhaps the exception of Hatam Askari). It is also the first album in which Shajarian extensively explores his lower register, perhaps partially under the influence of Ostad Dadbeh. The album also shows a new attention to detail and subtlety: careful and complex articulation, a more abundant use of glissandi, ghost note initial attacks, a wider gradation of dynamics, and strategic use of rests and silence. Persian musicians generally associate dastgah Nava with mysticism—it is the most mystical mode, the mode of clarity—and the performance begins with a calm, subdued feeling of stasis that supports this. However, it also exhibits an undulating contour that alternates and juxtaposes opposite "energies": there are four separate *oj* sections, some in rapid succession, that contribute to making it the most complex intensity curve of those reviewed in this study (Simms and Koushkani 2012).

The recording is also unique in being accompanied exclusively by the ney, the mystical instrument par excellence. The accompanist is Mohammad Musavi, a fellow student of Dadbeh. While there are private recordings of *majles* that feature Shajarian singing long performances accompanied by ney, this is the only one released by Delawaz. Aside from the symbolic and austere ambient effect, performing *morakab khāni* with ney accompaniment presents its own challenges. The ney has its own idiomatic logic and restrictions in terms of possibilities for modulation—one of the main points of the album—which is quite different from the transpositional conventions of stringed instruments and vocalists; Amir Koushkani notes other important technical considerations regarding tuning below. Following the ensemble introductory piece, the first thing to strike the listener is the extreme "slap back" echo applied throughout the *saz o avaz*. While this was fashionable in Iran throughout the 1960s to 1980s, especially among ney soloists, nothing comparable appears on other Delawaz albums.[18] Perhaps it was meant to enhance the mystical atmosphere, providing a sense of space and otherness.

The album cover (photo 7) explicitly emphasizes interiority: a long view of inside a traditional stone house facing an open balcony that is barely visible due to the sharp angle; it appears to be sunny and verdant outside through the peek. The walls and floor of the house are entirely bare and beige, with cool blue overtones. While this plays nicely into the theme of mystical retreat inward, given the date it may also allude to being forcibly cloistered as an artist and citizen, exiled within the four walls of one's home. The gatefold opens to include yet another room with a traditional *takht* couch/platform upon which a daff and setar sit in silence. As pointed out by Amir Koushkani, the multiple rooms depicted in the foldout also allude to the practice of *morakab khāni*, to the potential for moving between musical spaces within the house of the radif.

While Shajarian emphasizes the mystical layer of *iham* in the poem, a political one figures quite prominently, as expounded below. The beyt numbering indicates their order in the original poem.

Sa'di ghazal #437[19]

1. Let us pass before Your face
Serruptitiously to look at Your good aspect

2. Joy there is in separation and difficulty in sight
That difficulty is better, for the endurance of Your joy we have not

3. If You do not face our face, the command is Yours
Come back so that we can spread our glance upon your footsteps

5. *You said the followers of my love are more than the dust*
We are not more than dust, we are less than dust

4. *Our vows to you are in such that if the people of my time*
Turn into foes and behead us, we will carry on our vows

5. *You said the followers of my love are more than the dust*
We are not more than dust, we are less than dust

6. *We are with you and without you at the same time, very strange!*
We are in a ring-shaped circle with you and we are also like a ring on the door

7. *Neither do we sense the scent of kindness from You, oh wonder*
Nor the face to cultivate the kindness of another

8. *From enemies are taken complaints to the friend*
Since the Friend is an enemy where and to whom shall we complain

9. We, ourselves, do not go running into anyone's noose
He takes us, within whose noose we are caught

10. Sa'di who are you? For in this noose's circle
So many have fallen that we are a meager catch

Sa'di ghazal #439

We are the paupers of the King's army
We are the citizens of the Beloved's breath

The bond-slave has not his own name
Whatever title they give us, that we are

Whether they spurn us or forgive us
We know not the way to another place

Since the peaceful-heart strikes the sword
We lose our heads and turn not our face

Friends, while in the mood for speaking of the beloved,
Throw gold and we throw our heads

To the God of intellect and knowledge
Say: don't criticize us for we know not

Any new flower which comes into the world
We are to its love as a peacock

Those with limited sight look towards the fruit
We are the spectators of the garden

You look at the beauty of someone
We are bewildered by the evidence of creation

Except the tales of the beloved whatever we have said
We regret it all, all the time

Sa'di, without the talk of the beloved
This whole world is meaningless

Sa'di ghazal #404

1. Should I suffer the sadness of the times or the separation from the Beloved?
With the endurance I do not have, which weight shall I bear?

3. Neither the power to look for a way past Him
Nor the strength to put Him aside in jest

2. Neither the hand of patience can I put through the sleeve of intellect
Nor the feet of intellect can I put through the skirt of rest

4. Since one can endure with patience the oppression of the enemy
Why should I not be patient to endure the oppression of the Beloved

5. Having drunk from the cupbearer's wine in the pure cup of union
I must suffer the headache of the drunkard

6. If a flower, like your aspect, should be found in the grass
I shall bear the thorns as I secretly watch it

Baba Taher dobeyti

Oh God ignite my soul with the fire of love
From that flame set a spark to my bones
Like a candle enlighten me from the fire of love
In that fire burn my heart like a moth

Thousands of sorrows upon my heart have I
In my breast, a burning fire, have I
With one sigh at dawn, from my aching heart
Thousands of pretenders, deafened have I

Interlinear translation of transcription:
Mā rā sari-ist   bā   to   ke gar khalq ruzgar
We * pledge-is with you that if ring   world
Our vows to you are such that if the people of our time

Dushman shavand   o   sar beravad ham bar ān sarim
Enemy   they became and head goes   also on that pledge
Turn into foes and behead us, we will carry on our vows

Gofti   ze khāk bishtarand ahl   'eshq-e man
You said that dust   more-are people love-of me
You said the followers of my love are more than the dust

Az   khāk bishtar ne ke   az   khāk kamtarin
From dust more   not that from dust smaller
We are not more than dust, we are less than dust

Mā bā   toim   va   bā   to nehim nist bo 'ajab
We with you-are and with you aren't isn't strange
We are with you and without you at the same time, how strange

Dar halq -im   bā to   o chun halqe bar darim
In   ring -we are with you and as   ring on door-we are
We are in a circle with you and we are also like a ring on a door

Ne buye   mehr   mishenavim az   to   aye 'ajab
No scent-of kindness we hear   from you oh   surprise
We neither see a sign of affability from you, and how astonishing!

Ne ruye ānke mehre   digar kas   bepervarim
Not on   the kindess-of other people we are following
Nor do we care to nurture anyone else's love

Az dushmānan barand shekāyat   ne dushmān
from enemies   takes   complaints not enemy
One takes his complaints from enemies to his friends

Chun dust   dushman ast shekāyat   kojā barim
When friend enemy   is complaints where take
When friends are the enemies, where can we take our complaints?

Nava (Morakeb Khani)

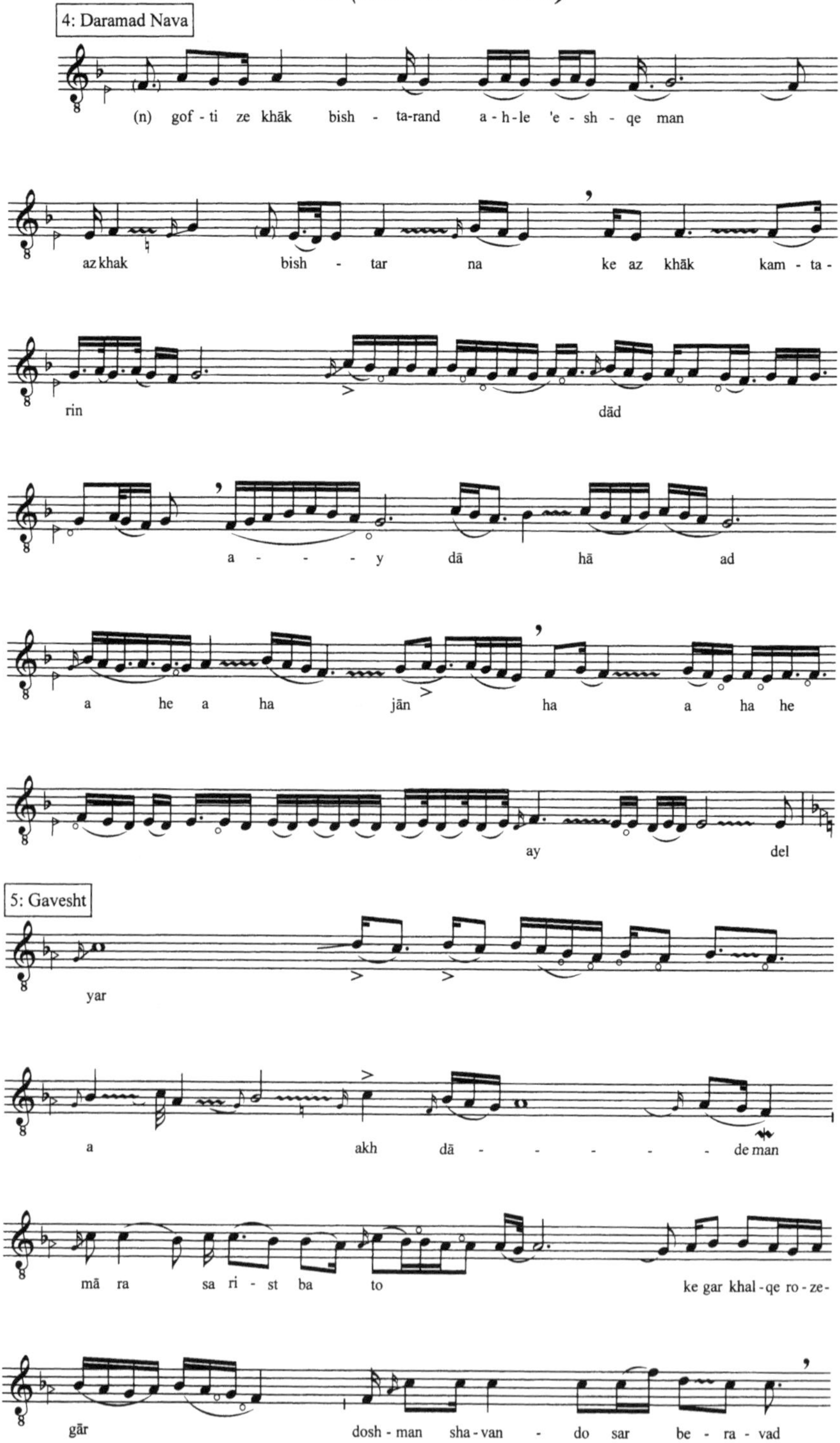

ham   bar - ān   sa-rim   a   yi

(forud)

hā   hā   hā   hā   hā - akh dād   a - mān   a   akh

dād   dā   ha   yi   ha

a   ei

6: Bayate Raje

kho-da   -   ye   del   ha

e   a   ha   akh   dā   ha - a - yi

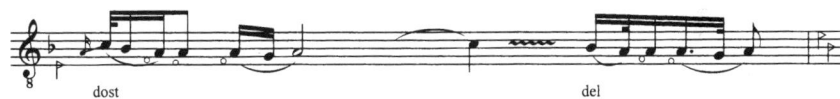

dost   del

7: Oshaq

mā - ra   sa-rist   bā   to   ke gar khal - qe   ro-ze-gār   dosh-man sha-van

do   sar   be - ra - vad   ham bar ān   (n)   gof - ti   ze khāk

bish - ta - rand   a - h-le   'esh - qe man   (n) gof - ti   ze khāk

bish - rand   a - h - l 'esh - qe   man   az khāk

bish - tar   na   ke az   khāk   kam - ta - rim

hā   hā

a   akh   a - man   i   n

ay ³   dād

9: Razavi

ma   ba   to   im   o   bā   to   ne - yim

int   bol - a - jab   dar   hal - qe - yim   -   ba   to

chon   hal - qe   bar   da - rim   na   yi   dād

wa

(The complete example is posted at www.yorku.ca/robsimms/shajarian)

AK

In my view, *Nava (Morakab khani)* marks an important turning point in Shajarian's avaz: there are so many changes, fresh approaches, and exploitation of potential held in the traditional materials that he opens up here. While Ostad Shajarian himself assigns the practice to his later albums *Yad e Ayam* and *Payam e Nasim* (early 1990s), *Nava* marks a decisive move toward integrating instrumental idioms into his singing: many tahrirs display an instrumental character, and he chooses to perform the gushe *Naghme*, which is traditionally an instrumental gushe with a rather unlikely vocal melody. Shajarian really mastered *morakab* modulation because he performed the avaz on this album with ney, which is quite daring because you can easily go out of tune on the ney without a string instrument to maintain a reference for pitch level. Musavi is of course a great master. We don't have so many ney players compared to other instruments because it's a technically difficult instrument to begin with and it's hard to stay in tune—there's a margin of pitch flexibility of at least a semitone. I don't know how they did it, but in this masterpiece *Nava (Morakab khani)* they stayed in tune very well. I also don't know how much preparation they had in making this recording but Shajarian often prepares the modulations on the album with a tahrir of vocables so they can lock on to the new mode; it's easier to establish a gushe without having to deal with the pressure of the text. The whole point of *morakab khāni* is to show a range of sudden changes and these tahrirs may have been deliberately included to help Musavi follow him; Musavi is clearly following throughout most of the performance. It also helps to prepare me as a listener to follow them both; the tahrir functions like a preview to the gushe that is about to carry the text. As always with Ostad Shajarian, the tahrirs also function to set the atmosphere and feeling of the text, contribute an abstract, left-brain musical gloss of the words.

There's an interesting symmetry and reversal of energy in the way Shajarian arranges and performs the third and fourth beyts—he sings them in order and then goes back to repeat the third beyt but presents it very differently. The third beyt is used to frame the fourth. He composed this structure in a deliberate way to make an oblique claim that is one of the most powerful examples of his word painting.

> You said the followers of my love are more than the dust
> We are not more than dust, we are less than dust

This framing beyt brings out nuances of meaning in Persian of the work *khāk*— dust, dirt or earth. The first misra uses it as an image of infinity, boundlessness: you (in a spiritual sense, God or the universe) told me that you have more beloveds than there are particles of dust. The second means "We are the lowest of your lovers, lower than dust, which is the lowliest thing on the planet." *Khāk* in Persian can connote servitude, so "we are your servants." Sa'di is playing with extremes of value, boundlessness, and lowliness through the image of dust.[20] His

initial rendering of this line expresses passive humility, just like the first appearance of the fourth beyt.

> Our vows to you are such that if the people of my time
> Turn into foes and behead us, we will carry on our vows

In the fourth beyt Sa'di plays with two meanings of *sar*, in the first *misra* it
refers to a vow, in the second, to your physical head. Shajarian is referring to himself here: "even if the government or other people are against me, I will keep my
promise, my pledge to service." And we can say now, almost thirty years after he
made this recording, that he has done this. The opening tahrir creates a mysterious atmosphere and he recites the first line in a passive manner, very matter-of-
fact. The terminal tahrir is a good example of his instrumental style, it's long,
florid, and unpredictable, quite outside of the cliché phrases that singers generally use. Though maintaining the same style he establishes a very different feeling
in the next section with the tahrir in Bayate Raje—using the word *Khoda*, God—
and repeats the line, though more forcefully. His first rendering was passive and
referring to the pledge but the second time here he's focusing on the enemies. He
then quickly turns to the next beyt that he sang directly, out of order from the
original but here deliberately framing the beyt we were just discussing.

Following this shift of energy and posture given to the fourth beyt on its repeat, he goes back to the third beyt with a feeling of more pressure and force,
which changes the emphasis of the meaning. He underlines the *gofti* ("you said")
here, as if reminding people of the original message or perhaps shifting the meaning to reminding hypocrites about their original message and pledge. It's less
passive and more of a claim or declaration. The meaning of servitude is not so
clear here: perhaps certain people who should be of service, aren't anymore, and
have lost their humility while others are being used. Or perhaps, according to
very subtle cultural sensibilities, he's speaking directly to someone or some
group, restating his humble pledge and then emphasizing their statement—I
didn't say this, you did. He then reaffirms that he is nobody, a servant, but responds with a hidden claim, as if to say "don't look at me like that, see what I can
do!" It's a challenge. The terminal tahrir is more aggressive and athletic, it picks
up the tempo and uses crisply detached articulation compared to the previous
ones, which featured a more smooth legato. So his tahrirs are really multitasking
in this work: they establish modes musically, set the atmosphere of the lines, and
are an expression of force. On a bigger scale, he's also backing up his claim by
showing his power of how he can work with *morakab khāni* as a singer on this
album. This is very deep and quite difficult to explain unless you've grown up in
this culture but Persians have learned to be humble and yet, meanwhile, they're
not humble! The way he sings these lines the second time around is not exactly
humble. This feeling continues and builds throughout the performance until he is
shouting at "them."

> We are with you and without you at the same time, very strange!
> We are in a circle with you and we are also like a ring on the door

The word *halqe* (ring) appears twice in the second misra, the first refers to sitting in a circle in the context of a Sufi meeting, the second to a door-knocking device. So the first is inside, intimate and connected, the second is outside requesting to come in. In the old days, doors traditionally had two kind of knocking devices, one for men (called *lingar*) and the other for women (*halqe*), each with a different sound so that you would know just from the knock the gender of whoever was outside. So the second use of the word expresses alienation by being outside the circle but perhaps also by being a woman in a patriarchal society. Listen to how Shajarian delivers these lines—he's very forceful, he's complaining. These beyts build up on each other into a growing outrage at being toyed with.

The following beyt uses the word *mehr*, which we know has a very loaded importance for Shajarian and other people. The ninth beyt speaks of betrayal and asks "what kind of a friend are you?" This claim has a specific meaning in Persian culture: basically you are against God. Of course, among other things there is an obvious political meaning to all of this. I think the climax, Shajarian's punchline—which I really love—is in beyts 9 and 10 of the second poem:

> Except the tales of the beloved whatever we have said
> We regret it all, all the time

> Sa'di, without the talk of the beloved
> This whole world is meaningless

It's a message of priorities and also to just retreat and remain silent unless you're going to address what really matters: love. Everything else is a mistake. This is a message from those old, trusted masters: in times like this, you should be quiet, this is the best way "to fight" for freedom and unity. Yes, make your claim, state your case, but then sit back and let it be, don't overdo it with words. This is one meaning of Mowlana signing off his poems with *khamush*, "silence." Direct that energy to paying attention to your internal enemy, your ego and your selfishness, because that will ultimately divide people. We all know who the real enemy is but there is also an enemy inside of each one of us.

Performance Example 5: *Dastan*

Looking Outward, Westward

OS

Dastan *was a project to showcase Persian music outside of Iran, and was per-formed four or five times in Europe by the* 'Aref *ensemble with Meshkatian. The poetry was more social and emotional and for the first time I designed some* gushes *and performed them: the* Masnavis *that I sang were very unique.* (2009)

RS

The paralyzing conditions for musicking in Iran by the late 1980s provoked Shajarian to seek performance opportunities outside of Iran. This was a time of silent, ferocious brutality. Nineteen eighty-eight witnessed the wholesale execution of an estimated 5,000 political prisoners,[21] a sickeningly sinister crime that is little known to the outside world—through secrecy, apathy, ignorance or all of these. Recorded in 1987, *Dastan* marks a decisive shift outward, whereby Shajarian's international tours began to get irrevocable traction beyond the initial "one-off" gigs, which were heuristic forays into this new domain. Discussed in greater detail in chapter 3, his bona fide tours constituted a new macro-occasion wherein he presented with the same piece throughout the tour.[22] The *Dastan* tour primed the pump and paved the way for longer and more regular tours, most of which also yielded live album releases on Delawaz. The touring-recording routine was a fruitful feedback mechanism for creative production and advancing his career through ever expanding territory. European gigs really took off in 1989 with a spring tour (accompanied by Pirniakan and Andelebi, performing works in Abu Ata and Mahur), and again in the fall with Meshkatian and the 'Aref Ensemble (performing Afshari and Nava). A concert in Paris on the latter tour resulted in Shajarian's first international wide-distribution release (on Ocora), which was probably also his first release on CD format. Beginning with *Dastan*, he would never look back careerwise. The precise transliteration of the title is *Dāstān*, which is a poetic form of *Dāstān*, "story, tale, fable" (Haim 1961:289, 302); it generously and unequivocally corroborates the narrative paradigm of avaz assumed throughout this study.

A few words are in order regarding the gushe designations of Bozorg and Masnavi Segah given on the track index of the Delawaz release. Bozorg is a gushe in Shur characterized by a repeated note gesture on the upper octave tonic and 7th degrees. The gushe is listed as occurring at the beginning the Masnavis (tracks 6 and 7) but there is nothing at these locations in the recording that would seem to resemble a transposition of Bozorg as it is conceived in the radif. Moreover, the two excerpts in question have the same name but bear no resemblance to each other. Perhaps the name, which means "big," is meant simply to emphasize the significance of the Masnavis, which Shajarian noted as being original compositions (and are discussed by Amir Koushkani below). We consider the designation Masnavi Segah to be a printing error, as the piece in question (indeed, the entire performance) is unequivocally set in Chahargah.

The excerpts discussed here are from the Iranian version of *Dastan* and include the avaz sections 1–2 (Daramad), 7–9 (Mokhalef), 11 (Masnavi Mokhalef), and 16 (Masnavi), the latter two sections presenting quite different settings of the same beyt.

Sa'di ghazal #374[23]

When you entered the door, I lost myself,
It's as if I had gone from this world to the next!

My ear to the ground, I wait for news from the friend,
When the messenger came I lost my senses.

I said that if I saw her again, it would still my eagerness,
But when I saw her I became even more filled with longing.

Like dew I fell before the sun,
My sun died and I rose up to the stars!

My hands had no strength to reach the friend,
At times I would rush to her on foot, and at times on my head.

To see her, and listen to her words,
I became all eyes and ears.

How can I avert my gaze from her,
It is to her that I owe my eyesight!

It was she who would not accept my offering;
It was I who wished to be her prey!

They say, Oh Sa'di, who has made your red face yellow?
The elixir of love mixed with my copper and I turned to gold!

Sa'di ghazal #130

Last night, far from your face, my soul burned out of grief for you,
The clouds of my eyes flooded my face because of melancholy over you,

Not from reflection of the intellect did the beggar see the inn of patience,
Not from the distressed heart did the love-crazed eye fall asleep,

The impression of your name praised the existence of the altar's heart,
Until dawn the praise-sayers kept the spirit in the altar,

I'd seen him leap—but they said to me: "Don't look at the face of the Friend!"
In the end I made it known that s/he was in the mercury,

My wheel of fortune lulled love, but the witness seemed missing,
I then remembered that the witness had pure, contaminated poison.

Sa'di, this road gets rough—the painful hypocrisy of love,
The first and the last had a bit of shallow patience.

Sa'di ghazal #492

The Heavenly Candle has risen in the East
O Saqi, pass me the ruby drink of dawn.

Take away reason, what use is it now?
I won't wake—let me dream and forget the world's strife.

Take my heart as a shield when stones rain from the sky,
Take my heart as a target when the arrows of evil tongues aim at me,

Like the Sufi and the corner of solitude, Sa'di wanders,
The artist doesn't make excuses for the dull and ignorant.

Interlinear translation of excerpts:
Az   dar darāmadi u   man az   khod be dar shodam
From door entered   you I from self   to door became
When you entered the door, I lost myself,

Gui   kaz in jahān be jahān be dar shodam
It says that this world to world   to door became
It's as if I had gone from this world to the next!

Gusham be rāh tā   ke   khabar midanad ze   dust
ear-my to road until that news   I knew from friend
My ear to the ground, I wait for news from the friend,

Sāheb   khabar biyāmad   o man bi   khabar   shodam
possessor news   came   and I without awareness became
When the messenger came I lost my senses

Man chashme zu che gune tavānam negāh dasht
I   eye   to   that sort I'm able glance had
How can I avert my gaze from her,

Ke avval nezar be didane u   dide   ur   shodam
that first look to seeing him/her sight him/her became
It is to her that I owe my eyesight!

U-rā   khod eltefat budesh be seyed-e man
He/she* self   favour   was   to prey-of me
It was she who would not accept my offering;

Man khishtan   āsire kemand nezar shodam
I   self   captive snare   look became
It was I who wished to be her prey!

Dush   dur   āz   ruyat   ay jān-e jānam az   qam tāb dāsht
Last night far from your face oh soul-of my soul from grief burnt had
Last night, far from your face, my soul burned out of grief for you,

Abre   chashmam   bar rokh az sodāye   to
Clouds my eye   on face from melancholy you
The clouds of my eyes flooded my face because of melancholy over you,

Ne   az   tafarkar 'aqle   maskin pāy-e gāh-e   sabr   did
Not from meditation intellect beggar foot-of place-of patience saw
Not from reflection of the intellect did the beggar see the inn of patience,

Ne   az   parishāni del-e   shuride chāshm-e khāb dāsht
Not from distressed heart-of frenzied eye   -of sleep had
Not from the distressed heart did the love-crazed eye fall asleep

Dastan

Daramad

az dar da - rā - ma - di (y)u man az khod be dar sho-dam

a   az dar da-rā - ma-di

yu man az   khod   be   dar sho-dam   (m) gu - i

ka - zin ja-hān be ja-hān   bi dar   sho-dam   a

akh   da

15: Masnavi Mohkalef

dush   dur   āz   ru - yat ay   jān   jā - nam az

qam   tāb   dasht   ab - re chash -   mam

bar rakh az   sho-dā - ye to   sey-lāb   dasht

16

(na) naz ta-fa - - - kar   (a) 'aq - le mas - - - -

kin   pā - ye gā - he   sabr   did

naz pa-ri   shā- ni   de-le shu-ri-deh   chash-me khāb

dasht   a

21: Masnavi

dush   dur   az   ru - yat   ay   jān   jā-nam az qam tāb   dāsht

ab-re chash-mam bar rokh az   so - dā-ye to   sey - lāb   dāsht

22

(n) naz   ta - far   kar   'aq - le mas - - - - kin

pā - ye gāh - e   sabr   did

naz   pa-rish-ā - de-le shu-ri - de chash - me khāb   dāsht

(The complete example is posted at www.yorku.ca/robsimms/shajarian)

AK

The first beyt of *Dastan* is very rich in meaning. The most obvious meaning of the word *dar* in this beyt is door, but it can also mean freedom in Persian literature (*rahāyi*). The translation from the CD that we adapt here is a very simple reading of the surface. Here is an esoteric interpretation of the first *misra*: my ignorance was a door and when you passed it, you opened it so that I could see you and at that moment I became free. It's not about you, it's about my consciousness; this becomes clearer later in the performance with passages that mention the Sufi path. He repeats this opening *misra* with slightly different emphasis but both times highlighting *dar* by leaping up to it. Then the next *misra* begins with *gui*, which literally means "saying" but here means something like "in other words" or "this really means" that because of this incident I've moved from one state of consciousness to a higher one.

This is "news," an important announcement. As Shajarian himself says, Chahargah is a heroic, epic mode, so it's a great vehicle, better than any other dastgah, for delivering news: the 6–5–6–5–6 . . . 1, 6–1 leap up to the tonic that is definitive of Chargah is announcing "Everybody listen to this." Shajarian really suspends the word *gui*, which you would normally gloss over quickly when reading. He tags it on to the first *misra* and then ends the phrase as if this really belongs to the idea of the first *misra*. He's saying "pay attention here, because this really means . . ." So the news is delivered through the words and then the tahrirs at the end of each phrase provide a musical, emotional commentary on the feeling and atmosphere of the announcement. This is an important general function of tahrirs, but in my view they also function to complete a melodic statement, fill in contours, goal tones and gestures that may not have appeared in singing the text, including features that are necessary to properly evoke the mode or gushe. It's a musical, modal consideration. So it makes sense musically but for me the feeling of this tahrir contrasts rather than supports the meaning of the poem. It launches upward and then immediately descends and gets stuck back on the tonic instead of moving forward, "onward and upward." The news is good, it has great potential, but as is so often the case with Chahargah, the news turns out to be an illusion, a dream—which is how I subjectively hear this. The forud of Chahargah always deflates the optimism built up, and unfortunately we are slaves to this. If Sa'di were listening to this he'd probably say "No, no, I want to go up!" The feeling is subtle at the beginning here but becomes more prevalent as the performance continues. The end result is a mixed message.

With regard to the gushe designations *Bozorg* or *Kuchek*, this can simply designate a "big or small" melody. A lot of names came into the radif after the Farahanis consolidated it; melodies were played in court and names probably got attached to the way certain performers rendered them: Javad khāni (i.e., "Javad singing"), Nasir khāni, Haji Hassani, Malek Hosseini, etc. So the musicians' names were used like a shorthand for their melodies and, as there was no concern with theory or objective description, the names stuck. Rather than developing a useful descriptive basis for Persian music, things went in the direction of complication by adding all of these names, which elevated it socially to some degree, showing that this is a complex sophisticated art.

When Shajarian starts singing the poem of Masnavi in section 11 it's like he's storytelling, which is a very different "voice" or approach than is usually used to recite Rumi's Masnavi. The traditional Masnavi style is quite static, constant, and continuous; there's no dynamic development or much in the way of contrast, and very rarely any leaps. It's pretty dramatic in section 12 when he leaps up to *"naqsha namat, karde del,"* his voice is amazingly expressive for these lines. When he injects such intense feeling in the words, it's like acting in *taz'iyeh.* He pays a lot of attention to expressive articulation of the words and melody. Because of this expression and the fact that he's in Chahargah it sounds a lot like *Shahnameh khani.* When he sings the *"Sa'di in rah moshkel oftad,"* the style is literally *rajaz* (the posturing oratory before battle[24]) or singing in a coffeehouse or *taz'iyeh.* I've heard this kind of singing but never in the context of avaz. The idiom and aesthetic is not from *asil,* it's from the other narrative genres.

The rhythm is also different from what you normally expect in a Masnavi because the *aruz* of his chosen poem is different from the standard one used for the Masnavis (i.e., *Raml:* - o - - | - o - - | - o -). Regardless of the difference in the actual rhythms from the traditional gushe models, you can nonetheless really feel the rhythmic energy in Shajarian's pieces, which is a defining feature of Masnavi and Rajaz. No one sings Masnavi like this!

The name Orjuze/Arjoze is synonymous with the more commonly used name Rajaz (the Mar'uffi radif; Miller 1999:79). Rajaz is not really a gushe, it's a style of "doing" Zabol and Mokhalef, a specific treatment but in the context of the rhythmic feeling of Masnavi. Using Farhat's terminology (1991), it's more in the category of a *tekke*—like Kereshmeh, Hazin or Zanguleh—but it's more restricted in terms of its distribution in different dastgahs (cf., Sufinameh, Hodi, Pahlavi). Hodi and Pahlavi are specific ways to treat Zabol and Mokhalef, respectively; Rajaz/Orjuze is similar to this.

The melody at the beginning of Shajarian's Masnavi (section 15) is totally original. I've never heard this before, it seems familiar, but I can't locate it precisely, it's new. It could be turned into a *zarbi* piece very easily, a tasnif in triple meter with a conspicuous upbeat. The glissando leap from E to B on the words *"qam tab dasht"* is completely outside the idiom of the radif and very dramatic and expressive. Shajarian later repeats the same beyts from the previous setting of Masnavi, which is paced faster here and evokes an entirely different feeling, opening up more possibilities of interpreting the meaning of the text.

I've been discussing specific features of these gushes but in terms of the bigger picture, Shajarian really breaks the usual progression of Chahargah—which can be annoyingly constant and monotonous—with a refreshing change of pace in these pieces. He visits Zabol and Mokhalef and also the same line of poetry but with a different feel and sense of movement. Shajarian composed these pieces: the melodies, their strong rhythmic character, the tahrirs with associated meaning, word painting, dynamics, leaps, repetitions creating a balanced form, etc. As they stand, there are no other pieces like them but his sources are clear. His composition is unique for avaz but it is not entirely new, it's an importation and hybridization. He's borrowing but he's really mastered what he borrows. If you played this recording for singers of these other narrative traditions they would say that it is a masterpiece of their art.

Performing Avaz and Oral Composition: a Comparative Demonstration

While it is always difficult to establish with any certainty the degrees and parameters of improvisation in a given performance, the technique of comparing "alternate takes" of recordings of a set piece, commonly used in the analysis of jazz soloists, provides some interesting insights into Shajarian's improvisatory practice (which is discussed in Simms and Koushkani 2012). Two versions of *Dastan* are available to us to make such a comparative study: a studio recording from Iran released on Delawaz, and another recorded live shortly afterward in Bonn in 1987 and released in 1991 on World Network (WDR LC–6759) targeting the then burgeoning Western world music market. Surprisingly, Shajarian was unaware of the existence of the latter release, one by which many Westerners were introduced to his music; such is the nature of the music business. The two recordings present the clearest empirical evidence that Shajarian conceives of his major works for touring and record releases as being very close to the notion of a Western composition—carefully constructed, repeatable, consistent, preset—and yet subject to great flexibility with regard to rhythmic and melodic details, ornamentation, inclusions and exclusions, and especially the creation of tahrirs. The program is not improvised avaz on the poetry of Sa'di set in dastgah Chahargah, it is "the piece" *Dastan*. On a given tour, he will repeat the piece each night, with performances likely featuring the range of variation evident in these two examples. In terms of the art of rhetoric, this is the creative-rhetorical process of *actio* of the same "argument."[25]

A comparative transcription of the opening sections of the two performances is given here, formatted to highlight their similarities and differences. The remainder of the complete performance is transcribed (twenty-six pages in total) and posted at www.yorku.ca/robsimms/shajarian. I have arbitrarily placed the German release on the top staff (titled DE), the Iranian on the lower (IR). As far as possible, I have aligned corresponding materials so they may be viewed simultaneously. The main objective has been to line up the phrases of text, which are sometimes set with varying musical phrases, juxtaposing similar melodic material, and aligning tahrirs, which are obviously of varying lengths. This necessarily involved occasionally distorting the flow of one performance in relation to the other, leaving spaces or compacting in one part so that each will align or "catch up" with the other. A blank space in one line indicates that there is no corresponding material in that performance. I have occasionally included arrows in such cases to remind the reader that the absence of a particular phrase does not mean that there is a gap (i.e., a *jawab*, or silence) but rather the immediate continuation of the next phrase; an arrow means that in realtime, the performance jumps straight to the following phrase. Avaz sections marked in squares in the margin are functional, and do not exactly correspond between the two performances: e.g., when viewed as separate transcriptions, the opening tahrir of Hesar (which is performed almost identically in both takes) is actually found at section 7 in *Dastan* Bonn and section 5 in *Dastan* Iran. Discrepancies such as this are due to extra *jawabs*, rhetorical repetitions, or tahrirs in one or the other performance.

My first impression of the two performances was their pervasive similarity. Shajarian's choice of gushes is the same in each, which are aligned identically in relation to the poems in the two performances. The instruments accompanying specific gushes and beyts are exactly the same. The overall form and shape of a gushe (which is both theoretically and practically open to variation) is the same. Often phrases are virtually identical or slightly varied but with the exact same pitch on a particular word (even syllable); melodic shapes and gestures, while varied, are almost always the same.

After more detailed study of the two recordings, however, the differences between the two performances seem equally striking. This is most evident in Shajarian's tahrirs, which are usually quite different in terms of centonic units, placement, and sometimes middle ground shape; they are generally more extensive in the Iranian version. While melodic material generally functions similarly in the two, there are many widely diverging phrases.[26] There are also many instances of material, usually tahrirs but occasionally other intermediary features, existing in one but not the other performance (again, indicated by blank spaces in the transcription). The German recording is in total ten minutes longer than the Iranian, which is due to differences in the tempos of composed pieces and longer *jawabs* in the live context of the Bonn performance. Also, section 20 of the German performance includes beyt that is omitted in the Iranian recording, showing another parameter of choice and variation in the process of *actio*.

Rather than describing the many variations here in the text, I will let the comparative formatting of the transcription speak for itself—designed as it is for detailed musical explication—and let the reader freely explore the similarities and differences of the complete transcriptions posted online in a performative spirit. One of the advantages of visual music notation is that it allows us to examine music "outside of time," in this case superimposed, which would be possible to construct through sound editing in an aural format but would be hopelessly messy and unintelligible. Repeated, detailed scrutiny of the comparative transcription gives a more accurate impression of Shajarian's range and degree of improvisatory practices than would aural editing or verbal description. Following the approach presented here, Shajarian's various renditions of the gushe Oshaq[27] would provide another productive field for gaining insight into his improvisatory practices that interested readers may wish to investigate.

When shown the comparative transcription and the differences in rendering the same lines, Shajarian responded, quite logically and understandably: "*It happens numerous times that I perform one phrase differently. Sometimes I give it a different expression right in that moment and I move on. . . . Most of the time, when I'm singing a tasnif, I have for example two bars to sing my tahrir. So depending on the occasion and my mood I will do different kinds of tahrirs.*"

Dastan
comparing two performances

2
gu - sham be rāh tā kha - bar mi - - - da - nad ze dust
gu - sham be rāh tā ke kha - bar mi - da - nad ze dust
sā - heb kha - bar bi - yā - mad o man bi kha - bar dam
sā - heb kha - bar bi - yā - - - mad o man bi kha - bar sho - dam (me de) a
3: Muye
gof - tam be - bi - nam - esh gof - tam be - bi - nam - esh
gof - tam be - bi - nam - esh gof - tam be - bi - nesh

ma - gar dar del - ti - āq sā - kan sha-vad
ma - gar dar del - ti - āq sā - kan sha-vad
(n)be - di - dam o mosh - tāq - tar sho-dam akh da
be - di - dam (o) mosh - tāq - tar sho-dam
(n) be - di - dam o mosh - tāq - tar sho - dam
akh da akh da
ha ei da jan

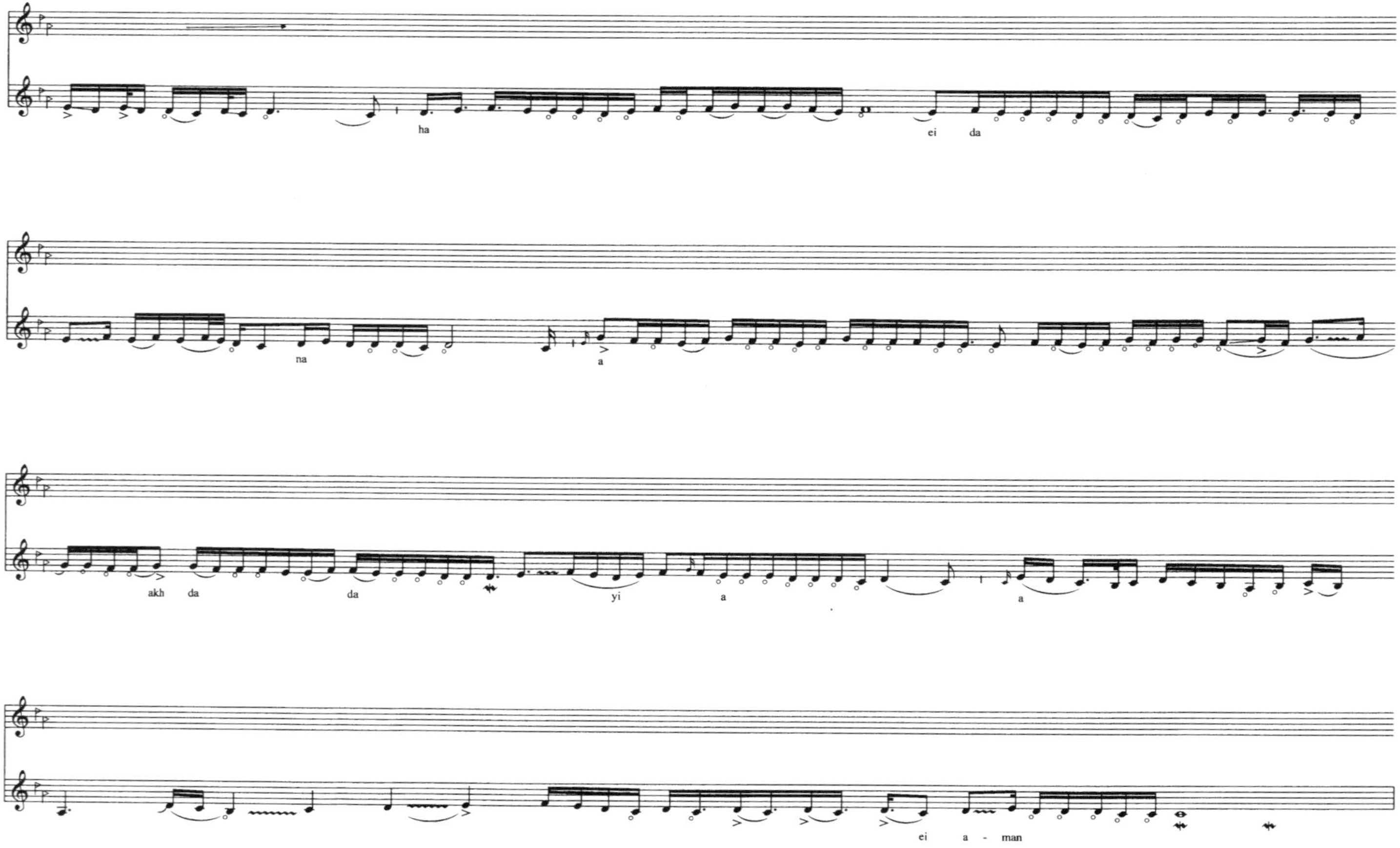
ha
ei da
na
a
akh da
da
yi
a
a
ei a - man

4: Zabol

Notes

1. See Simms (1996:289–303) for a detailed discussion and full transcription of this performance.
2. See chapter 2 of Simms and Koushkani (2012) for a full discussion and transcription of this famous recitation.
3. Our transcription method used throughout the study is discussed in detail in appendix 2 of Simms and Koushkani (2012). It generally follows the conventions of notating Persian music that have been established over the past half century, with a few added features. The ordinal numbers indicate sections of avaz between long instrumental jawabs and other breaks (tasnifs, composed ensemble interludes), which end with a barline. Dashes on the first line of the staff indicate larger phrases within the section; commas indicate shorter subphrases and pauses of relatively short duration. Beaming and flagging reflects both Shajarian's motivic vocabulary (discussed in chapter 4 of Simms and Koushkani [2012]) and rhythmic accent or stress, wherein the first note of a beamed unit receives a relatively stronger accent.
4. The numbering of Hafez *ghazals* throughout this book is from Correale (1980).
5. "Khezr is a mythical figure sometimes associated with the Biblical Elijah, believed to have initiated Moses in the ways of esoteric knowledge and guided Alexander through the realms of darkness to the fount of life" (Lewis 2008:34). Khezr is particularly associated with good fortune in Iranian culture.
6. A recording from one of these concerts was released by Delawaz in 1996 as the B-side of *Saz e Ghesse Gu* (sic) *& Konsert Bozorgdasht Hafez* ("The Speaking Lute & Tribute Concert for Hafez"). The period of these concerts corresponds with Shajarian's decisive move to Western tours as an outlet for dealing with the suffocating oppression in Iran.
7. A few examples include Shahr Ashub ("city disturber"), Koshte ("killing"), Shekaste ("broken"), Harbi ("warlike"), etc.
8. See our discussion of the role of tale, teller, and telling in Simms and Koushkani (2012).
9. Dabashi notes:

> The central thematic of ta'ziyeh as drama is the notion of *mazlumiyyat,* which is the defining aspect of Shi'ism itself. Mazlumiyyat constitutes the moral/political community in terms of justice and its aberration. Mazlumiyyat is the absence of justice that signals the necessity of its presence. For Shi'ites, the original promise of Islam to deliver earthly and eternal justice to the world is kept doctrinally alive in the charismatic figure of the Imam. In ta'ziyeh, Yazid and Imam Hussein, the two principal nemeses, have emerged as metaphoric representations of unjust power and the revolutionary mobilization against such tyranny. Mazlumiyyat is more an assumption than a notion. It means "having been wronged." Hussein's epithet is "Mazlum"; he is called "Hussein-e Mazlum," or "the Hussein who was wronged." But the trilateral Arabic root of mazlumiyyat, ZLM, means "tyranny" and "injustice" at one and the same time, combining the political and the moral. Thus two paradoxical principles are instantaneously summoned and metaphorically collapsed in the assumption of mazlumiyyat. First, it is a weakness that consti-

tutes power, a passivity that entails active agency; and second, it is a morality that surmises the political, a politics that summons the moral. (Dabashi 2005:93)

10. Both During (1991:68) and Zonis (1973:85) list Oshaq as essential to Homayun; Oshaq is found in all radifs of Bayate Esfahan, which is derived from Homayun.

11. *Hezāran* can also mean nightingales, a shortening of *hezār-dāstān* or *hezār-āvā*: telling a thousand tales or singing a thousand songs.

12. From Arberry (1962:97).

13. Shajarian uses this same modulation procedure on the album *Homayoun Masnavie*, recorded around the same time.

14. A term coined by Farhat (1991) to describe gushes with specific rhythmic and/or melodic formula that are generically transposed to various dastgahs throughout the radif (e.g., *kereshme, naghme, hazin, zangule,* etc.)

15. In an open air setting, as you can hear birds singing intermittently in the background from section 20 onward (in Dashtestani).

16. This layer of the *iham* is not unlike the concept of *mardomkhodāsāz* appearing in the mission statement on the Persian Delawaz website (www.delawaz.com).

17. Translation of both Hafez ghazals by Avery (2007); #45 is #461 in Avery.

18. This presented considerable difficulties for the transcription process and occasionally compromised the resulting accuracy of the transcription, which the reader should bear in mind.

19. Numbering of all Sa'di ghazals appearing in this book are taken from Mohammad Ali Farughi, ed. *Ghazāliyyat Sa'di*. Tehran: Qaqnus, 1382/2003.

20. The word and imagery of *khāk* take on increasing significance for Shajarian in the following decades, as discussed in chapter 3.

21. Claire Colley's book review of *Letters to my Torturer* by Houshang Asadi (Oneworld Publications) in *New Internationalist* 434 (July/August 2010), 33.

22. A fact I was not aware of in my 1996 study.

23. Translations of the poems are adapted from the World Network CD notes.

24. See chapter 2 of Simms and Koushkani (2012) for a discussion of *rajaz*.

25. See Simms and Koushkani (2012) for the relationship between rhetoric and avaz.

26. The *foruds* for Hesar (in section 6), especially in relation to the text, are rather different. This section was problematic to align; I ended up relating a small fragment of the Bonn performance to two different parts of the Iranian functioning as a pivot in a "double context."

27. Included in this volume and more comprehensively in Simms (2012).

1—With Hasan Kasa'i and master calligrapher Morteza Abdolrasuli, ca. 1980. Ostad Shajarian has generously given permission to use this photograph.

2—L-r: Sa'idi (singer), Ostad Shajarian, Reza Kasa'i, Ostad Jahansuz Dadbeh, Taj Esfahan, Hasan Kasa'i, Manouchehr Ghaouri (ney-player) in Esfahan, 1980. Ostad Shajarian has generously given permission to use this photograph.

3—*Original cassette cover for* Khalvat Gozideh, *recorded in 1980. Ostad Shajarian has generously given permission to use this photograph.*

4—*Original cassette cover for* Bidad, *released 1985. Ostad Shajarian has generously given permission to use this photograph.*

5—L-r: Jamishid Mohebi (tonbak player), poet Javad Azar, Shajarian, Ostad Bikchekhani, Parviz Meshkatian, ca. 1984. Ostad Shajarian has generously given permission to use this photograph.

6—Original cassette cover for Astan e Janan. Ostad Shajarian has generously given permission to use this photograph.

7—Original cassette cover and gatefold for the album Nava (Morakab khani). Ostad Shajarian has generously given permission to use this photograph.

8—Ubiquitous publicity photo, ca. 1987. Ostad Shajarian has generously given permission to use this photograph.

9—With Meshkatian and Pirnikan. Datsan European tour, 1987. Ostad Shajarian has generously given permission to use this photograph.

10—Questing for hāl with Pirnikan and Andelibi, early 1990s. Ostad Shajarian has generously given permission to use this photograph.

11—With Lotfi in Germany, 1997. Ostad Shajarian has generously given permission to use this photograph.

12—Crossing cultures with Homayoun and Azerbaijani Habil Aliyev in Tehran, 1991. Ostad Shajarian has generously given permission to use this photograph.

13—Performing at Shajarians presentation ceremony for the Picasso Medal in Paris, 1999. Ostad Shajarian has generously given permission to use this photograph.

14—Publicity photo for the Masters of Persian Music, 2000. L-r: Hossein Alizade, Kalhor, Ostad Shajarian, Homayoun Shajarian. Ostad Shajarian has generously given permission to use this photograph.

15—Soprano and bass sorahis. Ostad Shajarian has generously given permission to use this photograph.

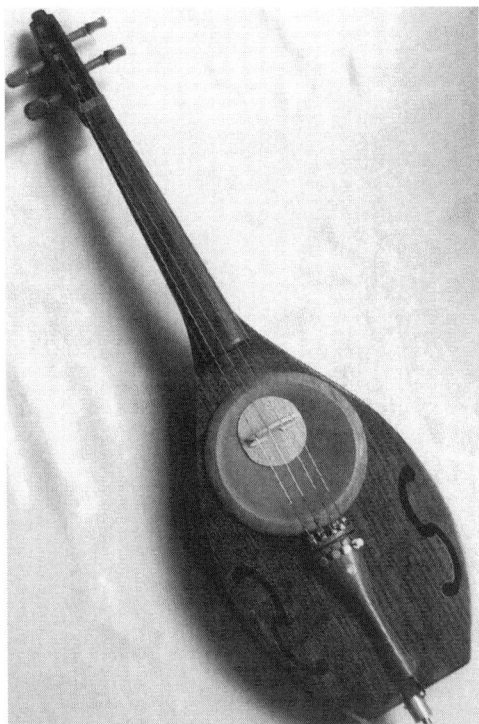

16—Sabu. Ostad Shajarian has generously given permission to use this photograph.

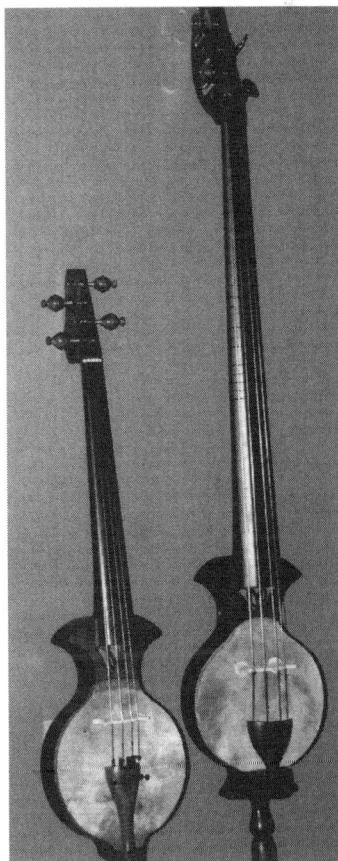

17—Sahbang and Shahnavaz. Ostad Shajarian has generously given permission to use this photograph.

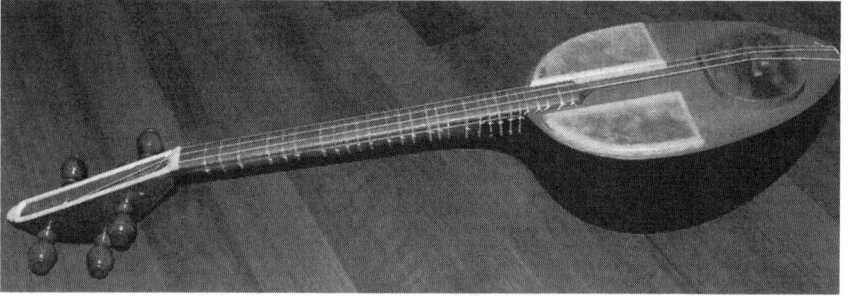

18—Saghar. Ostad Shajarian has generously given permission to use this photograph.

19—Kereshme. Ostad Shajarian has generously given permission to use this photograph.

20—*Ostad Shajarian's calligraphy for the Hafez ghazal sung in* Bidad, *1985. Ostad Shajarian has generously given permission to use this photograph.*

21—Touring the world with Derakhshani (to the right of Shajarian), daughter Mojgan (to the left), and the Shahnaz Ensemble, 2010. Ostad Shajarian has generously given permission to use this photograph

3
Around the World

Following a brief introduction contextualizing aspects of globalization in general as it pertains to Iran and Persian music, this chapter examines Shajarian's career and musical production through the 1990s and 2000s, when he made the decisive leap to being a global musical and public figure.

Globalization and Persian Music

RS
For at least the past three decades, a large contingent of scholars from various fields (e.g., Wolf, Weatherford, and Nederveen-Pietres) have demonstrated how the contemporary notion of globalization is merely the most recent phase of a human process that has been in continuous operation for millennia. Networks of connection, mutual arising, and codependency are buried under constructed notions of "pure" identity—racial, ethnic, cultural or national—and an insistence on the autonomous existence of "us and them." Iran's long history is largely predicated on a parade of such cross-cultural encounters and relationships, and Dabashi notes the crucial role a small group of young Iranians that spent time studying in Europe (particularly England) in the early-nineteenth century played in shaping modern Iran (2005:32ff.), to say nothing of the very direct political machinations of Russia, Britain, and the United States throughout the twentieth century. Viewed thus, the discussion of "East-West/traditional-modern" polemics and revolutionary ideology underlying this chapter, along with what follows in the concluding section, is somewhat of a red herring. It is nonetheless instructive to shift the perspective from "the musical culture in Iran" to the globalized context of Persian music in the twentieth and twenty-first centuries.

Persian music is the contemporary branch of music whose roots trace back through a densely complex web of cultural interchange—various Iranian peoples, Arabs, Turks, Central Asians, Chinese,[1] Indians—whereby it is often impossible to say with confidence (barring nationalistic axe-grinding) "who got what from whom." There is always some other angle to look at, an earlier period to consider, and a pervasive lack of reliable sources on all sides. Nettl hypothesized that the late-nineteenth-century formation of the radif may have been in some measure a response to Western influences (1978: 158–59). We also noted in our companion volume (chapter 3 of Simms and Koushkani 2012) the key role of French military music and infrastructure in the nineteenth century, as well as Vaziri's wholesale importation of Western musical approaches to Iran in the 1920s and beyond through Khaleqi and others. Aside from Vaziri's important branch of Western hybridization, there is a large and significant contingent, if not a majority, of Iranian musicologists and ethnomusicologists publishing research on Persian music who were trained in the West beginning in the second half of the twentieth century. Like Vaziri, some of them returned to Iran, such as Mehdi Barkeshli (1912–1987), Mohammad Taghi Massoudieh, and more recently Azin Movahed and Amir Pourjavadi. Others live in (or divide their time between Iran and) Europe and North America, such as Khatschi Khatschi, Hormoz Farhat, Manoochehr Sadeghi, Dariush Tala'i, Hossein Omumi, Amenah Youseffzadeh (whose primary work centers on *bakhshi* music), and Laudan Nooshin.

As the bibliographies of our study illustrate, since the 1960s there are many non-Iranian scholars researching Persian music. The growth of research on Persian music by American ethnomusicologists through the 1970s, frequently as part of their doctoral research, was facilitated by the cozy political relations that existed between the Shah and the American government. This wave of research from the 1960s through to the revolution coincided with the first wide-distribution releases of recordings of Persian music (featuring many of the top artists frequently broadcast on Iranian radio) on Western labels such as Folkways, Nonesuch, Lyrichord, and Barenreiter, which were staples of library collections and brought an awareness of the music to an unprecedently wide non-Iranian audience. Following the general growth of ethnomusicology in the United States, some of the first concert tours and artist-in-residence programs in the United States (and Europe) featuring prominent Persian musicians occurred during this period, marking a noticeable two-way flow of cultural traffic between Iran and the West.

The revolution effected a mass exodus of political refugees to various countries around the world but especially to Europe and North America, with particularly large clusterings in Paris, Cologne, Los Angeles, and Toronto. Replanted grassroots activities sprung up rapidly around the new diaspora: local community newspapers in Persian, various organizations, small businesses importing Persian books and recordings, night clubs, and community-based concerts of local as well as visiting Persian musicians. Among the large migration of Iranians, many Persian musicians, both amateur and professional, live and are actively musicking outside Iran. As a case study, Toronto's Iranian community grew from virtually nothing before the revolution to around 100,000 by 1990 and has doubled since then. There were three Persian weeklies published in the early 1990s and several outlets selling cassettes (often grocery stores with sizable collections). When Shajarian performed with Lotfi and tombak-player Ghavihelm in Toronto in 1997, it was strictly a community-based event organized by a few private individuals, held in a small college auditorium and only advertised in the local Persian papers; the audience was consequently entirely Iranian. But subsequent returns of Shajarian in the early 2000s were held in large, prestigious concert halls, produced by a professional production company, and featured prime promotion in the city's main media outlets. While the audience is still overwhelmingly Iranian, Shajarian and other big-name Persian artists attract an increasing number of non-Iranian concertgoers as well. It is likely that this kind of progression up the ranks of Toronto's music scene occurred in other diasporic centers as well.

This rapid establishment of a large Iranian diaspora coincided with the boom of the "World Music" market in the 1980s, in which Persian music played a relatively modest role but nonetheless provided artists such as Shajarian, Shahram Nazeri, and Alizadeh with an additional boost among Western audiences through CD releases on European labels. Persian music is now featured fairly regularly on premiere stages throughout North America, Europe, Japan, Russia, and continuing a longstanding historical tradition, neighbouring "maqam cultures" of West and Central Asia and North Africa. This newly globalized context takes on yet another historically unprecedented yet entirely natural turn. The increased exposure to Persian music (both live and recorded) among non-Iranian audiences in countries outside of Iran combined with the transplanted residence of skilled Persian musicians in these countries over the past three decades has resulted in a growing contigent of non-Iranian musicians who study the performance of Persian music (following the pioneering efforts of Jean During, Lloyd Miller, and others)—though their performance activity is presently restricted to a very local or private level. And of course the Web has burst open torrential access to world music on all fronts for anyone with a service connection—for the highly Internet-savvy Iranians to explore the music of other cultures, while the world has access to the incredible wealth of material on Persian music available online.

Shajarian played a major role in establishing this global audience for Persian music and indeed may be regarded as its first global representative.

OS
Question: How do you feel about avaz and its present global context?
I like to have more listeners, especially listeners from other cultures and to introduce them to our culture. We like to be sympathetic, understanding, and care for each other, just the way a family cares for each other. Therefore our people

*can be introduced to the people from other countries and I, in general, look at
the whole planet as a big family.*
Boroumand once told Bruno Nettl that "you will never understand this music."
(No response).
Do you think he perhaps meant on a more theoretical level?
Yes, it was.
There are different listening needs for everyone—those living in Iran, and the
global audience—how do you handle that?
*In general, the needs of the people are very transparent. We know that everybody
wants the same thing or very similar things but each of them use their own "lan-
guage." Perhaps Boroumand meant a specific part of the music, because it is not
like that. Music is an international language. If you listen to it carefully you can
take anything out of it. It is only the poetry that other cultures cannot understand. For example we cannot translate Hafez's poetry.*
Rumi is now the best selling poet in North America.
*You can translate Khayyam, Rumi or Attar but you cannot translate Hafez or
Sa'di. This requires someone who is purely Persian, very familiar with the English language, and knows all the little details of this culture and what each word
in every place means, because sometimes a single word can have ten different
meanings. Hafez has used language in a particular way, so that you have to understand the Persian language very accurately and at the same time be very familiar with Hafez's personality. There are many Iranians who do not even understand Hafez. So you cannot understand Hafez unless you are fluent in the
Persian language. But Persian music can be understood by anyone.*
Nusrat Fateh Ali Khān's music eventually became geared more towards the pop
industry while your music is geared towards the classical sector.
*Yes, my work is completely classical and my audiences are classical music en-
thusiasts as well. I mean when they come to our concerts, they sit in absolute
silence the whole time. They don't shake any part of their bodies and stay in total
silence the whole time as if they are listening to Western classical music. (2008)*

AK
My teacher, Dariush Pirniakan, was accompanying Mr. Shajarian on his tours in
the late 1980s and through the 1990s. Shajarian was working on expanding his
professional activities, figuring out an entirely new system that he had never
encountered before: playing for immigrant communities outside of Iran. Making
this transition was a demanding task that required a lot of learning on his part—
how to travel, international business regulations and systems, protocols, networking, etc.—everything required to make this new context of presenting the
music happen successfully. He had to establish reliable contacts and started
doing this on a "one-off" basis, one concert out and then back to Iran. He met or
knew someone from a particular city who would make grassroot arrangements
to present a concert within the local community. Everyone loves Mr. Shajarian,

so the concerts were successful. The earliest concerts were with Meshkatian and quite large ensembles in the late 1980s, but he realized that it was difficult to travel with so many people and soon reduced the group to a small chamber ensemble: Pirniakan, Jamshid Andelebi (ney), and Mortaza 'Ayun (tombak), who was actually living in Europe at the time, which helped to facilitate the concerts.

With expanded contacts and experience, he realized that he could turn these one-off concerts into a tour, which he first did in Europe and then the United States. Everything would be new for him: dealing with new people, people who were living outside Iran but still connected to their culture, new cultures, and environments. His ability to succeed at this illustrates his willingness to learn, his flexibility, and knack for fitting into different social groups and occasions. It's important to note that Shajarian functioned as a grass-roots link between these expatriate communities and Iran. No one else could present that calibre of Persian music in the diaspora and bring the local communities together the way Shajarian did. He was one of the pioneers in Iran for touring like this, and other musicians began to follow the path he opened up. For sure, other musicians were doing this—like Lotfi, Alizadeh, and Omumi—but not on the level that Shajarian brought it to. They didn't have singers.

The marked increase in subsequent activities you see with other musicians was largely inspired by him, and it was multidirectional. For example, Kalhor was living in Ottawa at the time but started to link up with musicians in Germany, playing concerts and asking Iran-based musicians like Nazeri and others to get involved. On a practical level for Iranian musicians, these tours made a lot of sense because it was very difficult to put on concerts in Iran, never mind making a living from it, and the tours usually proved to be financially successful.

Shajarian's Musical Activities in the 1990s

RS

In emphasizing Shajarian's increasing global profile and activities in the 1990s, it is important to remember that, despite his more than ample opportunities to live anywhere he wished, Iran continued to be his principal residence. This is still the case today, and as a result, he is in touch with an extensive network of Iranians and Iranian culture both in the country and around the globe. He is directly affected by, and experiences firsthand, events and changes that occur in Iran.

The Iran-Iraq war ended in August of 1988 and Khomeini died in July 1989, thus ushering in a new era for the Islamic Republic. Whereas Khomeini wielded sweeping, chilling powers, this was not the case for his successors. The subsequent discussion of contemporary Iranian history cites Iranian presidents as convenient period markers. While this dynamic of symbolic/iconic leadership of a President or Prime Minister operates similarly around the world—a natural

penchant for having some individual in charge (or assuming that the person dele-
gated to be in charge really is)—it is not the case in Iran. The post-Khomeini
period began with Rafsanjani's *relative* easing of the social lockdown, though
this did not pertain to the political domain, which remained under tight wraps.
The devastation of the war with Iraq necessitated focusing attention on Iran's
domestic economy, where initial signs of growth were followed by serious economic crisis: debt, inflation, and recession triggered riots in large cities through
1992, and in Tehran in 1995. Conservative vigilante groups still propelled by
revolutionary zeal pushed back in the mid 1990s, targeting the press, writers,
artists and arts organizations, and women. Mohammad Khatami's election in
1997 brought the first glimmer of reformist hope and thaw amidst the severity of
almost two decades of ruthless revolutionary social engineering. But the country
continued to be sharply polarized and after some modest initial gains, conserva-
tives reorganized to stymy reformist initiatives with renewed vigour through the
courts.

The path of Shajarian's Western tours initiated by *Dastan* in 1987 gathered
momentum through 1989. Nineteen ninety began with an invitation from the
mayor of Barcelona to perform in that city for two evenings; Daiush Tala'i and
Hossein Omumi accompanied him on this unprecedented occasion. Shortly
afterward, by special invitation of the Ministry of Culture and Art of Tajikistan,
Shajarian attended a music conference and ceremonial unveiling of a statue of
the historical-mythical musician Barbad in Dushanbe and performed two
concerts. While his diasporic touring was hitherto restricted to Europe, the
summer/fall of 1990 marked the beginning of his regular touring of North
America, accompanied by the small ensemble of Pirniakan, Andelebi, and
'Ayun. The tour resulted in a trio of live recordings that were released in 1991 on
Delawaz: *Payam e Nasim* ("Message of the Breeze"), *Del e Majnun* ("Insane
Heart") and *Sarv e Chanan* ("The Strutting Cypress").[2] Performances of the
former two programs were released on video in 1991 by Delawaz as *Persian
Music & Poetry: Mohammad Reza Shajarian in Concert.* American tours
followed in the fall of 1991 and late August-November of 1992, again with
Pirniakan and Andelebi but now with Shajarian's teenaged son Homayoun (b.
1975) on tombak. Further live recordings from these concerts were released:
Asman e Eshgh ("The Sky of Love") in 1992 and *Yad e Ayam* ("Memory of the
Old Days") from the 1992 tour in 1995. Shajarian regards *Yad e Ayam* and
Payam e Nasim as definitive of his mature style, revealing "all of his
techniques." *Yad e Ayam* is discussed in detail below. Amidst this busy activity,
during the period 1991 to 1992 Ostad Shajarian also experienced a major and
difficult transition in his personal life, separating from and divorcing his wife of
thirty years and marrying Katayun Khansari.

While in Los Angeles during the 1990 American tour, Shajarian performed
a benefit concert to raise relief assistance for the devastating Manjil-Rudbar
earthquake that struck the northern region of Iran in June of that year. His involvement in benefit concerts for various charitable causes continues regularly to

the present. In the spring of 1992 he participated in concerts in honor and support of the impoverished citizens of south Tehran and the innovative initiative of the Bahman Center (see Sadighi and Mahdavi 2009), which he later declared to be the most powerfully moving performance experiences of his career (Honar e Daftar 2003:2073). We noted in our companion volume (chapter 3 of Simms and Koushkani 2012) that there is a tradition of engaging Persian music toward charity extending back to the early twentieth-century and some of the earliest public concerts.

By the early 1990s Shajarian had established a routine of regular tours of both Europe and North America (from 1997 the latter expanded to include Canada) that he has maintained, almost annually, to the present. Additional live recordings from these tours and other concerts were released by Delawaz through the 1990s. His 1995 summer tour of Europe with Lotfi featured the dastgahs Segah and Rast Panjgah, a particularly spirited performance of the latter in Paris was released as *Cheshme-ye Nush* ("The Heavenly Fountain") the same year. Another outing with Lotfi, performing Shur in Köln in 1997, was released the same year as *Moammaye Hasty* ("Enigma of Life"). Dariush Tala'i accompanied Shajarian in several concerts through the 1990s, including a performance of Mahur in 1997, released the same year as *Shab e Vasl* ("Night of Union"). Shajarian would later note that, following Lotfi and Tala'i's aesthetic sensibilities, these latter two recordings "express the presence and mood of the Qajar era" (Shajarian et al. 2004:314). Pirniakan probably accompanied Shajarian in more concerts than anyone else through the 1990s, resulting in further live releases: *Rosvayie Del* ("The Disgraced Heart") recorded in Dubai in 1996 and released the following year, and *Aram e Jan* ("Quiet of the Soul") recorded in 1998, released in 1999.

Shajarian performed infrequently with Meshkatian in the 1990s, but a European concert in 1994 resulted in the attempted release (the date is unclear but likely the following year) of *Ghasedak* ("Dandelion"). The chosen texts by Sa'di, Attar, Rumi, Baba Taher, and Nima Yushij launched a devastating criticism of the current political situation in a manner reminiscent of *Bidad*, inspiring the authorities in Iran to ban the cassette by denying it a license for release (ibid.:313). Set in Mahur and Dashti, the work projects deep darkness and despair. In 1995 Shajarian and Meshkatian performed a concert of the *Ghasedak* program in England; in a radical departure from concert protocol, they both dressed in black.[3] It was to be one of their last performances together, as plans for further collaboration in the late 2000s were preempted by Meshkatian's sudden death in 2009. Some translated excerpts from the avaz of *Ghasedak* follow that likely caused alarm with the censors. The first Sa'di excerpt was surely flagged. In fact, Shajarian reset the same ghazal two years later and was permitted to release it as the album *Rosvayie Del*, but the offending *beyt* was missing:

An assembly said that looking (at something pleasurable) is forbidden
They forbade looking and yet murder (*khun–e halq*) is lawful

> If I have a foot in the grave, (that's alright because)
> A hundred thousand others better than I have perished[4]
>   (Sa'di)

> I am writhing with a wave of passion alone through night til day
> If you will, care and have mercy; if you will, go and be cruel
>   (Rumi)[5]

Here is the text by Yushij of the program's terminal tasnif *Ghasedak*, the dark signature of the album that Meshkatian subjected to a hauntingly dissonant setting:

> Dandelion, Messenger of the Field, what is the news you bring?
> For whom . . .
> And from where . . . a message?
> May you be the bearer of the sweet message . . . but,
> Your turning around me, my dwelling and my door is fruitless.
> I don't expect a message,
> From a lover,
> From anyone,
> From anywhere . . .
> Oh Messenger of the Field, the clouds of the whole universe
> weep in my heart night and day.
> Oh Messenger, in my heart everyone is deaf and blind.

Shajarian's concert format follows the conventions and proportions established by Darvish Khan earlier in the century (see appendix 1 of Simms and Koushkani 2012), an evening's performance consisting of two such "suites" in different modes separated by an intermission. Cassette releases either divide one long suite between two sides or, less frequently, include two shorter suites, one on each side. *Bahariye* ("Springtime") documents an interesting live performance at the Iran-Japan Cultural Institute of Tehran in 1994 (though not released until c. 2000) of what appears to be a demonstrational program; the concluding applause suggests an intimate audience of a few dozen people. The program opens with Pirniakan playing a very short tar solo nominally in the daramad of Mahur but actually making a strong case for Rast Panjgah before heading into a short *chaharmezrab*, accompanied by Homayoun Shajarian on tonbak. Ostad Shajarian then begins a thirteen-minute section of avaz to Pirniakan's accompaniment that undertakes a novel modal journey: the first half establishes Mahur in a conventional fashion before abruptly shifting to Chahargah, and then Shushtari before returning to Mahur. Pirniakan and Homayoun conclude with another short *chaharmezrab*. This condensed yet adventurous presentation of avaz (which is also included on the cassette *Gonbad e Mina*, issued in 1995) is followed by a five-minute demonstration of various rhythms on the tonbak by Homayoun, and another five-minute performance featuring the tonbak maestro Nasser Farhang-far, who sings Dashti to his own solo tonbak accompaniment. The program concludes with a series of four santur solos in dastgah Homayun by Meshkatian, accompanied by the tonbak of Homayoun Shajarian in all but one.

Reflecting the overall tendency of his Delawaz recordings, the overwhelming majority of Shajarian's performances from the 1990s released were live recordings. The 1992 release of *Delshodegan* ("Lovers") is unique in Shajarian's oeuvre in being the soundtrack to the 1991 film of the same name, directed by Ali Hatami. Centering on the story of a group of musicians in the late Qajar period and their attempts to make a recording, the majority of the soundtrack was composed by Alizadeh and consists of tar solos, Persian ensemble pieces, pieces written for orchestra in a polyphonic "East-meets-West" style (occasionally including Persian instruments and an uncredited female vocalist singing solo and in [an overdubbed?] chorus), four tasnifs, and two five-minute sections of avaz. The avaz includes Shushtari and a Hafez ghazal sung unaccompanied as a Masnavi of Bayate Tork. The penultimate track of the album, "*Marsh 'Azā*/Mourning March," features the polyphonic layering of various avaz soloists (both male and female), while the final track, *Gol chehre*/"Face of the Flower" has the same voices homophonically accompany Shajarian's prominent line of avaz. Alizadeh's deployment of this polyphonic approach to avaz—which he develops further in his later works—can be very effective and, in my view, holds great creative potential.

The album *Shab, Sukut, Kavir* ("Night, Silence, Desert") is another unique work in Shajarian's discography. It began as an independent project of Kahan Kalhor, who composed an instrumental work that combines various folk music traditions from Khorasan and Persian *asil* instruments. Bringing together musicians from both classical and folk worlds, Kalhor declared (in the liner notes to the American release) that "the overall theme is simply the merging of two styles." Kalhor completed the instrumental tracks in 1994 but later approached Shajarian about integrating a vocal part into the piece, which Shajarian agreed to and recorded in 1997. The resulting effort was released on Delawaz in 1998 and the American label Traditional Crossroads in 2000. Complementing the attempted merging of musical styles, the added poetry features a mixture of classical and modern poets—Attar, Baba Taher, Mo'Allem, and Ebtehaj.

The recording provides a rare insight into Shajarian's longstanding research of Khorasani music (discussed below), here as in other areas of his research, presented in the form of an artistic work as opposed to musicological or theoretical discourse. The album is also unique in having as its main impetus a work that was already conceived to which Shajarian adapted a vocal part, a relatively unusual creative process that he would repeat a few years later with Alizadeh on the album *Zemestan Ast*. As far as I am aware, *Night, Silence, Desert* is the only published documentation of Shajarian's decades-long work with folk music.

Shortly after completing the project he noted that *"the style of avaz* [on the recording] *is completely folk, sung in the Gornamānj (Kermanj) style . . . and is completely different from my other work. . . . We worked on this album for almost three years. I actually performed the vocal part at one time, but felt that the result was too distant from the authentic folk style. So I did further research for two years regarding those styles of singing we rerecorded it. . . . I always have a concern for the future and like working on fresh, new productions, though of course, we also rely on our ancestors* (Shajarian et al. 2004: 313).

I'm unable to comment on how Shajarian's self-described Kermanji style of singing compares with traditional Khorasani styles but from my limited knowledge of the subject feel that his singing, while noticeably different from his classical avaz, is considerably more refined than that of most folk singers I've heard on recordings and lacks the exaggerated theatricality and animation often characterizing the latter. The album features Shajarian singing a fairly strophic style of avaz on three tracks along with two metric songs that are essentially folkstyle tasnifs. Compared to his classical style, Shajarian's avaz here features wider vibrato, "wilder" glottal ornaments, along with a nasality, articulation (especially portamento play), and use of vocables such as *"lelele"* that are alien to *asil* music. In terms of modality, much of Shajarian's avaz on the album evokes the atmosphere of Dashti, clearly illustrating Kalhor's statement in the liner notes (of the American release) connecting the ultimate source of the radif to folk music. Performance example 7 below looks at a short example from this album in greater detail.

His two other studio efforts of the 1990s that followed were of a more conventional nature but stand out as being noteworthy for quite different reasons. *Dar Khiyal* ("In the Imagination") featuring Majid Derakhshani's tar accompaniment and excellent ensemble compositions, was recorded (apparently in the studio) in 1995 and released the following year; to my ears it distinguishes itself as one of the strongest of his many recordings from the 1990s. *Ahang e Vafa* ("Tune and Faith"), recorded in 1999, marks Homayoun Shajarian's debut performance as a singer in duet with his father. Homayoun accompanied Ostad Shajarian on tombak regularly since the 1991 American tour when he was only 16 years old, appearing on the album *Asman e Eshgh* ("Sky of Love") and virtually all releases afterward.

The 1990s were the peak decade for Delawaz releases, featuring a wide range of material both recent and from Shajarian's extensive archive. The second half of the decade was especially prolific, coinciding with Shajarian setting up a second residence in Vancouver, Canada in 1998. Spending a good portion of each year there until around 2000, he also moved Delawaz's production and publishing operations to the city, where they remain. Some of this material had been previously released but with only very narrow distribution; many fans were aware of these recordings and appreciated the wider reach and accessibility of the Delawaz editions, which were generally reissued under different titles from the original. Reissues from the 1970s included *Rast Panjgah* and *Chehre be*

Chehre ("Face to Face"), his now famous appearances at the Shiraz Festival with Lotfi in 1975 and 1977 performing Rast Panjgah and Nava, respectively. At the time these dastgahs were quite marginalized repertoire and given a major, strategic boost of interest among musicians through these recordings.

A number of Shajarian's recordings with Payvar from 1979 and 1980 were also among the wave of reissues: *Raz e Del* ("Secret of the Heart") from his last appearance with Payvar in Rudaki Hall, along with the studio efforts *Entezare Del* ("The Waiting Heart") and *Khalvat Gozide* ("Voluntary Seclusion"). The A-sides of *Entezare Del* and *Khalvat Gozide* were released again as a single cassette in 1992. *Saz e Ghesse Gu* (sic) & *Konsert Borzorgasht Hafez* ("The Speaking Lute & Tribute Concert for Hafez") combined an A-side featuring studio work with Payvar from the same period with a B-side of the infamous Rudaki Hall concerts with Pirniakan of 1988 (marked by the mass calling for *Bidad*). Other material recorded in the 1980s and released in the 1990s included *Eshq Danad* ("Love Knows"), the likewise infamous concert with Lotfi at the German Cultural Center in 1981, the studio duet with with santurist Mansur Sārami, *Homayoun Masnavie* ("Masnavi in Homayun"). The orchestral works *Gonbad e Mina* ("The Azure Dome") and *Jan e Oshagh* ("Soul of Love") were issued in various configurations. Finally, in 1999 he released two volumes of Qur'an recitation recorded between 1979 and 1982, dedicating it to the memory of his father (*Be Yad e Pedar*), who died in 1996.

On top of a busy schedule of concertizing, recording, and producing during the 1990s, Shajarian was also engaged in research projects and cultivated ties with various scholarly circles. He gave addresses at scholarly conferences and published articles on avaz and profiles of senior Ostads in various Persian journals (such as *Kelk*, *Āvā*, *Hamshahri*, and *Honar-e Musiqi*), some of which are reprinted in Habibi Nezhād (2004). Throughout the 1980s and early 1990s Shajarian had been collecting data and researching the vocal repertores of both *asil* and Khorasani folk musics, investing considerable time pursuing and interviewing rare and vital informants throughout Iran. According to Nooshin (2001), his interest in Khorasani folk music began in his childhood. During the 1980s and 1990s, if he heard about unknown, obscure singers who knew a particular gushe or piece of folk repertoire that he was unaware of, he would seek them out and meet with them to learn their material (personal communication, Siamak Shajarian, 1995). As usual, his methodology and goals were practical—to learn to sing through precise imitation, so that the material would become a part of his musical consciousness—but plans for making his research available to others were afoot.

Since the 1980s, musicians in the Persian music community have awaited a comprehensive recording of Shajarian's radif materials, which would be a historically significant and invaluable resource for both performers and scholars. While he considered doing this himself at one time, by the early 1990s he felt that students could consult Karimi's authoritative and widely available radif to obtain an adequate grounding in the fundamentals. Wanting to offer something different and recognizing the difficulty students have in performing *morakab khāni*, Shajarian seriously considered recording an instructional program of this art (personal communication, Siamak Shajarian, 1995). Aimed at advanced students who already have a fundamental understanding of the radif, his performance would illustrate idiomatic modulatory possibilities using specific pivotal (*pul*, "bridge") gushes. Another project was mentioned in a 1993 interview: "*I have been busy for some years with research and writings concerning the dastgahs of traditional Persian music, especially gushes that have become forgotten; my aim is to work on a presentation for singing avaz and tahrirs that have as yet not been documented*" (Shajarian 1993: 45). While work commenced on these projects, they were not completed and by the 2000s he had shifted his research interests to instrument design and felt that his performance recordings contained all of his knowledge regarding matters of musical repertoire and modulation (see Simms and Koushkani 2012), simultaneously serving pedagogical and artistic purposes.

As mentioned above, Shajarian was invited as an honorary guest to the Symposium of the 1400th anniversary of the legendary Sassanian musician Barbad, held in Dushanbe, Tajikistan in April, 1990. Aside from his performances there, he clearly had his own research and networking agenda, and arrived with a fair amount of familiarity with the music of this area already (Kasmai & Lecomte 1991:252–53). During his American tour of the same year he made addresses to students and faculty at UCLA, UCSD, Berkeley, Columbia, Harvard, and the University of Chicago.

Performance Example 6: *Yad e Ayam*

OS

If you want to document my style of avaz and show why it is different from others, you should listen to Yad e Ayam *in Shur and also my performance of Abu Ata on the album* Payam e Nasim. *The way I construct sentences and link them together is evident in these recordings—this is what separates me from other singers. (2010)*

Hafez ghazal #205

He came last night and his face was all aglow,
How the sorrowful heart had burned!

The custom of love slaying and the way of the riotous city
Were the garment sewn upon his figure.

*Although he said: "I'll kill you cruelly," I saw
That secretly his glance at me was heart-burned*

He regarded the souls of lovers as the rue of his own face,
For this work he kindled the fire of his cheek.

The heart held much blood, but the eye poured it out,
God, Oh God! Who was wasted and who saved?

The blasphemy of her locks struck the way of faith and that stone heart;
The torch of that fiery face was in his way.

Don't sell the friend even for the world:
Those who sold Joseph for debased coin didn't profit much.

He said, and said well: "Go burn the robe Hafez!
Oh Lord, from whom did you learn this knowledge of base coin?"

Hafez ghazal #346

You made thousands of holes in my faith with your black eyelashes,
Come! Out of your languid eye I'll pluck thousands of pains.

Behold the companion of the heart that your friends forgot,
May none of our days include a moment without remembrance of you.

The world is old and baseless, deliver us from this slayer of Farhad,[6]
Its conjurying and deception made me weary of my sweet life.

If you choose a stranger in my place, he is the judge.
May I be unlawful if I choose my life in the place of the friend!

Interlinear translation of transcription:
Gar che migoft   ke zārat bekosham mididam
Although he said that desires I killed   I saw
Although he said: "I saw desires and killed them,"

ke   nehānesh nazari bā   man-e del   sukhte bud
that secret   look   with me-of heart burnt was
My burnt heart saw his concealment.

Jān 'ushaq sepande rokhe khod midānest
Soul lover   rue   face   self he knew
He'd known the soul of love, the rue of his own face,

V   ātesh chehre bā   in   kār   bar   āfrukhte   bud
And fire   face   with this action on   lit   was
The fire of his face was emphatic with this.

Del   basi   khun   be ham   āvard   vali dide berikht
Heart   much   blood   to also brought   but   eye   poured
The heart brought   much blood, but the eye poured it out,

Āllah āllah ke   talaf   kard o   ke   āndukhte bud
God   god   who waste   did   and who   saved   was
God, Oh God! Who was wasted and then saved?

Kofre   zolfesh   rah-e   din   mizad ān   sangin del
Blasphemy her locks way-of religion struck   that stone   heart
The blasphemy of her locks struck the way of faith and that stone heart;

Dar rahesh mesh'ale   az   chehre bar āfrukhte bud
In   way-his   torch   from face   on   lit   was
The torch of that emphatic face was in his way.

Ba   mozhgāne siyah kardi hezārān rakhne   dar   dinam
With eyelashes black did   thousands holes   in   my faith
You made thousands of holes in my faith with your black eyelashes,

Biyā kaz chashme bimārat hezārān   dard bar chinam
Come that   eye   languid a thousand pain on   I pluck
Come! Because of your languid eye I've suffered thousands of pains.

RS

Recorded live in the United States (Los Angeles?) in 1992, *Yad e Ayam* is a concise performance of Shur, having the lowest proportion of avaz in relation to the entire album. After the cogent opening tahrir in Daramad Khara and first beyt in the Daramad, Shajarian draws our attention to the third beyt in what he identifies on the album index as the gushe Razavi, a designation that would be easily missed. His rendition exhibits the profile and progression of Razavi but is transposed to descend from the fourth degree to the tonic, as opposed to the usual seventh degree to the fourth, definitive of Razavi proper. Shur is characterized by an instrinsic ambiguity of similar melodic materials centered variously on the tonic and the fourth degree, which Shajarian seems to be exploiting here. It is indeed unconventional for Razavi to occur directly after the Daramad. Shajarian's interest in this excerpt, however, concerned the terminal tahrir:

Yad e Ayam

4: Razavi

gar che mi - goft ke zā - rat be - ko - sham

(m)mi - - di - - dam ke ne - hān - nesh

(n) na - za - ri bā ma - ne del - sukh - te bud ha

da

ja - - - - na

na yi ya

5: 'Asheq Kosh

jā - ne 'u - shā - - (q) se - pan - de ro - khe khod mi - dā - ne - (ne) -

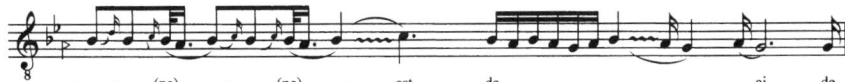

- - (ne) - (ne) - est da ai de

6

(n) ja - ne 'u - shāq se - pan - de ro - khe khod mi - dā - nest (a)

vā - ta - she che - h - re be - din kār   bar ā - frukh - te

(tahrir Naghme)

bud   de   ya   ha   akh   na

ha   ha   na   yi

u   a   ha

ha   a yi a   da

7: Salmak

gar   che mi-goft   ke zā - rat   bi-ko-sham

(faster)

mi - di - - - dam   a

na   ho   e   dad

8

(n) gar che mi-goft   ke zā-rat bi-ko-sham   mi - di - dam   ke ne-hā-mesh

na-za-ri   bā   ma-ne del-sukh-te   bud   da   az da e yi ya ha   da   he a he a   he a

a hi a he a he   he   a he a   ya   yi a

he   i   a

9: Qarache

del ba - si   khun bi (ke)(a)vard   va - li   di - de berikht

du ya da

10

(n)del ba - si khun be kâ-vard   va - li   di - de be-rikht

ā - llah ā - llah (n)ke ta-laf kard o   ke ān-dukh-te bud da

af da   ha

(The complete example is posted at www.yorku.ca/robsimms/shajarian)

Now this line that you are going to hear, you have to compare it to the older
Ostads and the earlier singers from the point of view of sentence construc-
tion and phrasing. None of the older masters have ever done such a tahrir.
In the older styles the tahrirs were pretty predictable but in my recording
you cannot predict what the tahrirs are going to be. The sentence construc-
tion in the older tahrirs was obvious. (2010)

Section 5 introduces the gushe designated as 'Āsheq Kosh on the album index. This gushe is exclusive to Mirza Abdollah's radif, where it is a satellite of
Shahnaz—indeed an alternate title for the gushe Shahnaz-e Kot ("short/brief
Shahnaz"). As it continues to unfold through the sixth section, however, Shajarian uses the natural fifth degree as opposed to the *koron* found in the radif and
definitive of Shahnaz. As Shajarian knows all the major radifs inside out, the
liberties taken here (and above with Razavi) are compositional initiatives, highlighting flexibility and creative application over theoretical, canonical correct-
ness. Perhaps Shajarian is simply attracted to the provocative name 'Āsheq Kosh
("Lover Killed"), which is particularly poignant in relation to the image *jān-e*
'ushaq ("soul of love") in accompanying the beyt of this ghazal so marked by
conflict. Shajarian again pointed out the significance of "tahrir Naghme" in section 6 and the terminal tahrir of section 7 in Salmak: *"These are sentences that*
the older masters never performed. These tahrirs are like an instrument, I am
bringing in the sentence construction of the instruments here; I am bringing in
instrumental melodies."

From Salmak, Shajarian proceeds onward to Qarache and Razavi proper in
a background progression that is wholly conventional. He specifically highlighted
the melodic variation brought to his two renderings of the first *misra* of Qarache as
well as the words *"an sangin del"* in Razavi. A brilliant rendition of Hosseini
followed by a forud closes this fifteen-minute block of *saz o avaz*, after which a
tasnif by Pirniakan is performed.

The following *saz o avaz* of section 15 remains entirely within Shajarian's
modal creation of 'Āsheq Kosh but is rendered in his low register in a subdued,
otherworldly manner reminiscent of Dadbeh's Dashtestani style. This
dramatically contrasting subterranean quality introduces and emphasizes the
beginning of a new ghazal, and conjures the darkness of the beyt ("You made
thousands of holes in my faith"). Parts of this and the following sections verge on
the threshold of audibility. This supremely quiet, rarified, and pensive ambience
accompanies the brooding second beyt, which longs for a glimpse of contact,
immanence. Shajarian returns from this descent to the underworld to his normal
register at section 18, where the text ("The world is old and baseless") brings us
back to this world as well. After the final beyt Shajarian returns to quietly intone the
words *"yād-e āyām"* on the fourth degree in his bass register. The upper-neighbour
D-*koron* points to Shahnaz/Salmak, thereby ending the avaz on ambiguous modal

footing. The *forud* to the tonic is accomplished by the concluding tasnif, a similarly suspended formal strategy used in the album *Khalvat Gozide* (recorded in 1980).

Compressed into less than eleven minutes of singing, *Yad e Ayam* contains key elements of Shajarian's style, personal toolkit, and approach to avaz: rhetorical repetition and variation (opening up great potential for word painting); unpredicatable tahrirs; use of instrumental idioms; an extremely wide ambitus that exploits dramatic potential; and compositional freedom with regard to gushes and large-scale form.

AK
This poem is difficult to understand without knowing the Sufi tradition; it's a very Sufistic poem. An important layer of *iham* concerns the notion of a test. In high levels of initiation in Sufism, a master will give a specific test to a disciple in which there is no help offered, the disciple is on his own. The first beyt of the excerpt could mean that the master doesn't care about me, the disciple—he is angry and would even kill me—but I can sense beyond this outward appearance that he is paying attention to my inside, my broken heart. Having a broken heart in Sufism, to see yourself as lost, a loser, is mandatory for being a good disciple. For me, the ambience Shajarian creates in his delivery of this line (in this first appearance) is one of sorrow but also contains a glimmer of hope. The fantastic tahrir supports this polarity with its free movement: hope inside a very dark situation where nothing is going well; hope that there is a reason for this suffering and that God can see the depth of my heart, which is essentially good. Shur is perfect for this expression, delivering this message that is really a kind of advice.

The following beyt ("*jān 'ushaq . . .*") compares disciples to the old tradition of putting rue seeds into a fire, whereby the smoke it creates protects an initiate against the evil eye. This burning, this sacrifice is for their benefit. The first time, Shajarian sings this opening *misra* (section 5) in a way that is announcing sad news, giving information; the repetition, that goes on to complete the beyt (section 6), is sung in a manner that is more like making a claim, presenting a rationale for the news. Section 7 goes back to "*gar che migoft*" and creates a lot of tension and expectation through the sustained notes on the words "*migoft*" and "*kosham*"—you're waiting to find out what's going on. The concluding tahrir and *forud* bring some resolution and sense of hope. Of course, we can extrapolate the meaning of this beyond the master-disciple relationship to reflect in general the struggles in our lives. We go through difficult experiences that may last a long time and need to make sense of them.

Qarache expresses great regret here ("*del basi khun*"), especially evoked through his use of portamento. This is a classic signal in Persian culture for sadness, it's similar to the way a *rozekhan* will elicit sadness and crying in his listeners. However, it's not good for disciples to complain about the pressure, sorrow, and pain they are experiencing during their "test." If you're showing that, you're losing a lot of potential benefit in the path of love and enlightenment. Pain in this path is fuel for spiritual progress. The poem says: "With all of this pressure, my heart sank in blood, but unfortunately my eyes lost some potential for spiritual growth by releasing this energy through crying." Your potential achievement can be lost through your fears, so you shouldn't show this discomfort. The *iham* here can be read as declaring that we made a mistake: on a personal level, or between a master and disciple, or perhaps in a political sense. It is a conflict between the eyes and the heart. The eyes have done something against the heart: my heart captured pain but my eyes lost it. Eyes are a symbol of material life while the heart symbolizes spiritual life. Shajarian's expression of the second misra, "*Allah, Allah,*" embodies and conveys this loss very intensely. The date is 1992, and look at the title of the album: *Yad e Ayam*, Remember the Good Old Days. Amidst this bleakness, however, I subjectively still hear that glimmer of hope in Shajarian's voice.

This is a very spiritual poem filled with contradictions. Hafez was not an orthodox Sufi and actually presented a lot of criticism toward some of those traditions. The beyt sung to Razavi ("*kofr-e zolfesh*") is observing all the contradictions of the master—he is a conduit to higher spiritual states but his behaviour doesn't align with this. This is not right. Shajarian's vocal tone, high register, and terminal tahrir are complaining and criticizing. He's angry and no longer sorry.

In the second poem, set in 'Asheq Kosh sung in his low register ("*be mozhgāne siyah*"), Shajarian's word painting really helps to evoke the ideas of contrast and contradiction that are so central to this Sufi poetry. *Din* is religion but it is also your level of consciousness, your *maqām* (spiritual station), your principles and system of belief, everything that you cling to to hold your life together. Your master is destroying that, you have to lose it so you can move further upward.[7] Shajarian's performance highlights the contrast between your former principles and losing these in the path of love, which is something most people can relate to in their personal lives.

Performance Example 7: "Rain" from *Night, Silence, Desert*

RS
Track 5 from the American release of this album, entitled "Rain," begins with a soaring and boisterous solo by Ostad Ali Abshuri on the *qushme*, a double-clarinet of the Khorasani Kurds, which settles into a drone over which Shajarian sings a short introduction before rendering Kalhor's ensemble arrangement of a popular song in 6/8 meter. The Delawaz edition of the album divides these three continuous sections into separate tracks and identifies the basis of the first two as the piece (*qit'a*) *Dornā*. Recordings of *Dornā* by Sima Bina and Mahsa & Marjan Vahdat[8] feature the same melody as Kalhor's tasnif arrangement but employ different texts. The poem set to the tasnif section of "Rain" is by the contemporary poet Mohammad Ali Mo'allem (b.1942), lending the track an interesting meeting of

tradition and modernity. The following translation of this poem—a desperate, agitated lament—is taken from the liner notes of the American release; Shajarian selects a few lines from this text (in italics) for his free introduction, which appear in italics.

My pierced heart, bleed sorrow!
Spill on the mountains, plains and deserts
As crimson lovers' lips,
In remembrance of lovers in this land,
Branded with the memory of the unknown.

Pour! Oh rain, downpour!
Shed tears with my heart, bleed rain!
Lover's tresses as dark as night,
As Majnoon did for Leili—Rain, weep!
Pour! Oh spring's cloud.
Follow my heart in yearning for the Beloved's locks,
My, oh my, what an age!
The moon has bestowed to the dark nights,
Pour! Oh rain, downpour!
Shed tears with my heart, bleed rain!
Lovers' tresses as dark as night,
As Majnoon did for Leili—Rain, weep!

As usual, Shajarian takes liberties with the ordering of lines, which he re-arranged as follows in this interlinear translation:
bebār aye abre   bahār
pour   oh cloud-of spring
Pour! Oh rain, downpour!

bā   delam   be havā zolf-e yār
with my heart to   air   lock-of friend
Follow my heart in yearning for the Beloved's locks,

dad   o bidad   az   in ruzegār
justice and injustice from this world
My, oh my, what an age!

māhu dādan be   shabhāye tāre bārun
moon gave to   nights of dark rain
The moon has bestowed to the dark nights

Bar koh   o   dasht   o   hāmon bebāre bārun
on mountain and desert and plain   pour   rain
Spill on the mountains, plains and deserts

Shajarian performs the introduction as an overdubbed duet with himself in which phrases are repeated antiphonally with varied ornamentation and a brief dovetailing of the end of the "call" with the beginning of the dubbed response (as is common practice in vocal traditions worldwide). The transcription below only provides the call for each phrase, which indicates the basic melodic contents of the piece.

Shajarian's articulation is punchy throughout the short introduction and features a vocal tone that is somewhat edgier and more nasal than that of his classical avaz. His *tekyes* (glottal appoggiaturas) are rougher and the descending glissandi from G to E are slower and more exaggerated here when compared to his usual avaz. The mode emphasizes the seventh and fifth degrees before making a Phrygian descent to the tonic. Most of the melodic material Shajarian sings is paraphrased from the framing *qushme* solo and tasnif, a performance practice commonly applied to both avaz and *zarbi* pieces in the radif (and employed in neighbouring West Asian modal traditions). The A section is paraphrased from the main theme of the *qushme*, while the C section, with its opening polyrhythmic implications, seems to be a slower variation on the *qushme*'s grupetto figure that prolongs the fourth degree before descending to the tonic. Singing in Khorasani dialect, Shajarian's articulation of both the text and melody of this terminal descent (*bar koh o dasht*) is quite distorted and "shakey" by the standards of classical avaz. The ending phrase of the A' section (*bā delam . . .*) alludes to a key gesture in the tasnif, as does the last phrase of the B section (*māhu dādan . . .*). The antiphonal descending sequence that occupies the first three-quarters of the B section seems to be the only phrase unrelated to the framing pieces. The literal translation of the line sung here includes the idiom "*dad o bidad*," which (not surprisinglying) proved irresistible to Shajarian when choosing from the full text.

AK

Sima Bina, who is a great authority on the style of music presented on *Night, Silence, Desert*, describes *Dorna* as a mystical (*'erfān*) Sufi song from Quchan about a particular kind of bird; the melody remains consistent but is set to various texts (personal communication, 2011). She really liked the arrangement and presentation of the album. In terms of these traditional styles, she felt that Ostad Shajarian's dialect (*lahje*) is not as convincing on the track *Dorna* as it is for other tracks on the album that feature the Mashshadi dialect, which is what one might expect, given his background. She makes the excellent point that a big part of the effect for listeners is that we're not used to hearing this kind of singing from Ostad Shajarian, so it catches us by surprise and challenges our assumptions. I personally feel that he is overqualified to sing this music, and it results in this new kind of style. This is actually what Kalhor was trying to achieve, a meeting of the two streams.

"Rain" (Dornâ)

Musical Activities in the 2000s

The 1990s closed with a familiar sense of foreboding. In July of 1999 violent attacks by fundamentalist vigilantes on student demonstrators at the University of Tehran led to riots that were brutally suppressed by security forces. This violent event marked the swift retreat of the already considerably eroded reformist movement through the early 2000s. Khatami's impotence in negotiating the complex network of firewalls and booby traps built into the postrevolutionary structure of governance was confirmed. It was both a lost opportunity and a chilling insight into the reality of the situation, the unforeseen extent of the revolutionary systemic stranglehold. The tipping point came when the lower classes, which faced the brunt of recent debilitating economic policies, began rejecting the reformist agenda en masse, paving the way for the rise of the old-school hardliner, Mahmoud Ahmadinejad, and his subsequent election as president in 2005.

The public performance of both obedience and resistance became increasingly complex through the late 1990s and 2000s: women wearing their headscarves slipped back to expose substantial bangs, extensive blogging, nightclubs having watchguards and "licit music" ready for quick shifting from what people were really listening to in the event of an inspection, and shouting "*Allahu Akbar*/God is Great!" from rooftops at night during the 2009 election crisis. Public and private personae and behaviours, always different in any culture, became and remain radically contrasted for most Iranians.

As Iran teetered back into the haze of a very tired, ossified and, for the majority of Iranians, suffocating betrayal of revolutionary ideology, the eve of the new millennium propelled Shajarian to a new level of international recognition with his receipt of the Picasso Medal from UNESCO in 1999. He continued the routine established in the 1990s but with a much higher profile and cultural cachet, performing in the most prestigious concert venues in the West. His accompanists through to about 2008 were Alizadeh, Kalhor, and his son Homayun, the ensemble was presented under the name *Masters of Persian Music* in North America for concert tours and domestic recording releases. The group toured Europe and North America in 2000 to 2001 performing a program of Nava and a setting of modern "neopoetry" in a modal invention of Alizadeh, which were released as two separate albums in 2002. A recording of the Nava portion of the concert was issued as *Bi To Besar Nemishavad* ("Without You Being is Not") on Delawaz and simultaneously on the American label World Village (an extension of the World Music Institute, New York) as simply "Without You." A California performance of the other half of the program in early 2001 was released on Delawaz as *Zemestan Ast* (discussed below). A live recording from the North American tour of 2002 featuring Rast Panjgah and *morakab khāne* resulted in the release of the double-CD *Faryad* ("The Cry") on both Delawaz and World Village. The poetry Shajarian chose to sing on *Faryad* is very graphic, the thinnest veil imaginable:

From the poison that has swept across this land, it is
A wonder that there remains any fragrance in its flowers,
Or any color in its fields

(CD I/Track 6: Hafez[9])

My house is in flames.
They burn furiously every thread that I painfully sewed,
Every leaf that I patiently grew, as I run fruitlessly
From corner to corner, and cry out, cry out.

From their rooftops, my enemies rejoice, pouring their
Ruthless laughter down at this destruction, as I witness
This injustice, and cry out, cry out.

With blisters on my hands, I overcome one flame
As another rises. Will my kind neighbours awaken even,
From their deep sleep, to lend a helping hand?

As I cry out, cry out.

(CD I/Track 8: Akhavan Sales)

I have lost my way in this dark night. Hear my call and rise,
Oh bird of guidance

(CD II/Track 5: Hafez)

I pound my fist on the door, scratch my fingers on the window
I am suffocating in this dead air.

Let me scream out loud. Let me breath the open air of
The hills and the rooftops.

I want to scream out, so all of you will hear my voice.
Will any of you, "the sleeping masses," join my cry?

(CD II/7: Moshiri)

The ancient city of Bam in south central Iran, a UNESCO Heritage site on account of its unique mudbrick architecture, was hit with a devastating earthquake on December 26, 2003 that killed tens of thousands and flattened the city. As he had done with previous disasters in Iran, Shajarian organized a benefit concert the following month which is documented on the DVD *Hamnava ba Bam* ("Compassion for Bam") released on Delawaz. The government had donated the use of a three thousand-seat theatre in Tehran but after the concert, in which Shajarian sang Akhavan Sale's transparently critical *Faryad* (translated above) and the protest anthem *Morghe Sahar,* the group's equipment was impounded with a $40,0000 release fee (Alavi 2005:236). Ney Davud (1900–1990) set a melody to the famous text *Morghe Sahar/*"Bird of Dawn" of the great dissident poet Mohammad Taghi Malek al-Shoara Bahar (1886–1951), composing an iconic tasnif that was banned by Reza Shah. A translation follows:

> Bird of dawn, cry out,
> Refresh my pains,
> Break this cage,
> Bring forth a transformation!
> My tangled-wing nightingale,
> Break out of this cage!
> Chant the anthem of freedom of humanity
> With every breath for the soil of this land and its inhabitants . . .
> The tyrant of the tyrants . . .
> Who have relinquished our home to the winds.
> O God! O Universe! O Nature!
> Make our darkest night dawn.

Unphased and keeping his eye on the ball, Shajarian and a group of his friends initiated plans to create an artistic center—consisting of a library, amphitheater, and garden called the Bam Art Garden—that would serve as a beacon of hope and inspiration to the surviving citizens in the lengthy recovery and reconstruction process. The project received support from citizens across the country. Shajarian elaborates:

> *We believed that raising the spirit of people is of the first priority and also that art can bring life back to them. We consulted others and decided to construct an art garden where artistic activities, research, and education can take place. We were thinking of accomplishing many social and cultural activities and construction of the buildings was only the beginning. We did not intend to simply build a structure. My colleagues and I were planning to take the art and cultural potential of our society to the city of Bam.* (Tehran Times, 2009)

Unfortunately the project got bogged down when, unbeknownst to Shajarian, officials of the provincial government switched contractors, who proceeded to use the funding to construct totally unrelated buildings. Shajarian withdrew from the project in May 2009 (ibid.).

In the last production of the *"Masters of Persian Music"* ensemble, a Tehran concert of 2007 was released as two separate albums the same year: *Soroud e Mehr* ("Song of Mehr") and *Saz e Khamoush* ("Instrument of Silence"). The same year Shajarian and Majid Derakhshani founded the *Shahnaz Ensemble*—named in memory of Ostad Jalil Shahnaz—as a vehicle for highlighting the talent of young Iranian musicians and as a dialectical outlet for developing musically the new stringed instruments that Shajarian had been designing and crafting over the past several years (discussed below). Two thousand and seven also saw the release of *Ghoghaye Eshghbazan* ("The Tumult of Lovers") recorded in the studio (the date is unclear) with Derakhshani and a small ensemble of traditional instruments.

Shajarian toured North America and Europe with the Shahnaz Ensemble in 2008, Europe in the fall of 2009, and then an intense sweep through England, Australia (for the first time?), and North America in the spring of 2010. Perhaps precipitated by the 2004 Bam concert, during his 2008 tour it spontaneously became *de rigeur* for Shajarian to sing *Morghe Sahar* as an encore in concerts, a ritual that he is called upon to maintain wherever he performs. Singing this song has become a symbol of resistance, refueling the flame of hope with each performance. A Tehran concert with the group in the fall of 2009 was recorded and released immediately as *Rendan e Mast* ("Drunken Rends"). Following in the wake of Shajarian's very public denouncement of the Iranian government in the aftermath of the election crisis, it became a huge hit in Iran and around the diaspora, depleting Delawaz's entire stock within months.

Ah Baran ("Ah Rain"), an album featuring orchestral arrangements by Mazda Ansari with Farhang Sharif accompanying the avaz, appeared in 2009; the date of recording is unclear but probably quite recent. The number of Delawaz releases in the 2000s dropped markedly from the prolific 1990s, and consisted mainly of issuing recent concert recordings shortly after their performance, often the same year. Two archive recordings were published during this decade: *Bouye Baran* ("The Smell of Rain") from the 1970s and the 1984 duet with Farhang Sharif *Peyvand e Mehr* ("Relation of Mehr") were both released around 2000.

Performance Example 8: *Zemestan Ast*

OS
Zemestan ("Winter") *features a different method of doing avaz with neopoetry. I thought about it for many years, about* Zemestan, *to come up with an original style of avaz only for neopoetry. (2010)*

In the Zemestan *concert, like the poem, I try to express the connections with coldness through the language of avaz. Of course, this is not an unusual invention in this field. But the basis for the existence of such a thing is [latent] in our music and—of course, with a little change—we took into account two gushes from different dastgahs for this work. I must also mention that the piece* Dad o Bidad *had been devised by Mr. Alizadeh. He proposed that I find a suitable poem for setting avaz in the new mode. I started to think about which ghazal might work with it but after some time I thought about incorporating Akhavan's poem "Zemestan" with this mode in avaz. We had one or two practice sessions, and realized that it is going to be a good work for presenting at the beginning of the concert; then we recorded and released it. (Shajarian et al. 2004:230)*

To be honest I was very moved by the poetry of Zemestan, *to such an extent that I confess that no other concert has ever moved me as much. Sometimes, when the concert was over, I would feel the coldness of winter and the ceiling of the sky in my own being. This is how much poetry moves me. The feeling that was ignited in me on the stage was the same feeling of those who were bearing the difficulties of winter, and I felt that I am one of them too. (ibid.:223)*

I think Zemestan *is the best example of how to perform a neopoem with avaz.*

Question: So why didn't you continue exploring neopoetry?

Well, it's largely dependent on what one wants to say and what message one wants to pass on. I have other works that are also based on neopoetry and I will perform them in the future.[10]

I like Akhavan a great deal . . . he didn't hold back in his struggle and is very direct.[11]

AK

There was a movement of musicians attempting to set avaz to neopoetry that started long before Shajarian's *Zemestan Ast.* For example, Lotfi composed *Darvak* with the poetry of Nima Nushij, which Mr. Shajarian sang, Meshkatian's tasnif *Ghasedak* was neopoetry, and there were attempts by other singers but these weren't successful according to many musicians and connoisseurs. Nazeri performed *Zemestan* in 1981 and later (in 1987) *Dar Golestaneh* to Sohrab Sepehri's poetry; Sepehri's poetry was (and still is) very popular because he has a spiritual message that speaks to people and what they've been enduring during these past decades. People were trying to compose and sing with the new style of poetry but Shajarian was the real leader in this movement and everyone was wondering how he would set neopoetry to a form of avaz.

Shajarian seems to be using an adaptation of the style of *naqqali* or *rajaz*[12] in *Zemestan Ast.* Traditional singers use this style in various contexts, especially narrative ones: in epic recitation, eulogies, sacred histories, *taz'iyeh*, etc. It is not a new style but has a long and deep history in Iran. They're singing in a dastgah but they're not developing it musically in the same way one does in avaz; they want to make it very serious. They take out the ornamentation and tahrirs, and exaggerate the articulation—detaching notes, making both micropauses and long pauses—to make it more speech based, like a heightened form of talking, which is exactly what *rajaz* is. The delivery is very rhetorical and dramatic. So Mr. Shajarian is using the tools that he has inherited in a secular context, removing it from the religious context of *taz'iyeh* and toward the goal of making artistic and social commentary in delivering the narrative contents of the poem. In order to present this neopoem of Akhavan in a classical manner, Shajarian needed to practice these words a lot so as to deliver them in a dignified, effective way. This is something that is new for him, he's not used to it. He actually becomes like an actor of *taz'iyeh* in *Zemestan Ast,* but the context is totally secular. It's not a joyful poem—it's winter, everything is dark and cold, everyone is cold. This is the environment of Iran.

But Shajarian is of course expanding the traditional *rajaz* and being more creative in *Zemestan Ast*; he's really creating an ambiance. That is one of the main features of Alizadeh's music and style: he creates an ambiance. It's a style called *fazā sāzi*, which is literally "making space/environment." So Alizadeh created the background environment that Shajarian applied very effectively to the text of Akhavan's poem. Certain words are emphasized to capture the feelings of the listeners. Ostad is deeply affecting their feelings through his setting of the words but he doesn't use much tahrir because he's very aware that this would evoke an entirely different feeling and ambience. He sets and paces this brilliantly but it is really based on creating a powerful ambiance on a scale that really only Alizadeh's music can. Without that ambiance I'm not sure that this would work and I couldn't see him working further in this direction with other musicians.

RS

Avaz is synonymous with classical poetry, which is definitively structured on the meters of *aruz* and various patterns of rhyme—in turn these constitute the structural fabric of avaz.[13] Nima Yushij (1896–1960) is considered the father of modern Persian poetry, specifically the free verse style of *she're no* ("new poetry," commonly translated as "neopoetry"). He dispensed with the conventions of *aruz* and rhyme and focused on contemporary issues rather than the traditional imagery and subject matter of the classical poets while targeting a wider, more popular audience than the courtly elites who fostered most classical poetry. He began exploring this new idiom in the 1920s but most of this work remained unpublished and little known until the late 1930s. One of the most brilliant proponents of this movement was the Mashhad born Mehdi Akhavan Saless (1928–1990), who assumed the penname *M. Omid*, "M. Hope." Saless was imprisoned after the fall of the Mossadegh government—infamously orchestrated by the British and Americans—and shortly afterward, in the winter of 1955, published the poem *Zemestan* describing the chilling shroud of alienation that enveloped Iranian society. It is one of the most popular and famous neopoems ever written. The poem found a renewed resonance with Iranians after the revolution, and still again when the impotence of Khatami, the reformists, and the divided foundation of society were put in clear focus following the 1999 student riots. This marked the return of yet another Ice Age after the brief hope of a thaw through the mid 1990s.

Shahram Nazeri sang parts of the poem in M.R. Darvishi's 1981 work *Zemestan*, scored for Western orchestra and solo vocalist, where the avaz functions more like another line within the orchestral texture—one that, given the anchoring in a Western harmonic idiom, seems likely to have been provided by the composer with Nazeri contributing occasional ornamentation. Short tahrirs aside, the vocal idiom seems quite tenuously grounded in Persian avaz.

Shajarian first recorded avaz using neopoetry in 1975 on *Golhāye Tāze* #77, setting Moshiri's *"Por kon piyāleh rā"* ("Filling the goblet") to Mahur with the violin accompaniment of Habibollah Badi'i (Shajarian et al. 2004: 67); the recording was later reissued on the album *Jām Tohi* (see the appendix). However, his approach on this recording was quite close to conventional avaz, the poetry seemingly grafted onto the conventional style: slow paced, using gushes from the radif and including tahrirs.[14] *Zemestan Ast* present a very different style of singing that marks an unmistakable departure from convention while remaining within the aesthetic realm of Persian music.

Shajarian's European and North American tours of 2000 to 2001 with the *Masters of Persian Music* lineup featured a setting of the poem in the first half of the concert, documented on the CD *Zemestan Ast*[15] from a California performance in 2001, published by Delawaz the same year. The recording is remarkable in many respects: it is a powerful, moving performance; it is unique as Shajarian's first major foray into singing neopoetry as avaz; and it is also unique in terms of Shajarian's usual working process, which usually begins with a poem that spawns the music. In this case, as stated above by Shajarian, the music came first. Alizadeh's 1998 album *Raze No* ("New Mystery") featured a thirteen-minute track entitled *"Dad o Bidad*/Justice and Injustice," a new modal invention described as a combination of the gushehs Dad (from dastgah Mahur) and Bidad (from Homayun), set to a brooding groove and a marvelously swirling polyphonic combination of male and female soloists. Despite the atypical arrangement and polyphonic texture, the poetry sung on this track is classical (by the Qajar-era poet Mirza Nasir Esfahani) and the individual strands of avaz are entirely conventional. The following three-minute track continues with the same poem and mode, *saz o avaz*, with Alizadeh's tar accompanying a male solist, whose style of avaz likewise continues in a conventional style, quite unlike Shajarian's adaptation of Akhavan's poem to Alizadeh's ambient backdrop in *Zemesatan Ast*.

Given its date, it's tempting (though probably incorrect) to read into the recording some kind of a deliberately commemorative timing: new poetry and a new style of avaz to kickoff a new millennium (if only according to the Christian calendar), one in which Shajarian entered a new level of global recognition with his recent receipt of the Picasso Medal. The audience seems somewhat caught off guard on the recording, with the artists getting their usual raucous, California style welcome of hoots, hollers, and whistling as they took the stage, while the concluding applause—usually the same kind of football game roar overlapping the final notes—enters tentatively and remains markedly subdued after six seconds of silence. An unpublished recording from a European date on the same tour features a similar delay. Perhaps this speaks more to the powerfully introspective and sobering atmosphere that the performance induces. I felt somewhat indifferent to the recording upon first hearing it but quickly tuned in to its profoundly moving spirit; more than most of Shajarian's recordings, it richly rewards repeated listening. In retrospect, the concert recording seems presciently frozen in history, as the performance was early in 2001 and no one had a clue as

to the catastrophic cold front and prevailing darkness that would soon descend upon America and subsequently the entire planet. A new world order.
Translation (transcription excerpts are in italics):[16]

(Dad)
They are not going to answer your greeting,
their heads are in their jackets.
Nobody is going to raise his head,
to answer a question or to see a friend.
The eyes cannot see beyond the feet,
the road is dark and slick.
If you stretch a friendly hand towards anybody,
he hardly brings his hand out of his pocket,
because the cold is so bitter.
The breath which comes out of his lungs,
becomes a dark cloud,
and stands like a wall in front of your eyes.
While your own breath is like this,
what do you expect from your distant or close friends?

(Bidad)
My gentle Messiah, O, dirty dressed monk,
the weather is so ungently cold.
You be warm and happy!
You answer my greeting and open the door!
This is me, your nightly guest, an unhappy gypsy;
this is me, a kicked up, afflicted stone,
this is me, a low insult of creation, an untuned melody.

(Iraq)
I am neither white nor black.
I am colorless.
Come and open the door, see how cheerless I am.

(Dad)
O, my dear host, your nightly guest is shivering outside.
There is no hail outside, no death;
if you hear any sound, it is the sound of cold and teeth.
I have come tonight to pay up my loan.
I have come tonight to leave my debt beside my mug.
What are you saying, that,
it is too late, it is dawn, it is day?
What you see on the sky,

is not the redness after dawn,
it is the result of the winter's slap,
On the sky's cheeks.
And your universal sun, dead or alive,
is hidden by the long coffin of the dark.
O, partner go and get the wine ready,
the days are same as nights

(Shushtari)
They are not going to answer your greeting,
the air is gloomy, doors are closed,
the heads are in jackets, the hands are hidden,
the breaths are clouds, the people are tired and sad,
the trees are crystallized skeletons,

(Homayun)
the earth is low-spirited
the roof of the sky is low,
the sun and moon are hazy,
It is winter.

Dad and Bidad:
the air is gloomy, doors are closed,
the heads are in jackets, the hands are hidden,
the breaths are clouds, the people are tired and sad,
the trees are crystallized skeletons,
the earth is low-spirited
the roof of the sky is low,
the sun and moon are hazy,
It is winter.

Given the unique declamatory style and lack of rhetorical repetition in this performance, I forego the interlinear translation of transcription presented hitherto and here simply align the transliterated text with the translation:

salāmat-rā nemikhahand pāsokh goft
They are not going to answer your greeting,
sarhā dar garibān ast
their heads are in their jackets.
kasi sar bar nayārad kard
Nobody is going to raise his head,
pāsokh goftan o didār yārānrā
to answer a question or to see a friend.
negaha joz pishe pārādid natavānad

The eyes cannot see beyond the feet,
ke rah tārik o laqzān ast
the road is dark and slick

havā bas najavanmardāne sard ast . . . āy . . .
the weather is so ungently cold . . . oh . . .
damat garm o sorat khosh bād!
You be warm and happy!
sālamam-ra tu pāsokh gu yi dar bogshāy!
You answer my greeting and open the door!
manam man, mihemāne har shabat, luli vashe maqmum
This is me, your nightly guest, an unhappy gypsy;
manam man, sangi tipā khordeye ranjur
this is me, a kicked up, afflicted stone,
manam, dushnāme paste āfarinesh naqmeye nājur
this is me, a low insult of creation, an untuned melody.

na az ruman na az zangam hamān birange birangam
I am neither white nor black. I am colorless.
biyā bagshāy dar bagshāy deltangam
Come and open the door, see how cheerless I am.

Harifā! Mizbānā! mihmāne sāl o māhet poshte dar
O, my dear host, your nightly guest is shivering outside.
tagargi nist margi nist
There is no hail outside, no death;

sedāyi gar shenidi soh bete sar mā o dandān ast
if you hear any sound, it is the sound of cold and teeth.
man emshab āmadastam vām bogzāram
I have come tonight to pay up my loan.
hesābatra ke nāre jām bogzāram
I have come tonight to leave my debt beside my mug.
che migui ke bigah shod sahar shod bamdād āmad?
What are you saying, that, it is too late, it is dawn, it is day?

salāmat-rā namikhahand pāsokh goft
They are not going to answer your greeting,
havā delgir darhā baste sarhā gar garibān,
the air is gloomy, doors are closed, the heads are in jackets,
dasthā penhān
the hands are hidden,
nafashā abr, delhā khāsteh o qamgin,

the breaths are clouds, the people are tired and sad,
derakhtān eskilit hāye balur ākin
the trees are crystallized skeletons,

zamin delmordeh safer āsmān kutāh,
the earth is low-spirited the roof of the sky is low,
qabār āludeh mehr o māh zemestān ast
the sun and moon are hazy, it is winter.

Alizadeh's skill as a composer for film is clearly demonstrated in *Zemestan Ast*, where he creates a paradoxical sense of stasis and movement (so characteristic of Iranian cinema), often through the means of circuitous minimalism. In a unique and powerful synergy, Shajarian adapts to Alizadeh's foundation by overlaying an equally paradoxical narrative of avaz that restlessly goes nowhere. Where Alizadeh's original 1998 recording of "Dad o Bidad" remains within the compounded modality that he invented, the form of *Zemestan Ast* is considerably expanded through a progression of gushehs identified on the track index as: (tar intro–*pishdaramad*)–Dad–Bidad–Iraq–Dad–Shushtari/Homayun/Dad and Bidad. The very liberal usage of these designations suggests a more narrative, dramatic deployment of the semantic associations of these titles as opposed to a concern for technically precise modal nomenclature. The compound mode "Dad o Bidad" of Alizadeh's original 1998 recording is designated as Dad or Bidad alone until the very end of *Zemestan Ast*.

The described compound nature of Alizadeh's beautiful invention is not particulary obvious (see "Dad," on the first page of the transcription). The radif of Abdollah Davami (with whom Alizadeh studied) juxtaposes a short phrase entitled Dad within his Bidad of Homayun but this bears no resemblance to Alizadeh's creation. Shajarian follows this with phrases that somewhat abstract the leaning, descending gestures—"sighing" gestures by European baroque *Figurenlehre* standards—along with the Ionian tetrachord definitive of Dad in the radif, which is mirrored in its return after 'Iraq (i.e., beginning with somewhat "Dadish" gestures [transcription page 3] before closing in the distinctive "Dad o Bidad" with its flattened second degree). Similarly, the central Bidad section is actually in Qarache and Razavi of Shur, Shajarian's most frequently used modulation. While the gushehs that cluster around Bidad include a modulation to Oshaq, to which Shajarian generally attaches Qarache and Razavi, there is nothing here evoking Bidad proper. The inclusion of 'Iraq buttresses the Mahur association of Dad, but the appearance of Shushtari and Homayun in the penultimate section of the performance ground the piece in Homayun, the modal homeland of Bidad while the coda recapitulates the ambiguities of Alizadeh's Dad of Bidad. The motif with which the work reaches its fading conclusion actually evokes the atmosphere of Shur. In terms of modality and form, *Zemestan Ast* is a novel and creative use of radif materials that illustrates the latter's flexibility and intrinsic creative potential.

Zemestan Ast

"Dad"

sa - lâ - mat - râ   ne - mi - kha - hand   pâ - sokh go - - - - -

o - - - - oft sar - hâ dar ga - ri - bân ast   sar - hâ dar ga - ri - bân

ast   sa - lâ - mat - râ   ne - mi - khe - hand   pâ - sokh

goft   sar - hâ   dar   ga - ri - bân   ast

ka - si sar (va dam) na - yâ - rad kard   pâ - sokh gof - tan o

di - dâ - r(i) yâr - an - râ   ne - ga - ha joz pi - she pâ - râ   di - (du) nat - vân - ad

ke rah tâ - rik (o) - laq - zân ast   ke rah   tâ - rik   o laq - zân   ast

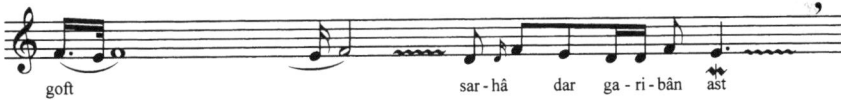

"Bidad" (second section)

ha - vâ   bas na - ja - van - mar - dâ - ne   sard   ast   â - - - - - y

(n) da - mat   garm o so - rat khosh bâd   sâ - lam - am - ra   tu pâ - sokh gu   yidar bogshâ - ay ma-nam man   mi-he-mâ- ne har sha-bat   lu-li va-she maq-mum

ma - nam   man   san - gi   ti - pâ   khor - de - ye   ran - jur

ma-nam   dush - nâ - me pas-te â   -   fa-ri   -   nesh

(n) (naq - be-nam)dush-nâ - me pas-te â - fa-ri-nesh   naq - me-ye nâ- jur

naq - me-ye nâ   jur

Shushtari

sa - lam-at - râ   na - mi - kha-hand   pâ-sokh goft

ha - vâ del-gir   dar-hâ bas-te   sar-hâ   gar ga-ri-bân

das-hâ   pen - hân   na-fas-hâ   a   br del-hâ khâs-teh o qam-gin

de-rakh-tan   es - ki-lit - ha - ye   ba-lur   â - kin

(The complete example is posted at www.yorku.ca/robsimms/shajarian)

Of course, the juxtaposition of the semantic polarity of Dad o Bi-dad/Justice-Injustice, is powerfully provocative in the same way that 'Āshiq Kosh is in *Yad e Ayam*. As mentioned, Dad and Bidad occur together in Dava-mi's radif but the words are more commonly used as an extratextual voca-ble/filler for tahrirs and musical phrases. Shajarian employed it repeatedly near the end of *Astan e Janan* while reciting *dobeytis* of Baba Taher. And by 2001, inclusion of the pronoun "Iraq" carried quite specific connotations in this regard, though very differently for Iranians and Westerners. Again, while its inclusion was doubtlessly coincidental, the prescience of this is chilling, given the un-thinkably ruthless injustices that still awaited Iraqis at the time of the recording. Occasionally art can resonate with larger historical patterns that may lie outside the deliberate intentions of its creators. In many ways the modal nomenclature seems to make *Zemestan Ast* function like a sequel to *Bidad (Homayoun)*, partic-ularly in its recapitulated evocation of restless stasis and frigidity, heightened by the fifteen years that passed since the appearance of the latter album.

Shajarian's declamatory style engaged here allows him to deliver the text much more quickly than with his usual style of avaz; the rather long poem is deftly paced (including repeated sections) through the use of this idiom. For the most part the rhythmic setting fits surprisingly close to a linear relationship on a steady pulsed grid, much more so than the fluid, messier ratios encountered in his conventional avaz (to say nothing of the complexities of the *Rabbana*). There are no tahrirs, save for some occasional short flourishes and little in the way of melodic development. Variation and interest is generated through a quasi-dramatic change of vocal timbre, vocal grain, and dynamics resulting in the im-pression of a change of characters or emotional-psychological states. Do these varied characters represent a collage of vignettes of different individuals? A con-versation? A narrative of struggle (collective and/or individual) through time? The rambling inner dialogue of a divided self? A vivid nightmare? All of these possibilities are simultaneously implied in this one-man opera. Shajarian brings colorful shadings, variation, and progression to the monochrome bleakscape where time plods on but one goes nowhere. His constant hesitation and short, fragmented phrasing create a sense of uncertainty and edginess, underlined on a larger scale by the nervous alternation of various instrumental interludes that make for an exhausting, mercurial winding up and down of energy.

Shajarian surely succeeds at his goal of evoking the cold alienation of the poem. Venturing deeper into the dense *iham* of his setting of the poem, a narra-tive strand of the process of grieving seems entirely plausible. The stages of grieving impending death as posited in Elisabeth Kübler-Ross's famous model—denial, anger, bargaining, depression, and acceptance, which others have sup-plemented with shock, upturns, loneliness, and hope, etc.—are seemingly visited in Shajarian's journey through *Zemestan Ast*, albeit with some variation in the ordering.

Shajarian's vocal character in the opening of the presentation of "Dad" is withdrawn, dejected, blasé, and indeed cold, the long-held notes of the opening immediately introduce listeners to the stasis pervading the work. The following section (not included in the transcription), although continuing to describe the bleak atmosphere suggests a gentle, somewhat lighter, warmer and perhaps hopeful shift of perspective. The opening of Bidad marks a decisive shift of gears and energy, modulating to Shur and building in intensity. Shajarian's vocal character is no longer passive but now agitated and aggressive, there is a clear sense of distress, desperation, and panic as the person/persona wildly addresses a possible saviour.

This energy culminates in 'Iraq, where Shajarian sings the existential text slightly out of sync with the 3–3–2 ostinato/groove, dramatically entraining with it only at the last word "*deltangam*/my cheerlessness or longing." The vocal character here is strident and seemingly angry, pushing back at obstacles. Akhavan's claustrophobic, rhetorical repetition of "*bagshai*/open," the keyword of the demand to "open the door" and "open my cheerlessness/longing" is further heightened by Shajarian's setting. Very interestingly, the setting of 'Iraq in the unpublished European performance mentioned above possesses none of this aggression, and rather understates this key portion of the poem in the lower octave with a relaxed vocal tone and quick delivery. It is a remarkable example of the flexibility of Shajarian's composition of avaz; the variation of this potentially climactic moment alters the whole form, and cumulative dramatic/narrative effect.

Following on the heels of the frenetic energy of the instrumental interlude propelled by 'Iraq, a decidedly more "Dad-ish" side of Dad emerges in a vocal character that is coming back to its senses and, as the poem relates, is accepting its fate, paying its debt. The Ionian ambience here is one of solemnity, peace, and nobility at this moment of surrender. The section following the excerpt continues on this path but steers back towards the cold desolation of the Phrygian "Dad o Bidad" cadence. The driving *zarbi* interlude following this is suddenly derailed and arrested with the appearance of Shushtari. Sung in his low register, Shajarian's vocal character here is stark, dark, frozen, seemingly comatose. The text recapitulates the opening lines along with some key motifs of the poem before turning to an image of crystallized skeletons. Is this death? It does not last long, for he immediately ascends the octave and assumes an entirely different vocal character that seems very matter-of-fact, like a reporter or narrator (or the ancient Greek Chorus) standing outside of the tale: these are the facts, this is what happened. The "punchline" of the poem, its final line, is repeated four times: it is winter.

The stage is powerfully set for the curtain to now drop on Akhavan's icy tragedy. But the poem belongs to Shajarian at this time, not Akhavan. Shajarian resets the lines in vocal character we have not yet heard but somewhat resembles the dignified, peaceful voice we met in the return of Dad (page 3 of the transcription, after Bidad), here cast amid an ethereal instrumental drone and echo from his son Homayoun. It evokes visions of an entirely different level or dimension of reality, emotionally neutral yet leaning towards calm. Is this the afterlife? After-death? Time seems suspended but the performance fades with unmistakable, restless movement forward, whispering "it is winter, it is winter . . ."

Shajarian's Public Role and Position

In Iran

OS
Question: How do you see your role in the artistic world before and after the revolution?
I have always had a role in our society and in families but I am not alone, there are a few other singers who have assumed this role as well. But I know that since singers get more exposure, they automatically become more influential. This is basically the artist's credit. When I first started singing, this art was considered forbidden, motrebi,[17] *and was frowned upon. People regarded all artists as drug addicts, but of course not all were like that. But because one or two were addicts or displayed inappropriate behavior, everyone concluded that all artists behave this way. So families were afraid of artists and were afraid to send their children to learn art and music, because they thought they may turn into drug addicts. But I proved that you can stay in the arts and remain clean and this had a very great influence and outcome in society. Of course, I was not alone in effecting this, there were a few others too. But I think that I was more influential because I had more exposure. So families told each other "Look, there is Shajarian, too—how come he hasn't been corrupted?"*

If you look at the families in Iran in the present day, you see that every family wants their children to at least play one instrument. In my time they broke the instruments over the heads of their children, but that is not the case anymore. Today families even force their children to play an instrument. This is all due to the work that we did and the way we behaved. We proved that an artist can have a good place in society and can be likeable and trustworthy. So I see this as a very important point, that we were able to have such influence on our society and basically took that wariness away from families. Once I was in court to see a judge and there were some other people there from the government. One of them, whom I think was an ayatollah, came to me and said, "My son wants to learn how to play the setar, can you recommend a good school for him?" Do you know what this means? It means that the very people who had called the music harām/"forbidden" *are now accepting it. When I was young it was never this easy, we always had to hide everything. (2009)*

AK

When people listen to Shajarian's voice, they have two choices: one is to look at it as entertainment. But you gradually come to realize that his music is very bad for a party or as background music because you have to really listen to it. If you don't listen attentively, it actually bothers you. I've noticed this so many times when Shajarian's music is on and people are talking. "What is this? Turn it off." Even musicians say turn it off in these contexts. There is another choice: you can look at it as a message. Some people are afraid of the message being conveyed, or do not understand it, or are not yet ready to understand it. A major change for Shajarian from before and after the Islamic Revolution was that he wanted his music to respond to society and become a message. So he made himself a messenger, sending a message from those people in Iranian society—poets, intellectuals, Sufis, writers, and artists—who have a deep understanding about what is going on. And he wanted to become a person who knows these things. That's why he responds to events happening in society. If you know what's going on in this society, you understand. You think "Oh my God, what an art!" It is saying "this is my belief" but you know that it's really true. So you get involved, you unite with other people. You actually became one with that art, along with many other people at the same time. I remember Mr. Shajarian once said something to the effect that: "What I like about my job is that, when I go to cities outside of Iran and notice that there are so many people who don't like each other, I know that because of me they're coming together to a "big house" and that they love each other. For that night, they know they have one thing in common: they like my voice and they like the poems I am singing."

RS

> The history of Middle Eastern music contains references to towering figures who were singled out by the shah and other potentates for special recognition or honour. The sharply hierarchical structure of society, headed by the figure of the king, seems in some ways to have been reflected in musical life. Middle Easterners, on the whole, do not respect musicians greatly, but they single out for special adulation a few of the best—the stars. (Nettl 1978: 156)

> After Aref Qazvini and Qamarolmoluk Vaziri, Shajarian is the most loved singer in the history of Persian classical music, and no one except him has exerted a deeper influence on the musical taste of Iranian audience (sic). (Musavi 2003:3)

> One of the few receiving nearly unanimous support from advocates of the ancient as well the modern, because he lives up to the public's expectation that he should not make concessions in his art, and who, in any case, has had no rival for thirty or forty years, is Mohammad Reza Shajarian. Had he wanted to, he could have known the media glory of Nosrat Fateh Ali Khan or of Alim Qasimov, but he decided to dedicate himself to his audience in his country which has at least saved him from compromising at all with world music,

even if, in the past few years, he has performed with instrumentalists closely linked to this trend. His position is due not only to his talent, but to the symbolic place of chant in Persian music, which is comparable to an immobile center around which instrumental music whirls. (During 2005:386)

Among both musicians and the general public, Shajarian is the most influential Ostad of Persian music in the late-twentieth-century, a position occupied by instrumentalists in the late-Qajar period. For musicians, Shajarian is an uncontested master of avaz based on both artistic and professional criteria. His technique, expressive and improvisational abilities, formidable knowledge of musical repertoire, and deep understanding of poetry have earned him a prestige reserved for the most respected, senior Ostads in the tradition. He is very much a "musician's musician." Likewise, he has no peer in terms of professional accomplishment and ranking within both domestic and international circuits of Persian music; he stands singular and uncontested at the top of his profession. Shajarian's musical cachet stems from his conservative yet tasteful and engaging mastery of avaz, funneling the best qualities from a range of sources within the tradition and presenting them with what many regard as technical perfection. While consciously following the creative vocation as a renovator, Shajarian had assiduously done his traditional homework and "would certainly be applauded by the Qajar Masters, which is probably not the case of the well-known 'creators' of our days" (During 2009: 126).

From the vantage point of the early-twenty-first century, it is apparent that Shajarian's brilliant consolidation of avaz style has become a pervasive model for the singers who followed him. Indeed, from the late 1990s onward his style may be also viewed as an overwhelming attractor that presents a crisis of its own to the present state of Persian music. While Shajarian is a more conservative renovator, the effect of his influence is akin to the reactions of musicians to the more revolutionary stylings of Charlie Parker in jazz or Paco de Lucia in flamenco, both of whom created a brilliant opening of possibilities along with an unintended, paradoxical closing due to the huge number of imitators they inspired.[18] The influence began as revolutionary but quickly moved from acceptance to *de rigeur*, to overbearing: stifling diversity and inhibiting individual expression. It is tempting, following from this, to view Shajarian's accomplishment as a phase transition of Persian music parallel to what bebop and *nuevo flamenco* represented to their respective traditions. While this analogy holds true for his tremendous effect on the propogation of his personal style among singers who followed in his wake, Shajarian's style is more like a further crystallization rather than a break from the Farahani radif, the creation of which clearly represented such a phase transition in the Persian tradition. A key difference in the present generation of singers is that Shajarian drew upon and synthesized numerous models while they evidently draw upon Shajarian alone.

Shajarian's rise to the top is surely a function of his extraordinary artistic gifts. But, alas, succeeding in the music business usually requires more than this and Shajarian's unprecedented professional achievement also speaks to other qualities he brought to bear—ambition, determination, political, and managerial sensibilities—while navigating the competitive, rough and tumble subculture of the professional Persian music scene (which wildly contrasts with the ethereal character of the music itself). His trailblazing success opened professional pathways for other Persian musicians. As is the case with musicians in all cultures, there are surely many brilliant singers of avaz who, active only privately or in small, restricted milieus, the world will never hear about: in many significant ways they are the very backbone of a tradition, whose values, conditions of performance, and significance are entirely different from those of the professional world.

In terms of more conventional, unmediated mentorship, Shajarian recently stated that he had seventy students and is clearly interested in supporting the next generation of artists: *"The lack of a large Persian musical instrument ensemble with new colours and textures performing new polyphonic arrangements on the one hand and the ever increasing number of extremely talented young music graduates who needed to be absorbed in classical Persian music ensembles on the other, were the main incentives for the formation of the Shahnaz Ensemble in 2007."* [19]

For the general public in Iran and throughout the diaspora, Shajarian is a national icon and celebrity, a role complete with concomitant stalkers, giddy women seeking personal postconcert photo-ops, chatty interviews, and lightweight coverage in Iran's popular press aimed at fans interested in his personal life, and so on. Like others in his position, to preserve his sanity amidst the bane and burden of celebrity necessitates the use of a formidable shield of go-betweens who filter the unending stream of requests and correspondence. He is extremely difficult to contact. In a 2001 interview he lamented: *"It is really difficult for a man to grow into fame. I am really ashamed [about the situation] of those true lovers of my work who speak about my work and want to meet me at least once and are unable to meet me. When the water overflows, it kills the man. When one grows famous he cannot respond to the kindness of all his admirers"* (Manateqe Azad 2001).[20] In addition to the marketplace clearly affirming Shajarian's public preeminence through his longstanding position as a top-selling recording artist, he has received many national awards for artistic excellence: placing first in a national competition of Qur'an recitation (1977), winning the National Radio and Television's "Golden Cup" (1977), being named "Iran's best classical vocalist" by the Ministry of Culture (2000), receiving the Nushin Medal, the most prestigious prize of the Critic and Theater Writers Society of Theater House (2008), and is currently Head of the High Council of Music of *Iran Musiqikhane*, the most prominent professional music association of the country. As occurs in all cultures, his considerable national cachet was boosted even further by receiving official international recognition (discussed below)—in Shajarian's case on an unprecedented level for an Iranian national in the contemporary world, let alone an Iranian musician.

As Iran's foremost musician, Shajarian embodies and symbolizes many things in Iranian society: national identity, Iranian tradition, *adab*, Sufism, *samā'*, and, following from the latter, subversion and resistance. Shajarian has performed concerts at all the important shrines and sites emblematic of Iran and Iranian identity: Persopolis, the shrines of Hafez, Ferdowsi, and Rumi, among others. As noted in chapter 2, Shajarian recorded some *sorud-haye enqelabi* in the optimistic haze immediately following the revolution but, as the true colours of the Islamic Republic became apparent, quickly and decisively distanced himself from overt political affiliation. But through a conscious and brilliant manipulation of *iham*, Shajarian made thinly veiled social commentaty that deftly sidestepped and simply transcended government authority, packing a powerful resonance. It was seditious yet expressed mass sentiment in the potent, frequently "forbidden" medium of music, which made it all the more attractive in the spirit of the mythological archetype of the "forbidden room" or "forbidden fruit." Its very restriction made it more seductive and, ultimately, powerful among a people under social seige. The revolutionary imposition of formally regulating religion, which was previously private and voluntary (eg., the maintenance of mosques) drove people to practice religion less publically and formally, and more privately. The resulting paradox was a secularization of "sincere religion" or spirituality due to its increased systemic empowerment and regulation by the government; a shift toward secularization resulted through sheer disillusionment (Abazari et al. 2008: 243, 250, 251). For many, Shajarian's avaz assuaged the struggle for sincere spirituality in the public sphere, people turning towards it to help fill the void left by bankrupt, hypocritical public religious figures. In this crisis of credibility and legitimacy, avaz increasingly served as a secular equivalent of *rowze khāne*,[21] uniting social classes in a common bond of belief and solidarity.

Shajarian's activity through the 1980s showed solidarity, daring defiance, shrewd intelligence, and integrity of leadership. He chose to stay in Iran when he could have easily left, as so many did—often with considerable effort and sacrifice. He remained musically active and visible throughout the period, as far as this was possible, pushing the envelope of meager opportunity to the limit by releasing recordings and performing live. He obliquely yet clearly criticized the government through the impunity of the great poets, ascending to a de facto, unofficial position of authority as a "truth teller" promulgating sincerity and truth in the face of hypocrisy.[22] The incident discussed in chapter 3 of the Vahdat/Rudaki Hall cancellations in 1988, with the overflowing hall calling for *Bidad* perfectly illustrates Shajarian's significance for embodying public sentiment, "real" Iranian spiritual values, and as a charismatic foil to Khomeini and his regime. In short, because of his music, his message, and his behaviour during these difficult years, Shajarian became a contemporary hero for a vast number of Iranians.

While the date of his first usage is unclear, Shajarian signed off the liner notes to the 1991 cassette (recorded in 1980) *Khalvat Gozide* as "The Dust on the Feet of the Iranian People" (*"Khāk-e pāye mardom-e Iran"*). *Khāk* ("dust, soil, dirt") signifies traditional values of humility and service in Iranian society. Variations of this theme would appear with frequency when signing off published statements throughout the following decade so as to constitute his quasi-*takhallus*: "The Dust on the Path of the People,"[23] "The Dust on your Foot,"[24] and "The Dust on the Foot of the People/Nation of Iran" (*"Khāk-e pāye melt-e Iran"*),[25] among others. It would figure very ironically in his high-profile denunciation of the government in the aftermath of the 2009 election crisis, discussed at the end of this chapter. This symbolic association combined with his often professed love of nature, his skill as a gardener, diligent study of birdsong, extraordinary singing ablilites, and the healing function that his music holds for many of his fans lends Shajarian some quasi-shamanistic archetypal qualities, albeit a decidedly modern, hypermediated, and enstatic highbrow shamanism.

Global Representative of Persian *Adab*, Transcultural Currents

Global connections figured prominently in Shajarian's activity and career even before he began regularly touring outside of Iran in the late 1980s. As noted in Simms and Koushkani (2012), he performed in concerts and television broadcasts with his mentor Ahmad Ebadi in Iraq, India, Afghanistan, and Pakistan, while other concert activities took him to Turkey, China, and Japan. From another angle, he performed and recorded in European embassies and cultural institutes of Tehran in the early 1980s, oases of diplomatic and international outreach within the rigid musical lock-down of the city at the time. While singers such as Taherzade, Qamar, and Banan were national icons of their respective periods, Shajarian was the first singer to achieve a solid international profile and become a global representative of Persian music. Many prominent Persian artists active as radio artists in the 1960s and 1970s were known outside of Iran through their appearance on anthology recordings released in the West but this was not coupled with a regular presence as touring concert performers, despite occasional appearances in Europe and North America. Moreover, the mediated reach of these artists outside of Iran was restricted to a fairly small audience with predominantly academic interests. This generation of Persian artists had neither the sizable, sustainable audience nor the need to pitch their careers outside of Iran at the time. Shajarian's initiative of undertaking regular tours to the West coincided with, and was facilitated by, both the general boom of World Music in the music business, as well as the huge swelling of the Iranian diaspora resulting from the mass exodus following the revolution. Shajarian—and immediately behind him Shahram Nazeri and Alizadeh—had both a ready made, welcoming audience and a meaningful new context for the music.

The occasion (*monāsebat*) for these Western tours was unique. Shajarian's earliest tours through to those of the late 1990s exclusively targeted and addressed the diaspora, which consisted almost entirely of political refugees from across the socioeconomic spectrum. Based on his fame on a national level before the exodus and the social premium placed upon avaz as a quintessential expression of the core Iranian values denoted by *adab*,[26] his concerts were likely among the largest and most diverse gatherings of expatriate Iranians within their respective transplanted communities. These gatherings would elicit a very different atmosphere and set of expectations than other large community events, such as political rallies or religious celebrations, and yet included aspects of these, striking a very deep chord of Iranian identity, solidarity, and nostalgia—the latter on both immediately mundane and potentially spiritual levels. The poetry Shajarian chose for these occasions usually acknowledged the difficulty of the refugees' position, and in a subtle form of protesting the pervasive injustice, called for wisdom and patience. The combination of this linear, rational message with the nonlinear, suprarational quality of Shajarian's presence with his fellow Iranians in exile, the powerful emotional force of his voice, the evocative medium of the dastgah, and the exquisite language of Hafez or Sa'di, produced a tremendous effect of heightening the present moment like nothing else could under the historical circumstances. Expatriate audiences on his tours include a wide range of age groups and social classes. Reactions from those attending his 2008 concert in Vancouver included weeping during the performance and comments afterwards such as: "He sings what we feel inside" from a young student, and from a senior, renowned architect in exile, "[The concert] makes me feel very close to this ancient culture—so full of content—but it makes me feel even more removed from this place" (Ditmars 2009:63, 64). Each expatriate community has its own character and Shajarian feels a particular connection with Iranian communities in San Francisco, Toronto, London, Köln, and Paris.

Shajarian's global profile moved into the mainstream music business through the release of compact discs—most of them live recordings of the kind of concerts just mentioned—on wide-distribution Western labels as part of the growth of the World Music market in the West. These recordings could be found stocked quite regularly in large mainstream record shops of Europe and North America, could be ordered through mail or the fledgling online sales of the time, and were acquired by a large number of university and public libraries. In short, they were visible and reasonably accessible to Western music consumers. The first of these releases were live recordings of concerts in Bonn and Paris.[27] The next releases were on the French label Al Sur in 1996, consisting of reissues of three influential recordings made in Iran from 1979 to 1984 and produced by Shajarian, including the iconic *Bidad (Homayoun)*. Also in 1996, Kereshmeh Records of Los Angeles released the concert with Lotfi made in the German Cultural Center of Tehran in 1981. His appearance on Kalhor's *Night Silence Desert,* released in 2000 on Traditional Crossroads, brought him wider recognition among a sector of the World Music audience with predilictions toward crosscultural fusions.

A series of releases in the first four years of this century by World Village Music (record label of the New York-based World Music Institute)—*Without You* (2002), *Faryad* (2003), and yet another reissue of *Bidad* (2005)[28]—were attractively packaged and the former two geared for sales in tandem with Shajarian's *Masters of Persian Music* tours, which moved beyond the exclusively diasporic promotion they received up to the late 1990s and were now marketed to the Western urban concert-going market at large. Given World Village's production of the American releases (they were simultaneously issued on Delawaz), it is probably not coincidental that both *Without You* and *Faryad* featured the poetry of Rumi, who is the bestselling poet in North America but is chosen by Shajarian with a noticeably disproportionate infrequency (see chapter 4 of Simms and Koushkani 2012). For those Westerners who discovered Shajarian through these CDs and were keen to dig deeper, it was not a huge leap to access his voluminous catalog of releases on Iranian labels through local Iranian businesses in many major cities or the Internet.

We have noted how Shajarian's Western concert tours and recordings initially targeted the Iranian diaspora but increasingly included a modest numbers of non-Iranian "locals." This was a logical move for business reasons but also more accurately reflected the social reality of Iranian émigré communities, who are generally very good at fitting into the mainstream of cosmopolitan urban life of Western countries, countries into which they had sunk solid roots by the late 1990s. The presence of non-Iranians increased at these concerts—which are still by far attended by members of the Iranian community—and made the occasion/*monāsebat* somewhat more complex, as most of them (in my experience) were attracted to the music but did not understand Persian.[29] Shajarian enjoys exposing avaz to non-Iranians in a humanistic, intercultural spirit but can do little to accommodate non-Persian speakers beyond translating the poetry into English (or French or German) in his recording liner notes; translations are not supplied in his concert programs.

Clearly, much is lost on these listeners without translation of the poetry and the impact of its coupling with the avaz, particularly given the great care Shajarian takes with regard to selecting poems and in wordpainting them. Perceptual differences between those who understand Persian and those who don't in the reception of his music are profound. Of course, non-Persian speakers who enjoy his music do so because of the expressive power of his voice and his superb technique, which is clearly evident to anyone with musical sensibilities. Indeed, perfecting and exhibiting this musical and technical aspect of his singing was Shajarian's primary aesthetic focus early in his career. While definitely not applicable to Shajarian's mature conception of avaz, Wright's conclusions regarding the subordination of the text to musical expression in avaz (2009:122–24) likely apply to many singers and Persian-speaking listeners. Moreover, many among the latter don't understand the poetry of Hafez or Sa'di to begin with, just as the genius of Shakespeare escapes most contemporary English speakers. The ostensibly iconoclastic composer Harry Partch was a staunch traditionalist when it came to such issues (1974: 15–17), noting the tendancy through Western music history of subverting the Greek intentions of supremacy of text (especially with regard to unintelligible engagement of Latin chants), calling for a "Corporeal" music that privileged the monophonic setting of intelligible text. Shajarian is clearly his ally in this regard, although in a global context his Corporeal intentions necessarily become abstract, they are still appreciated but quite off his intended aesthetic mark. The transcultural communicability of his brilliant singing, while abstracted, still allows him to fufil his more general socioaesthetic goal of "pleasing and uniting" people.

For Shajarian *"music is an international language. Maybe one cannot understand the words I am singing, but they know what I am talking about. They can feel it. When I am influenced by a topic and I am singing about it, they can feel that energy and understand it. I have seen it numerous times, but I also have to know my job and understand the poetry and furthermore have the tools to explain it."*[30] This accords perfectly with the central tenet of *iham*, whereby individuals, based on their levels of understanding, take what they can (or want to) from the multiple layers of meaning and significance encoded in the performance of the poem. Some might argue, to Partch's consternation, that the aesthetic experience is even broadened and enriched by not understanding the language and its prompted imagery, opening the range of responses to infinity (as instrumental music was regarded in nineteenth-century Europe). The situation is quite analogous to the many lovers of Western art song or opera who don't understand Italian or German; some will read an abridged summary of the lyrics for a general orientation, others will simply listen and enjoy the music.

My own encounter with Shajarian's music provides a microscopic and random but nonetheless informative contrast to this generalized discussion of his global profile, which focuses on the machinations of the recording and concert promotion business. As important as the latter are in shaping musical culture, underground, grassroots micronetworks that operate under the official radar of business and culture brokers also play a significant but less analyzable role. As a student in Winnipeg (central Canada) in the 1980s, I was part of a circle of "world music" enthusiasts who shared cassette recordings—yes, I confess that they were all bootlegs—of a wide variety of musics that we acquired very much randomly. It was a classic manifestation of pre-Internet, self-organizing, micromusical cassette culture (cf. Manuel 1993). Around 1987 two unmarked cassettes that arrived through untraceable connections captured my attention and fuelled my growing obsession with Persian music. The singing with sparse accompaniment was extraordinarily deep and moving, a fantastic message in a bottle. Few Iranians lived in Winnipeg at the time and it wasn't until I later moved to Toronto that I first identified the singer as Ostad Shajarian, playing the cassette for an Iranian friend who instantly said "Oh, that's Shajarian. He's kind of like Iran's Pavarotti." I cite this anecdote because I don't think it was entirely surprising that Shajarian's cassettes penetrated this esoteric circle of Winnipeg enthusiasts. Given Shajarian's significance in Iran, odds were heavily stacked in his favour that someone would pack his recordings along with their exile to cold central Canada and share them with the first Canadian who showed an interest. I can never know the real back story of the mysterious cassettes but they sowed the seeds for this book and a lifetime of exploring Persian music.

Over the past two decades of discussing Persian music with Iranians in Canada, their frequent surprise that non-Iranians would be attracted to this music at all has been equalled by my surprise at their considerable underestimation of its obvious transcultural appeal, its potential ability to move and enrich the human soul regardless of cultural background. Compared to many non-Western musics, Persian music does not present a huge aesthetic leap for Western listeners. Conversely, it doesn't in the least surprise me that many Iranians love Bach and Beethoven, for the simple reason that it is great music, period. Among other things, Shajarian represents a positive, attractive, and inspiring face of Iranian culture to small but significant non-Iranian audiences around the world. His symbolic role in this capacity is all the more important given the lowly public image Iran has as a pariah state in the West, where an ancient history of propaganda, stereotyping, and an appalling lack of basic knowledge among the general population makes this very easy to perpetuate. In my own case—as I imagine with many other non-Iranians worldwide as well—Shajarian's music was the hook that inspired me to embark upon an extensive exploration of all aspects of Iranian culture, particularly its poetry. Of course, many people, including Ostad Shajarian, now regularly traverse crosscultural bridges in their music appreciation.

OS
Question: What do you listen to in your solitude?
I listen to [Western] *classical music, and also Shahnaz, and Mahjoubi's piano— these people give me energy and motivation because both of them are very skilled in composition and creativity. I also sometimes listen to jazz to relax, like when I drive. One has to know why one listens to music. You cannot listen to one kind of music all the time.*[31]

When music, which is the language of humanity, comes out of the disposition of an artist who lives for humankind, the hearts of any nation will accept it. Although I am not familiar with the lives of any of the masters and artists that I am going to mention, I nevertheless enjoy their art and I feel that each one has a humanistic fire hidden in his heart. When I listen to the sitar of Vilayat Khan or Nikhil Bannerjee, I feel that it has summoned my whole being. When I listen to the sarangi of Sultan Khan and the shehnai of Bismillah Khan, it will move me. These are people who have not lived for themselves, but have lived for humanity and beauty. The voice of Um Kulthum moves me; when this artist passed away, she had a several million mourners, because she arose from the heart of the Arab people. The voice of Nat King Cole and the flute of Zanqi[32] also captivate me. Vivaldi's Four Seasons and many other Western classical works also give me pleasure. So you see that I do not have any prejudice towards my own music. I desire a voice that has risen from a humanistic disposition. We have to know this, that when our music is good, and the artist has followed it with love, and has spent time on it, and has obtained the required knowledge and confidence, and also speaks the truth, it will certainly make an impression on anyone. This individual can be Japanese, Canadian, an Eskimo, a black or a white person. (Qaneeifard 2003: 111–12)

Global Recognition and Awards
RS
Even as his career was secured in Iran, Shajarian was establishing an international reputation, receiving various awards and distinctions from foreign governments and organizations, a form of official global recognition that increased dramatically from the late 1990s onward. In 1974 he was among a group of artists chosen as "special guests" to travel to China and Japan, marking the opening of flights between Iran and these countries. In 1976 he received a prize from the speaker of the Turkish *majles*/parliament for his Qur'an recitation. Three years later he placed second in an international competition of Qur'an recitation in Malaysia. As noted above, in tandem with his regular North American tours through the 1990s, he was invited to make lecture-presentations at various prestigious American universities, including UCLA, Berkeley, Columbia, Harvard, Chicago, and the University of California at San Diego. We also noted his invitations from governing officials to perform in Barcelona in 1990 and Dushanbe in 1991.

The two awards from UNESCO brought Shajarian a level of global recognition reserved for the most elite artists in the world. In 1999 he received one of UNESCO's highest honors, the Picasso Gold Medal, awarded "to individuals or groups in recognition of an outstanding contribution to the arts or culture";[33] previous recipients included Shostakovich, Yehudi Menuhin, and Nusrat Fateh Ali Khan. And in 2006, following the likes of Elizabeth Schwarzkopf and Mstislay Rostropovich, he was presented with the Mozart Medal, awarded "for contribution to world peace through music and the arts."[34] The prestige of these awards lent incalculable political and artistic cachet to Shajarian in Iran, signaling his unprecedented position as a representative of the positive face of Iranian culture, and the admiration of the world for his art, compassion, and leadership. Shajarian represented hope. The gesture empowered him as an artist and public figure, and indicated an interest in the world-governing body to establish normalized relations with Iran, a bridge predicated on art, welcoming it into the world community through his embodiment of *adab*. It was a rare carrot offered to Iran via Shajarian after decades of confrontational stick diplomacy. It also empowered and further inspired Shajarian to continue his peaceful resistance of the Islamic Republic, which emboldened him to be unprecedently outspoken in the immediate aftermath of the election crisis of June 2009 and throughout his 2010 world tour, as we will see shortly.

In the period between garnering these prestigious UNESCO awards he was also recognized by the mainstream music business with Grammy Award nominations for "Best Traditional World Music Album" in 2004 (*Without You*) and 2006 (*Faryad*). While the nominations were in the name of *The Masters of Persian Music*, and the Grammys are more a recognition of business rather than artistic prowess, there is little doubt regarding his leadership of the ensemble, which would simply not have the public appeal without him—indeed the back of the CDs specify to "File under: World/Iran/Shajarian."

Still, Shajarian clearly accords with Grammy criteria in the sense that he racked up considerable record sales and commanded top performing fees for the concerts that these albums promoted, playing the most prestigious Western venues usually reserved for top-ranking Western classical musicians. His clout within the already waning World Music market was considerable throughout the 2000s. In terms of global recognition for Iranian nationals, only Shirin Ebadi's Nobel Prize of 2003 for her work advancing women's rights approaches Shajarian's accolades, which derive from a variety of unrelated institutions over an extended period of time.

Shajarian and World Music
Shajarian stands among a small group of singers of classical non-Western traditions who have received considerable renown within the amorphous marketing category of world music, a self-similar fragment of the larger historical-political discourse of "the West and the Rest" that effectively delegates the Majority World of "the Rest" to an unthinkably vast and subordinate ghetto of musical diversity. A facile definition of world music might be: any non-Western music, along with select Western folk musics, marketed for Western mass consumption. Since its official christening in the mid 1980s as a bona fide metagenre, the most commercially successful and widely known artists generally represent "folk" traditions, produced and presented with varying degrees of crosscultural hybridization (Western or otherwise), whether originally integral or concocted in the studio. As it peaked in its share of the overall music market during the late 1990s, the top World Music acts were by far the European "interior exotic" representatives of *rumba flamenco* (specifically the Gypsy Kings) and Celtic music. The former harkened back to very well-trodden grooves of gypsy music as a peripheral invigorator of Western classical music throughout the nineteenth century, the latter a resonance of the identity questing of post-World War II United Kingdom.

Among the many precursors of the 1980s phenomenon of world music, one of the most important was Hindstani classical music as embodied by the influential ambassadorial careers of Ravi Shankar and Ali Akbar Khan beginning in the 1950s through the crucial agency of Yehudi Menuhin and later, with an even greater populist impact, George Harrison. This early penetration of non-Western classical music into the mainstream music business—the release of multiple recordings on wide-distribution Western labels and a sustained touring presence in the West— paved the way for *oud* soloist Munir Bashir to become the first West Asian representative of the prenascent world music scene in the early 1970s, followed by *ney*-player Kudsi Erguner in the late 1970s and early 1980s. The activity of all of these artists dovetailed with and was easily subsumed, indeed boosted, by the world music industrial boom that followed in the mid 1980s. The fact that all of these artists were instrumentalists is noteworthy, perhaps indicating that instrumental music was more accessible to the ears of Western record buyers. On the other hand, surprise "hits" of the boom included the "folk"/"neofolk" vocal traditions of Bulgaria (Les Voix Mysterieux), Tuva (Hun Hurtuu), South Africa (Lady Blacksmith Mambazo) and later, polyphony of the Baka people of Congo. Naturally, colonialist differences continued to shape the new subindustry whereby the world music scene in Paris also accorded West African vocalists such as Salif Keita, Youssou N'Dour, and Mory Kante high standing relative to the Anglo-American market.

Through the crucial agency of Peter Gabriel's WOMAD and Realworld Records, the *qawwali* music of Nusrat Fateh Ali Khan was hugely successful and emblematic of the whole world music enterprise of the 1980s and 1990s. While accompanied by a large ensemble, the focus of the music was clearly on his virtuosity as a vocal soloisist, singing in Urdu. The earliest wave from his prolific output of world music recordings was traditional *qawwali* which quickly gave way to hybrid experimentation that grew increasingly less recognizable as *qawwali* and more an exotic thread within a pervasively Western popular idiom. Nusrat justified what many criticized as a compromised, watering down of his music in the latter recordings by proclaiming that his mission was to spread the Sufi message to the West. In this respect he was an extension and qualified fulfilment of Inayat Khan's pioneering mission, as directed by the latter's sheikh some eighty years previously. Among other things, Nusrat helped to establish "Sufi Music" as a subcategory of world music by the late 1980s (Bohlmann 2002), which had been percolating in another quarter during the late 1970s through Western tours of the Mevlevi dervishes and the work of Kudsi Erguner. Erguner was particularly influential as he spoke both English and French, cultivated a grassroots following in Europe through concerts, workshops and lessons, and released recordings with increasing frequency throughout the 1980s. Like Nusrat, his work included high-profile films (*Meetings with Remarkable Men, Mahabharata*) that exposed Sufi Music to an unprecedently wide audience.

While admiring Nusrat's vocal technique and ability to create excitement, Shajarian distances himself from his music on the grounds that it is limited in scope and limited in potential for development relative to avaz (personal communication, 2008). And yet he and Shahram Nazeri have undoubtedly inherited Nusrat's mantle as being the foremost global exponents of singing Sufi poetry. A large number of those Westerners interested in Shajarian's music will associate him with this function and Nusrat (e.g., Daftar-e-Honar 2002: 2225) whether Shajarian likes it or not. Yet, following During's remarks quoted above, Shajarian has made few compromises with his art in the face of the eclectic, hyperhybridizing impetus characteristic of the world music subindustry. His style and "branding" is consistently, unambiguously conservative and uncompromising compared with many world music icons. While he stretched borders somewhat in his work with Kalhor on *Night, Silence, Desert*, and performed with Azeri kamanche master Habil Aliyev in 1991, Shajarian really doesn't do world music.

Vocal soloists with successful careers in World Music circles abound from various cultures but very few of these represent classical/art music traditions. In the realm of maqam cultures Alim Qasimov and Lotfi Bouchnak stand out as classical vocalists with considerable profiles in the West, if not globally. There are, of course, many great singers who are very famous within the region and diaspora—Saba Fakhri being one of the most prominent among these—but who have not penetrated the larger platform of the global music industry and media. Likewise, Lakshmi Shankar and Pandit Jasraj are probably the most prominent classical Hindustani vocal artists globally, while the West African griots Kandia Kouyate and Dimi Mint Abba made an impact in the 1990s, especially in Europe. Reviewing this relatively rarified field of classical vocal soloists points to the likelihood that—despite the unquantifiable nature and questionable significance of such matters—Shajarian presently maintains one of the highest global profiles in terms of wide release recordings and a regular, global touring presence aimed (at least partially) beyond a diasporic audience. It is interesting to note that Shahram Nazeri also has a considerable international profile among this culturally diverse field, particularly in view of his association with the topselling poet Rumi.[35]

AK

I don't think Persian music has the potential for being world music in the way that, for example, Nusrat Fateh Ali Khan channeled *qawwali*. Nusrat had musical gesture in his voice, and the driving rhythm and clapping—all of that created an ambiance that people regarded as music for the dance floor or discotheque. But Mr. Shajarian's music is very culturally specific, it plays an important role in carrying and communicating the very deep meaning and message from the classical poets. Without any hesitation I can say that 90 percent of the audience of this music is Iranian, including immigrants living outside their country, but the music still functions for Iranians. Sometimes Shajarian changed the platform for presenting his concerts, like during the period he was working with the World Music Institute in New York (in the early 2000s). At that time his audience expanded somewhat and different people were paying attention; Kalhor really pushed the music of Alizadeh, whose music is prominently featured in the concerts and recordings of that period. You can really hear his style there. They pushed it to the level of being nominated for Grammys but it's not world music: it's Persian music, through and through, to the core.

As an analogy to the situation we could look at food, for instance. Cuisine from all over the world is available in restaurants in Toronto but they try to somehow domesticate that food for Canadian taste. The ingredients, recipes, and concepts are the same but they usually have to tone it down, make it softer than the original. The cooks and restaurant owners are concerned about what customers will like, so they have to think about what they are presenting and the experience newcomers have with this cuisine. But Persian musicians rarely think about this crosscultural experience, it's presented as is: undiluted, unadjusted, and undomesticated. In this sense you could say that it is "wild." If a non-

Iranian understands this music, they had to learn, had to teach themselves how to listen to it. It's like going to China and learning how to appreciate "undomesticated" traditional cuisine. There's quite a barrier that one would have to bridge or break through. But Persian musicians don't generally care about that kind of gap or what such an outside listener may be going through.

Persian music follows Persian culture and whatever is going on in Iran. That's why Shajarian can never leave Iran. He told me once that the source of the music is Iran and he couldn't understand how I could live here as a Persian musician. For my part, living in Canada and performing throughout North America, I have consciously tried to domesticate my music a little bit, adjust it to this new occasion. It was a pressure of learning, actually: learning how to combine things with my music and how to collaborate with musicians from various backgrounds. The situation demanded that I learn to do this.

Um Kulthum and Shajarian
OS
"Um Kulthum . . . is the best Arab singer. There will never ever be a singer like her again with a voice like that." (2008)

RS
On an entirely different level, Shajarian is often compared to the legendary Um Kulthum (1904? –1975), and with good reason. Um Kulthum is in a category of her own, both within West Asian musical culture and her contemporary global profile. Curiously, she was not directly a part of the historical paths traced hitherto in this discussion of the entrance of non-Western music into a Western, and then global, mainstream. Indeed, surprisingly few of her recordings have been made available through the media channels that conveyed Ravi Shankar or the later exponents of world music in the 1980s to wider audiences. Despite the fact that her last concerts were in the early 1970s while the first wave of "proto-world music" touring was well under way, her only concert outside of the Arab world was in Paris in 1967 (Danielson 1997:186). While little research seems to have been done on this topic, it seems that her legendary prestige and preeminence in the Arab world was transferred to a global audience more by a grassroots "word of mouth" grapevine of musicians (including some seemingly unlikely figures such as Bob Dylan and Robert Plant), critics, and music enthusiasts than by the conventional infrastructure of the globalizing music industry. Her global reception and prestige is all the more remarkable given its anomalous lack of industry machination.

Despite the many fundamental differences between Egyptian and Iranian cultures and musical traditions, Shajarian and Um Kulthum share a remarkable number of definitive artistic and cultural qualities, indeed, even biographical backgrounds. Both emerged from a provincial, clerical background—Um Kulthum was regarded as *min al-mashayikh* "reared among the sheikhs"—and began their vocal training as child prodigies of Qur'an recitation. In both cases, their fathers played a central role in their early musical development and in launching their public careers (ibid.: 21ff.). Both left the provincial back waters to further pursue their careers in "The Big City," where they eventually triumphed (ibid.: 24ff; 42ff). Like Shajarian in his mature style, from her earliest work Um Kulthum placed a high premium on the execution and evocation of the poetic text. A connoisseur in the 1930s noted that her "great value, in addition to her beautiful voice, was that she was educated (*adiba*) and understood what she sang. . . . She pronounces . . . all the songs in literary Arabic and she is almost the only one who penetrates the meaning and understands the secrets [of the poetry]" (Danielson 1997:97). Her skill at word painting, often accomplished through a judicious manipulation of shifting timbral colouring,[36] was widely appreciated by both music critics and devoted fans (ibid: 139ff). Of course, Um Kulthum was renowned for her prodigious, allegedly "perfect" vocal technique—her tone, powerful projection, control, flexibility, strength, and endurance—and her improvisatory skills, particularly her legendary ability to spin out endless variations on single lines or phrases of a song (ibid: 146ff). She preferred performing for a live audience, whom she greatly loved and appreciated, and whose feedback inspired her greatest achievements; she explicitly led rather than followed her accompanists (ibid:134, 136). All of these features and facts apply equally to Shajarian.

Moreover, both Um Kulthum and Shajarian are regarded as embodying quintessential traditional values of their respective cultures that resonate with a strong sense of national identity. Both artists consolidated key stylistic strands of their traditions while building upon, extending, and renovating them in a manner that emphasized continuity as opposed to wholesale innovation (ibid.:123, 197). Their work was emblematic of appropriately progressive cultural authenticity and admirable personal integrity, earning them an unprecedented sociocultural cachet. Both signified *adab* in very similar ways. Both became national icons, voices of national sentiment in their respective countries, though in very different political contexts and with completely opposite relationships to their respective governments. Both were renowned for performing in benefit concerts and national concerns (Danielson 1997:184ff), though again, in very different contexts—Shajarian's were largely in support of disaster relief until the election crisis of June 2009, when he attempted to muster national mobilization of an order quite different from Um Kulthum's rallying cause. Um Kulthum's concerts and broadcasts became legendary cultural events across the Arab world; some of Shajarian's concerts and recordings have had an equally significant impact in Iran and the diaspora. While Um Kulthum's music has been absorbed into the traditional Egyptian canon, "passing into *turath*" since her death, it seems quite clear that several of Shajarian's recordings (notably those discussed in detail in chapter 2) and certainly his consolidation of avaz style will be similarly incorporated into the Iranian musical canon. To further drive home the uncanny parallels between these two singers, the following quotes from the conclusion of Danielson's definitive study of Um Kulthum (1997) perfectly describe Shajarian's accomplishment and position among Iranians:

Umm Kulthum gave life to historically Arabic song in a commercial environment. . . . She emphasized her connection to the "folk" without recourse to folk music, associating herself with the more obviously learned traditional expressions.(p.196, 197).

Umm Kulthum was not . . . a politicized person, but she functioned in a political environment. (p.197)

She did not merely reflect social attitudes, she advanced them, promulgating a point of view, articulating a position, and feeding a strong and deep current of feeling. . . . After the entry of a song into the repertory of society, listeners used it for many purposes and moved its meaning through time and space. . . . This music, these songs, figured in the large-scale process of "acknowledging" within the society. They were taken in by listeners, learned, recited, performed, and replayed over years. They contributed to the popular construction of Umm Kulthum as one of them—a "real" Egyptian, an educated Arab.[37] (p.199)

A notable difference between the two can be seen in their creative working processes and participatory roles in the composition of their respective works. Um Kulthum relied on others to compose new poetry while Shajarian himself mined the classical poets for lines that expressed his intentions. Likewise, composers supplied all of the music for Um Kulthum, which she vetted, called for changes, adjusted to her own taste, and then memorized whereas Shajarian composed all of his avaz—melodicially, formally, and with regard to textual underlay—relying on a composer to supply framing zarbi pieces and tasnifs, though, as we shall see immediately below, Shajarian has also composed many of the latter himself. Lohman convincingly argues that Um Kulthum very consciously constructed her public image during the last years of her life in order to consolidate a legacy as an erudite, charitable, pious, politically-engaged nationalist. Egyptians rather unanimously embraced this image in the decades following her death (2010). By contrast, Shajarian shows more continuity throughout his career and, at seventy-one years of age, appears to have little need to engineer his image toward a targeted legacy. This is likely due to the very different political and historical contexts that formed the backdrops of their respective careers as well as differences in the personalities of these two great singers. Shajarian's musical-political activism dates back to the beginning of the revolution, before he achieved superstar status, with his nationalist *soruds* and his quick turn to veiled critique, which has remained his trademark *modus operandi* ever since. Likewise, his charity work covers several decades of sustained commitment, often due to the tragic regularity of major earthquakes in Iran.

Despite these differences, what Um Kulthum represents to the Arab world on the one hand, and the world of music in general on the other, is of a very similar order and magnitude to Shajarian's position among contemporary Iranians and global music culture.

Other Creative Output: Fine Arts Polymath

This study (including Simms and Koushkani 2012) has gone into considerable detail to illustrate how and why Shajarian is regarded as the unsurpassed master of the art of avaz and the vast literature for which it is a vehicle. A truly remarkable achievement in itself, Shajarian is an unusually talented individual with a wide range of interests and expertise; any accurate view of Shajarian the man and artist must include mention of this broader context of his consciousness, knowledge and abilities. This section will briefly review other creative work—musical or otherwise—to which he has devoted considerable time and energy pursuing and in which has attained a very high level of skill, lending him the distinction of being a rare "Renaissance man" of the fine arts.

Compositions Outside Avaz

AK
Ostad Shajarian began composing tasnifs in the late 1980s and was most prolific in the early 1990s; his output continued in the 2000s with new pieces as recent as 2009. In general, his style of tasnif derives from the lineage of Darvish Khan and Ney Davoud and follows the same school as his contemporary instrumental colleagues: Lotfi, Pirniakan (who composed more through the 1990s), and Derakhshani. Sheyda and Aref's tasnifs were simpler in structure but arguably more effective in impact because these men were both the poet and composer and could fuse those art forms together in a way that is more immediate and successful than with two separate individuals representing and trying to unite these domains. Table 3.1 below lists his tasnifs appearing on Delawaz releases.

Table 3.1. Tasnifs Composed by Shajarian

Title	Album	Mode	Poet
Sheydaye Giti	*Saz e Ghesse Gu*	Shur	Hafez
Sarv-e Chaman	*Sarv-e Chaman*	Mahur	Hafez
Khātr Hazin	*Sarv-e Chaman*	Mahur	Hafez
Be Hamzaban	*Sarv-e Chaman*	Mahur	Javad Āzar
Payam-e Nasim	*Payam-e Nasim*	Abu Ata	Hafez
Del Bordi	*Payam-e Nasim*	Abu Ata	Esfahani
Sanamā	*Del e Majnun*	Afshari	Mowlana
Del–e Majnun	*Del e Majnun*	Afshari	Mowlana

Y'ani Che	*Del e Majnun*	Bayate Tork	Hafez
Āsmān-e 'Eshq	*Āsmān-e 'Eshq*	Segah	Mowlana
Midanad (Be Garde Del)	*Āsmān-e 'Eshq*	Segah	Mowlana
Yad-e Ayam	*Yad Ayam*	Shur	Rahi Mo'yari
Kham Zolf	*Yad Ayam*	Shur	Baba Taher
Bar Man Sanamā (a.k.a. Motreb-e Del)	*Without You*	Nava	Mowlana
Faryad	*Faryad*	Dashti	Akhavan Sales
Dar Faraq	*Ghoghaye Eshqbazan*	Shur	Sa'di
Bād-e 'Eshq	*Ghoghaye Eshqbazan*	Afshari	Sa'di
Zaban-e Atesh	n/a	Dashti	Moshiri
Chashm-e Yarie	*Rendan e Mast*	Homayun	Hafez

Source: Delawaz recording liners.

There are various ways of composing tasnifs. Some artists compose a melody and then look for the poem but Shajarian's style of tasnif composition, like his avaz, is derived from the poem itself: choosing the dastgah, the gushehs for different lines, the phrasing, and rhythm. Previously, composers of tasnifs who didn't also write the poetry usually worked directly with the poet, who would customize the poem for the purposes of the tasnif and the two artists could craft the final work in mutual consultation. By contrast, Shajarian selects a finished poem, as is (though perhaps deleting and reording beyts) and works singlehandedly from that. His tasnifs are really a manifestation of his avaz with meter and he probably goes through a similar working process in the two genres. Of course, the metrical dimension adds certain constraints and conditions but he clearly uses his tools from avaz to create tasnifs. I perceive two different styles in his tasnifs. Some have a continuous, "flowing" style that keeps pressing forward, moving on in the progression of gushehs without returning to the daramad area or going back to earlier material until perhaps a recap of the first section to conclude (e.g., *Ba Hambazan*). Others, like *Yad e Ayam*, are more traditional, featuring a clear refrain, usually of daramad material and episodes in other shah gushes.

Shajarian likes to use an additive compositional technique where an idea is repeated and then extended with each repetition; this is also apparent in his Abu Ata Pishdaramad from the album *Payam e Nasim*. Whether extended or not, repeated material is usually subjected to some kind of subtle variation, which is probably improvised and different each time he performs the piece. Following the tradition of Darvish Khan, the instrumental refrains in his tasnifs repeat material from the vocal line (some composers, like Meshkatian or Payvar would include different material for such interludes). He specifies the placement of

interludes and the accompanists respond accordingly; there's frequently a noticeable hetereophonic element to these responses within the ensemble rather
than a clean unison. There's generally more elaboration, ornamentation, and use
of dynamics in Shajarian's rendering of the lines than in the instrumental responses. So the latter are more a matter of performance practice than composition
per se.

At any rate, in both approaches to form mentioned here his tasnifs have a
remarkable clarity in their setting and expression of the poetry. There's also considerable rhythmic variety in his songs: he uses both simple and additive meters
(especially seven or five beats) and his approaches to phrasing can range from
very square four-bar regularity (e.g., *Sarv e Chaman*) to more asymmetrical and
unpredictable groupings (e.g., *Yad e Ayam*). While Shajarian's composition of
instrumental music occupies a much smaller portion of his output, his pishdaramad in Abu Ata shifts between phrases of three bars (at the beginning) to
four-bar lengths.

Sarv e Chaman, Bi Hamzaban and *Asman e 'Eshq* are quite famous now and are
regularly performed by other musicians. As with his avaz, he has a knack for
picking poetry that is appropriate for the times, the broad historical occasion.
People love Shajarian's music and compared to his avaz, which is pretty prohibi-
tive in terms of performance potential for others, his tasnifs are beautiful and yet
accessible.

Sarv e Chaman (Hafez ghazal #187)[38]

1) Why does my cypress of the meadow show no inclination for the meadow?
It doesn't seek intimacy with the rose. It does not remember the jasmine.

3) In the hope of union with you, the heart is not at one with the soul:
In desire for your street, the soul does not serve the body

6) With all the folds of your gown, I wonder at the morning breeze,
That from wafting by you it does not make the dust musk of Khotan!

4) Once my vagrant heart entered the twist of his curl,
Because of its long journey, it does not make for its native place.

8) Though it were all dregs that my silver-thighed wine-boy were pouring,
Who is it that would not make the body into a wine-bowl, all mouth?

Sarv-e Chaman

sar - ve cha-mâ - ne man   che - râ   mai - le cha-man ne - mi   ko - nad

ham - da-me gol   ne - mi   sha - vad   ya - de   sa-man ne - mi - ko - nad

Del   be o-mi - de vas - le to   ham - da-me jan ne-mi - sh - a-vad

del   be o-mi - de vas - le to   Del be o-mi - de vas - le to

ham - da-me jan ne-mi - sh - a-vad   jan   be ha-va - ye ko - ye to

jan   be ha-va - ye ko - ye to

khed - ma te tan   ne mi   ko - nad   khed   ma te tan   ne mi   ko - nad

ba   ha-me at - re da - ma nat - â - ya dam az - sa bâ - a - jab

(The complete example is posted at www.yorku.ca/robsimms/shajarian)

Yād-e Ayām

yā - de a - yā - mi ki dar gol - shan fa - ghā - ni

dā - shtam dar mi-yā - ne lā - le u gol ā - shi - yā - ni dā - shtam

ā - shi - yā - ni dā - shtam ā - shi - yā - ni dā - - - - shtam

A' (interlude)

(5 mm.) **(saz)**

yā - de a-yā - mi yā - de a - yā - mi

A **A' (interlude)** **B**

ger - de ān sha - me ta-rab mi - sukh - tam par -

1.

vā - ne vār

2. **A**

vā - ne vār pā - ye ān sar - ve ra-vān ash - ke ra-vā - ni dā - shtan ash -

ke ra-vā - ni dā - shtan ash - ke ra-vā - ni dā - - - - - shtam

(The complete example is posted at www.yorku.ca/robsimms/shajarian)

Pishdaramad-e Abu Ata

from *Payam-e Nasim*

(The complete example is posted at www.yorku.ca/robsimms/shajarian)

Yad e Ayam (Rahi Moayeri)

Memories of those times when a song in the garden I had
A home amidst the tulip and flower I had
Around that candle of joy I burned like a moth
At the foot of the flowing tree, a flowing tear I had
My soul on fire, but my lip silent from complaint
A craving for the meaning of love form the tear I had
The pain of lovelessness has taken away my soul's endurance
Otherwise, I had calm while a calm soul I had
Like disgrace, from joy I kissed the earth of the threshold
Like dust, from joy I headed for the heights of the threshold
The nightingale of my nature is now silent from solitude
While I had one to speak with, many songs I had

Instrument Design and Construction

RS

Ostad Shajarian's achievement in designing and constructing stringed instruments is unique in many ways. In cultures around the world the invention of instruments is frequently explained by fantastic mythical stories involving supernatural beings; just as often, the original design and subsequent development of an instrument is acknowledged as having been accomplished by anonymous individuals. Famous musicians occasionally contribute to instrument designs. In the European tradition, J.S. Bach was a renowned expert of organ construction, invented an instrument that bridged the cello and viola, experimented with using gut strings on the harpsichord that produced the sound of a lute, and most significantly, worked on a prototype of the forte piano, which eventually evolved into the piano. Later designers of the piano consulted with performers and composers (Haydn, Beethoven, and Liszt among them) to improve the instrument. Changes in the instrument led to changes in the musical style and technique: Chopin's music sounds the way it does because of these changes in the design and construction of the piano.

While mythological origins of instruments abound in West Asian and specifically Iranian musical culture, there is also a long heritage of great musicians inventing and improving the design of instruments. The Sassanian court musician Barbad is credited with the invention of the lute *barbat* in some sources. Contributions to the improvement of existing instruments frequently take the form of strategically adding strings: Ziryab to the 'oud and Moshtaq Ali Shah (eighteenth century) to the setar. Ostad Elahi (1895–1974) added a string to the tanbur but also designed hybrid lutes. Long-necked lutes in twentieth-century Herat and Badakhshan underwent considerable transformation through the work of individual virtuosi (some known, others not). Again, changes in the design brought about changes in technique and musical style. What all of these examples have in common is that they involve a virtuoso of a particular instrument making changes to that one instrument.

By contrast, Ostad Shajarian—a great singer—has made original designs of several stringed instruments, some of these involve "family members" covering various ranges. These instruments feature innovative acoustical designs resulting in new timbres and greatly expand the range of the traditional Persian classical ensemble, opening up new possibilities for orchestration and polyphony. While Shajarian is not consciously doing so, he is following the archetypal footsteps of the legendary master musician/instrument innovators of Iranian music history mentioned above, but going considerably further than any of them. Should even one instrument from his large collection of inventions take root among musicians and become a standard instrument, his place in Iranian music history would resonate further beyond his unprecedented achievements in avaz. Indeed, his overall impact would be fairly unprecedented viewed in the larger context of contemporary world music history. One thinks of the example of the American composer Harry Partch, who designed and built a wide range of highly original instruments for his highly original music. But Partch's music is not played today and knowledge of the existence of his work is limited to a small group of scholars and composers; ingenious as they may be, the instruments never got traction beyond his own music. By contrast Ostad Shajarian has millions, perhaps tens of millions of listeners and is much more practical than Partch in his conception and goals as to how the instruments might be used. He was unaware of Partch but interested to see photos of his instruments, which I showed from Partch's manifesto, *Genesis of a Music* (see his comments below).

And yet the lofty matters of historical impact or legacy do not concern or motivate Shajarian in the slightest. Likewise, any conscious notions of seeking new challenges to take up, new artistic media to explore at this stage of his life, were quickly dismissed. His interests in designing and crafting instruments are purely practical and aesthetic: *"to either introduce new sound textures to classical Persian music or complement the sound of existing musical instruments used in classical Persian music."*[39] And his interests in this regard are longstanding, beginning when he was twenty-one. As soon as he had moved from under his father's house rules, he took up santur to deepen his understanding of musical structures and repertoire, and for pure edification. He continues to play the instrument but only for himself or in the company of friends in the privacy of his home (Shajarian et al. 2004: 281). His encounter with the santur led immediately to matters of construction—with limited tools and resources—and attempts at improving its sound. Lacking a source of tuning pins on his first santur, he very painstakingly drilled holes through seventy-two thin, generic metal rods.

Shajarian's working process in designing and crafting instruments reveals much about his personality and, indeed, shows how he honed his art of singing avaz. In addition to natural talent, his *modus operandis* is patience, focus, dedication, meticulous attention to detail, and hard work, along with a balance of enterprising autodidactic confidence and attentive mentoring from masters. While observing various craftsmen as opportunities presented themselves, Shajarian studied with the master luthier Ostad Ibrahim Qanbari in the 1980s. It is important to emphasize that Shajarian, even now with his considerable resources, doesn't dream up a design and then hand it to technicians and artisans to execute the plans: he both designs and crafts each instrument himself. According to Shabnam Ataei, an electrical engineer and R&D consultant for Delawaz, the evolution of Shajarian's designs were accomplished through prolonged experimentation: multiple cycles of envisioning the design, building a model, evaluating it, discarding models that didn't achieve his goals, and retaining any elements that seemed to work (personal communication, 2010). This is precisely the kind of empirical, intuitive methods that Stradivari employed to discover the acoustically optimal design of the violin. It is also reminiscent of the practice of ney craftsmen, who similarly make instruments with great intuitive industry and discard pieces that are in any way defective. This approach undoubtedly applies to Shajarian's acquisition of technique, repertoire, and synthesis of *sabk* that form the basis of his personal style of avaz.

Shajarian employed his typical tenacity in calculating the mathematical formula for the relationship between string length, diameter, and frequency in order to inform his designs. Totally unaware of the existence of this formula or the mathematics and physics underlying it, he made an arduously comprehensive series of empirical measurements on several pages of spreadsheets in pencil to calculate the formula himself—reinventing the wheel but realizing his goal, independently acquiring what he needed to do his work (Shabnam Ataei, personal communication 2010). Compare this approach with the following anecdote of wedging research into his busy work schedule: "*One day I travelled to Qazvin; I struggled with a tahrir from one of Banan's recordings until I lifted it. From Tehran to Qazvin I replayed that tahrir fifty times before I eventually learned it properly*" (Sabur 1992:213).

While Shajarian has been crafting instruments for almost four decades, this aspect of his creative work expanded greatly and took on a new significance since the mid-2000s and it now occupies a large portion of his time and energy. Indeed, such work cannot be successfully accomplished without a sense of sustained, single-minded obsession, as any good luthier will testify. Shajarian went to Qom and bought many tons of wood for his workshop from which to select the best pieces, and while on tour he invests much time, enduring ferocious traffic jams in cities around the world in search of quality strings (he is experimenting with various kinds), tuning machines, and other supplies. Shabnam Ataei notes that "he loves the instruments like they are his children" (personal communication, 2010). Having arrived at satisfactory designs for a number of instruments after an exhaustive refining process, he has been keen to present them to the public. This was one of the main factors behind his creation of the Shahnaz

Ensemble in 2007 and has led to several international public and academic presentations regarding his instruments since: the Conference of Interdisciplinary Musicology in Paris (2009), Griffith University (Brisbane), UCLA, Berkeley, and York University (Toronto) in 2010.

Shajarian emphasizes the dialectical, collaborative nature of this work—that the interaction with instrumentalists and composers is essential to the whole enterprise. As a singer he is in complete control of how the art unfolds but his work creating instruments involves a large degree of surrendering such control in order to create music of the quality he seeks. This deferral to other musicians and simply watching what they do with his vehicles seems to be part of the attraction. Shajarian specifically highlights the key role that Majid Derakhshani has played in directing and assisting musicians in their exploration of the technical possibilities hidden within the instruments and awaiting discovery. Who knows what kind of music may emerge? Shajarian is clearly interested in the polyphonic potential he is opening up with the resources provided by his instruments but totally leaves this in the hands of composers.

Since constructing his first instrument in 1961, Shajarian estimated in the early 2000s that he had made twenty to twenty-five santurs to date (Shajarian et al. 2004: 287). Right from the beginning he experimented with expanding the sonic possibilities of the standard instrument, and no doubt each of his two dozen instruments featured changes in design both major and minor. While the standard range of a santur is E (koron)3 to F6 (i.e, where middle C is C4), the instrument used for the 2010 tour shifted this range up to A3 to D7. The biggest departure and innovation in his santur work is the design and construction of a bass santur, which he calls tondar ("thunder"), possessing a range of A2 to G6 and a distinctive tone. The tuning pins of santurs are conventionally inserted to the side walls of the body, but due to the expanded range and the uneven distribution of tension across the soundboard, Shajarian mounted the pins on a ledge that slopes slightly down from the sides of the soundboard after the strings contact a raised side bridge. The interior of the resonating chamber is divided by interior bracing walls that create five separate sections fanning out from a central triangle. Conventional santurs use only unwound steel strings but the lower register of the tondar requires the use of wound steel strings.

The largest contingent within Shajarian's new ensemble of instruments is bowed lutes/fiddles featuring soundboards that are partially skinned. There are three basic types: the sorahi, sabu and shahbang. Sorahi (*sorahi* "wine glass") is a family of four-stringed instruments similar to the violin family covering enormous musical range (see photo 15). The soprano and alto sorahis have two sections of skin—a circular one under the bridge and another semicircular on the lower bout—but no f-holes. The tailpiece is mounted on the soundboard between these skin resonators (likewise for the bass and double bass instruments). Shajarian has designed the skin resonators in such a way that they may be changed quickly, enabling options for a wide range of timbres. The soprano is played between the knees while seated in a chair, the alto has a long spike and is played like a cello; both may be played with

either specially designed bows or regular violin/viola bows. The range of the soprano is G3 to E6, the alto A3 to C6. Shajarian explains *"I designed it and then I
thought about how to make it produce a different timbre, so that it is unlike any
other instrument. It is then that I put that flower pot-shaped design on it. . . .
Making the first instrument took a while, you really have to think hard so that it
is done accurately. But now that the design is established, I guess that it takes me
about a month to make one"* (2010).

The bam sorahi ("bass sorahi"), roughly twice the length of the alto, has an
elongated and deeper body, with the circular skin resonator located near the
neck; the lower skin resonator is divided into two "pie-slice" quarter circles, and
there are two f-holes. The lower portion of the neck is equipped with five movable frets. The shah sorahi ("king sorahi" or double-bass) is a remarkable instrument featuring only one skin resonator under the bridge, shaped like a stretched
circle; there are two small f-holes above this and two large rosettes below. The
soundboard of this instrument is uniquely two-tiered: the teardrop-shaped plate
with two small f-holes framing the upper end of the neck is overlaid with a circular lower plate covering about two-thirds of the body; this lower plate has two
large, elaborately carved rosettes. A short demonstration video I saw hinted at
the rich timbre and enormous range this beautiful instrument is capable of producing.

The sabu (*sabu* "crock, jar") is a fiddle with a design and tone colour that is
quite different from the sorahi (photo 16). The base of the instrument is flat,
resembling a bottle or bowling pin; the tailpiece is attached to this base like a
violin. Where bridges of the sorahi family stand directly on the skin resonator,
the bridge of the sabu stands on a small wood plate mounted on the skin, under
which is attached a conical-shaped extension or "speaker" pointing inside the
resonating chamber. There are two rather long f-holes placed close to either side
of the soundboard, framing the tailpiece The sabu has a range similar to the
violin—G3 to E6—and can be played either under the chin like a violin, on the
knee or between the legs.

The shahbang ("king cry/roar/sound") and shahnavaz ("king play, sound,
strike") differ from Shajarian's other bowed lutes in featuring necks that are
considerably longer in proportion to the size of their resonators, and soundboards
that are largely skin, which is stretched and glued over the edges (photo 17). The
elegant waisted shape of the instruments is reminiscent of various Central Asia lutes
that feature distinctive decorative "wings" at the top of the body (e.g., Uzbeki,
Pamiri, and Uyghur *rubab*s, the Dolan *rawap*), though they are considerably
subdued here. There is a triangular soundhole in the small wood portion of the
soundtable just under the neck attachment. The tailpieces are attached to a non-
resonating extension of the end of the soundboard. The string lengths and ranges
are identical to the cello (for the shahbang) and double-bass (shahnavaz); they
are equipped with spikes and employ the same bows and playing positions as
their Western counterpart. The shahnavaz has nineteen movable frets placed like a
tar or setar, while the upper reaches of the fingerboard are unfretted. When

considering these instruments along with the tondar, the bam and shah sorahi, Shajarian has contributed significantly to supplying the Persian classical ensemble with a very substantial, previously nonexistent bottom end.

Shajarian has invented two plucked lutes: the saghar and kereshme. The saghar ("goblet, cup"), which he completed in 2008, features a body shaped like a rather deep, inverted teardrop (or large tanbur, but with the narrow end at its base) [photo 18]. The mulberry soundboard is equipped with three skin resonators, the bridge standing directly on the lowest of these, while the other two large "windows" begin on either side of the upper end of the body, framing the strings halfway down the length of the soundboard. Six nylon guitar strings are arranged like the tar, in three double-courses each tuned in octaves, the courses are then tuned in fourths covering the range C2 to G5. Movable frets are tied in the configuration of a tar or setar.

Shajarian explained that the kereshmeh (literally "coquetry" but also the name of an important rhythmical pattern found throughout the radif) was inspired by the skin soundboard and sympathetic strings of the Afghan rubab (which in turn was derived from the Indian sarod) [photo 19]. The body is somewhat pear-shaped and rather shallow; the lower and larger portion of the soundboard is covered with lambskin while the upper portion is wood with two fairly large star-shaped soundholes framing the playing strings. Very uniquely, its back is also skin. The seven nylon (guitar) playing strings are tuned like the saghar but with the addition of a single-course bass string, providing a playing compass of G2 to G5; frets are tied in the regular tar-setar configuration. Whereas the tuning pegs of the saghar follow the design of the tar headstock, the friction pegs here are all inserted on the top side of a triangular head stock, which is visually compelling. Ten sympathetic strings (Persian *vakhun*) fan out from a hole beside the tailpiece across the left side of the soundtable and are attached to tuning pins mounted on the top side of the body after passing over a long side bridge attached to the edge of the body. The sympathetic strings are tuned to the pitches of the scale (*māye*) being performed. *"These strings give a very good sound to the instrument, a good harmony or resonance."* Ostad Derakhshani plays the kereshmeh held at chest level, aided by a strap. Both saghar and kereshme are played with a plectrum similar to that used for the 'oud, though Derakhshani occasionally shifts to his fingers, employing righthand techniques associated with the dotar or Kurdish tanbur.

OS
Question: Having mastered avaz, is your work designing and building instruments a new artistic medium for you to explore. Does it fulfill a creative need or challenge?
No, I am not thinking about that. It is more because in the past years I have noticed that we lack some sounds in our Iranian orchestras. That's the reason I started making instruments. I started with santur from 1961. I thought some parts of the santur don't have a pleasant sound, so I tried making one that was

more appealing. This continued year after year and I was not satisfied, so I worked even more until I reached this level. I worked on santur until 2007, and since fifteen years ago I have been thinking about working on a bass santur (tondar). I tried looking for strings and bridge. Since 2006, I realized that I had gained so much experience in instrument making and sound production that I began thinking about making a bowed instrument with a skin soundboard—something different from kamanche, because the sound of kamanche irritates me a little. The first string on the kamanche doesn't really satisfy me, so I wanted to make an instrument that is somewhat like kamanche but with a nicer sound. Then I thought about making its bass version, so that it makes up for what we lack in our orchestras. So in September 2008 I made my first sorahi.

It seems that you must devote a lot of time on these instruments.

Yes, a lot. I go to bed with the thought of instrument designs and I wake up with that thought.

I know luthiers often find their work relaxing and meditative, and that their state of mind at the time goes into the instrument.

Yes, absolutely. When I work on them, I don't think about anything else, I just think about the instrument. It gives me a lot of pleasure, especially when I am designing them. I have wasted so much paper just on design; the papers all have dates on them.

Now that you are satisfied with the design of these instruments are you going to make copies of them?

Yes, I want to reproduce them. For example, in the family of sorahi instruments I have made fifteen instruments for a stringed/skinned orchestra: eight sopranos, four alto, two bass, and one double bass.

Are you interested in polyphonic music?

Yes, very much.

Do you have any idea of the resulting music in your mind, polyphonic or otherwise, while you make these instruments?

No, not really, because someone else will arrange that.

What is it like for you to sit back and watch others "run" with your creations?

It gives me even more pleasure because I really like the sound of these instruments and can really relate to them.

Do you ever get surprised by what musicians come up with?

Well yes, sometimes. I mean when the regional (folk) musicians play with sorahi, I really feel fulfilled. These instruments haven't been in the hands of too many musicians. I think different musicians should work on them until someone comes along that understands the instrument better and can generate a better sound from it—that person has to discover the sound and bring it out. This is exactly like Hafez when he created his poetry and different singers took it and performed it differently. Therefore, different instrumentalists will bring different sounds out of these instruments. When different composers work on them, they will each find new things in them and it is then that the instrument will show its true colors and capacity. I make the instrument and I will try to provide all the necessary tools, like good strings and good skin, and the rest is up to the musician to discover and bring out.

Are you satisfied with the ensemble sound of your orchestra, with your instruments playing together as a unit?

No, not yet. Even Derakhshani says that he is learning more and more about these instruments as we go on and in the future he can take a better use of them. He has to find those sound colors and write for them.

I think you can surely get other composers interested in writing for them.

Yes, I mean the rest of the work is on their hands.

Can you see them functioning in a way similar to a Western string quartet or string orchestra?

Yes, the artists can do this, but they need to understand the instruments by picking them up and playing with them for a while. But they can play any piece of music with these instruments. You can play symphonic music that is written for string instruments with these.

But can you envision making a Persian music, perhaps drawing upon the techniques of Western string music?

Yes, very much so, but the composers have to do these things: which notes and phrases to write for each instrument and how to use each instrument. For example, Ahmad Pejman, a great composer who works in classical and film music— he is the best among the Iranian composers—was always looking into new synthesizers for new sounds. For people like him these instruments are good, since they all have new sounds.

Do you know Franghiz Ali-Zadeh, the Azerbaijani composer?

No, I don't, but the alto sorahi has a very special timbre that Azeri composers could really put to good use.

I really liked the big bass sound of shah sorahi featured on your demonstration video and think that has a lot of potential.

Yes, that is really good. When these bass instruments join the ensemble the whole thing changes. But, unfortunately the instrument wasn't included in our touring ensemble because it is so big, making its transportation very difficult. . . . Anyway, I want to make more instruments.

In any culture when the instruments change, the music changes.

Yes, and I am feeling that a certain kind of movement is taking place that can really turn big in the future and that other instrument makers will start to develop new instruments as well. And of course we will get there. Also, I will be working on just wood instruments without the skin soundboards because I have bought a lot of good wood for the tops of the instruments too. I will design them later; I think that will also make for another twenty instruments. I'm also thinking about modifying the qanun.

(Upon perusing Harry Partch's book *Genesis of a Music*.)

Well, you see here that he has to teach people how to play these instruments; only he himself can play these instruments, which is why they can't become mainstream. This person has worked hard, and has worked well, but there is no musician who can play with them. These instruments are big and hard to carry, they take so much space so they become like a piano. It takes a lifetime to master these instruments. New instruments have to be accessible, so that if a young musician wants, he or she can work on them and find a technique for them—it is only then that these instruments can show themselves. When I design my own instruments I think of my musician too, to see who can play them.

When people were developing the design of the piano in Europe they used to send models to Beethoven and other artists for their feedback.

When I made shahbang and shah sorahi I brought the musicians [double bassists] to the studio twice to look at them and give me their suggestions, which I followed, so that they can play them easier.

Do you have any future plans to work on wind or percussion instruments?

Well, I haven't had the time. I have put all my time on these instruments. It has been close to a year that I thought about wind instruments but I am not too familiar with wind instruments and how to make them. My work began with the santur and moved on from there into the wider realm of string instruments. So string instruments are my main base. (2010)

Calligraphy and Gardening

RS:
Scholars have noted the close relationship of Persian music with the traditional Iranian visual arts of architecture, miniature painting, and calligraphy (e.g., Ardalan and Bakhtiar 1973, Bakhtiar 1976, During 1982), to which one might add gardening. Modular structures, reconfiguration of preset patterns, and ornamental flourishes are evident in all of these arts. The spatial organization of the bazaar particularly corresponds to definitive features of the radif and conventional musical forms in both specific structures and the general tendency of restricting the possible routes of circulation. Like avaz, both miniature painting and calligraphy are dependent on a literary vehicle and, as the latter is usually already well known to the audience or readership, the aesthetic focus is given to "form over content, to manner over subject manner" and is devoid of subjective personal experience, typified by the blank stare of visages in miniature paintings (During 1982:80). We have used the visual metaphor of "word painting" throughout our analysis of Shajarian's avaz, carefully qualifying it in relation to the notion in Western art music practice, implying a bridging of artistic media.

Among the visual arts, calligraphy probably comes closest to avaz in terms of general purpose, structural correspondence, and immediacy:

> The way of encasing the song, of emphasizing it with a single note as with a stroke, of taking up a fragment of it like an echo, of seizing a motif in order to unfold it in arabesque before bringing it back into line, of framing its grand

moments, of organizing its punctuation and the layout...the poetic pearls are mounted with art in such a way that one no longer knows whether one should admire the jewel or its setting. (ibid.: 81)

Ostad Shajarian is a highly accomplished calligrapher—an art cultivated on his mother's side of the family—beginning his studies in the third grade, continuing in Tehran with the Association of Calligraphers and under Ostad Mirkhāni. He abandoned his formal studies in 1971 but, as a perennial student, continued to cultivate his skills and practice for the sake of his own growth. He often performs on stage reading from his own calligraphed manuscript of the poem being sung. Photo 20 is of Ostad Shajarian's calligraphy of the Hafez ghazal he sang for *Bidad*. On one occasion Shajarian corroborated Wright's objections that there are no such concrete links between these art forms but rather a vague parallel, one that for Wright reinforces stereotypes of a "spiritual orient" and other Orientalist reifications (2009:119–20). On another occasion (see below) Shajarian gives some credence to their interrelation.While his personal view in the former instance is significant and lends considerable weight to Wright's argument—few have Shajarian's extensive knowledge, experience and achievement in these disparate art forms from which to make an authoritative assessment—it is precisely the function of the "etic" perspective to examine dimensions or connections that may be operative and perhaps outside the concerns and awareness of practioners, whose goals are creative as opposed to analytical. There are undoubtedly other analogies drawn and dots connected throughout this book that Ostad Shajarian would reject. The question of their subsequent value and validity is left to the reader. It bears repeating here regarding Shajarian's skill at calligraphy that, above the beauty of his work and the obvious talent and hard work it embodies, it also illustrates his refined interpersonal skills, as the subcultural circle of calligraphers is one of the most difficult to penetrate in Iranian culture.

To round out this brief view of Shajarian's other artistic pursuits we will only briefly note that he has longstanding interests in photography and gardening. "Shajarian is in love with flowers and nature. He has purchased a big orchard in Hashtegard [outside of Tehran] and he often visits his orchard alone. . . . He knows every flower and is fully familiar with [horticulture]. He personally looks after his flowers and sings for himself" (Manateqe Azad 2001).

OS

I used to learn calligraphy from Master Mirkhāni but I didn't attend a master's course, as I had to write my dissertation. It was the custom for students to sit down and write down things that the instructors told them. Then the instructors examined our writings and gave their mark. At that time I wasn't writing badly but since I was in no mood to write a dissertation [nor the] incentive to receive a license in calligraphy, I gave up that art. I only wanted to improve my calligraphy. Calligraphy takes a long time to learn, like music. . . . Under special circumstances, calligraphy and music have common rules. From the point of view of flexibility, mood, style and enthusiasm I think music and calligraphy are very similar to each other. . . . [Mirkhāni] was a first-class player of kamanche and played it far better than the late Bahari but he didn't enter into the field of music. Nowadays there are many calligraphers in the country but one can [only] enjoy one or two real calligraphers. They write well but to tell the truth, none of them can match Mirkhāni. The mentality of a master plays an important role in calligraphy and one could easily notice the wonderful sense of calligraphy in Mirkhāni.

During my childhood I was less interested in painting than calligraphy. . . . During my high school years I used to receive the best mark (20) for painting, calligraphy, sports and discipline! . . . I didn't continue my painting. I started . . . oil painting and produced several paintings but I gave up because I lost my friend who used to encourage me to paint and in the interim I was transferred [as a teacher] to Tehran. I loved painting a lot and used to [draw] with pencil and I wanted to work with watercolours, but when I came to Tehran I only pursued my lessons in calligraphy and music. (Manateqe Azad 2001:2)

Question: Has your involvement in other forms of art influenced your music? Or have they provided you with a different way of looking at things?
Not really. They have all had their own place in my head and although it may seem that some of them are connected to each other, in reality none have influenced the other. My sense of aesthetics takes me on a journey to achieve the best possible outcome of any art form that I am attracted to. (2009)
"I like soil (khāk), it's like my lover, and flowers and plants come up from that same soil. I like to spend most of my time alone with plants and flowers." (Shajarian et al. 2004: 268)
Once I was asked: "If you were born again and could choose your profession, what would that be? I answered: "Agriculture. I like nature more than anything else." (ibid.: 314)

The Election Crisis of 2009: *Ostad-e Sabz*

In artistic work my actions are like those of a politician! I'm not saying that art isn't political; perhaps I'm saying that I can't place my work in the frame of political groups. It means I don't present music affiliated with political parties. But my art is political in the sense that I work for the promotion of rights, beauty, and humanity, and I'm opposed to anything that is against these. (Shajarian et al. 2004:141–42)

RS
We have seen that following the album *Sepideh* in 1980 Shajarian steered clear of direct political affiliation or commentary and instead chose the more subtle yet highly effective route of using thinly veiled political and social criticism in his avaz through the agency of the classical poets. But by 2008 he became increasingly

outspoken and direct in criticizing the government of the Islamic Republic. In a recent interview with Shajarian for a Canadian magazine, the interviewer commented that many in the West have a distorted view of Iranian society as being "almost *talabani* in its restrictions rather than a place of music, poetry and culture," to which he replies, "*Actually, if you compared the regime to the Taliban, you wouldn't be far off. They are only allowing a certain degree of musical expression— mainly on national radio and television, to lure listeners and viewers into hearing their own propaganda*" (Ditmars 2009: 64). Suspicions of widespread ballot fraud in the national elections of June 12, 2009 in Iran led to sustained mass protest in Tehran and across the country, in which literally millions of citizens regularly took to the streets in the following weeks. Police and security responded with brutal force that led to rampant violence and the deaths of both unarmed protesters and those caught in the crossfire. As rightly noted by Zillah Eisenstein while the events unfolded:

> Iran looks more democratic than the U.S. in at least one sense in these past weeks. When the people of Iran thought their election was fraudulent, they took to the streets. When the U.S. Supreme Court fraudulently ruled that Bush was our next president despite losing the popular vote, the public quietly obeyed. And, then the rest of the world, along with the U.S. paid a terrible price for the Bush-Cheney decade of fascistic democracy. (Bashi 2009)

Named after Green Party, who was seen as the main target and victim of the alleged fraud, the protest movement became known as the Green (*Sabz*) Movement. The world watched the seemingly unstoppable expression of unified protest against President Ahmadinejad and Supreme Leader Khameini who, through the uncompromising use of violence, miraculously managed to put the genie back in its bottle, stemming the tsunami of dissent. Amid the rhetoric used by Ahmadinejad to denounce the protestors he branded them as "*khas o khāshāk*"—usually translated as "dust and trash"[40] (figuratively, "riff raff"). Throughout the unfolding of the crisis over several weeks the state radio, *Seda va Sima*, played Shajarian's music, specifically his nationalistic *sorud enqelabis* (such as *"Iran, sarayeh omid"*) that he recorded immediately following the revolution in 1979. Just as the poem is no longer Hafez's in Shajarian's hands, his recordings were no longer his in the hands of government media, who spun, manipulated, and recontextualized them to their own ends. Just as Shajarian exploited the loopholes of censorship in the 1980s through his selection of poetry and gushe names, he craftily and boldly bypassed Iranian media control by interviewing on BBC and Voice of America, addressing Iranians at home—where many are well equipped with satellite dishes and some intrepid surfers manage to get around Internet filters to access Youtube—and the diaspora. In a telephone interview with BBC Persian during the first week of the crisis, Shajarian spoke with unprecedented directness and force:

Under such conditions when our people are trapped in tears and shock, and when "dust and dirt" are flying in the air due to the storm that Mr. Ahmadinejad has created, my voice has no place in the government-owned radio and television of the Islamic Republic. Therefore I am strictly asking them to stop playing my voice and stop making me upset and stop violating my rights and freedom. My voice is a voice of the "dust and dirt" and it will always remain a voice for the "dust and dirt." I have asked them numerous times in 1995, directly to the head man in charge, to stop playing my voice but they ignored my request and violated my rights and freedom.

My whole body shivers every time I hear my voice from these quarters and I feel humiliated. So I asked them again, quite strictly, to stop violating my rights by playing my voice on their broadcasts. These nationalistic anthems that I sang in 1979 were for the revitalization movement that people had ignited at that time and it was for that movement. But now I realize that they are slapping these anthems in my face and in the face of those for whom I have sung these anthems. This is the reason why I would not let them play these anthems—they do not have any rights to them nor to my voice.[41]

The words *"This voice is a voice of the dust and dirt and it will always remain a voice for the dust and dirt"* coming from the singer who referred to himself for decades as "Dust on the Feet of the Iranian People," broadcast over international airwaves and bypassing Iranian censors, became a bold, openly seditious endorsement of the protests. It wildly swept through the media (especially the Internet) and onto the streets among those who risked their lives in the protests. Shajarian pressed his demand with aggressive legal action against the government. An interview from Hannover with Voice of America on September 6 further and unequivocally explicated his position:

OS
You see, the purpose of radio and television is to serve the people and be their voice, quite contrary of the Islamic regime's ideology, which only represents one viewpoint and only for a particular kind of people. Not everyone necessarily approves of the programs that they show on the television; I certainly don't have the patience for watching anything broadcasted on national television. Furthermore, I don't like my voice to be aired on these media because they only represent one way of thinking, they are very one-sided. At the same time they are getting their funding from the people [i.e., tax payers] and their programs should be for everyone and not only a few. So this is the reason I told them that they should stop playing my songs and my music. The only thing I allow them to play is Rabanna for the month of Ramadan.

In the last thirty years, they haven't taken a single step towards music. They have only used music as a "device"; they have not even made a single music hall. In every part of the world, they make their churches, but they also make their music halls, and cinemas. But not here! We don't even have one con-

cert hall that is appropriate for performance. The Vezarat Keshvar (Ministry of State) *Hall is for meetings and is not a concert hall—the sound is terrible. No matter what you do, you cannot get a decent sound in that hall. Anyway, the radio and television only make a political use of music, and I don't like my voice to be treated in such a way. I asked them a numerous times to stop playing my music but they never listened. Therefore, I was forced to make a formal complaint and reach them through legal channels in order to get my message across. Until they change their views and change them for the benefit of their people, I will not allow them to play my music.*[42]

RS

In late July, *Seda*'s deputy head Mohammad Hossein Sofi announced that "Shajarian's music will never be played on the radio again . . . not even . . . during the Holy month of Ramadan."[43] Given the overall context surrounding the dispute and the government's aggressively defensive stance, it was a spectacular victory for Shajarian. That *Seda* unsurprisingly labeled him as unpatriotic only reinforced the façade.[44] Equally predictably, the government's poorly strategized ban on broadcasting his Rabanna during Ramadan in 2010 only served to strengthen Shajarian as an icon of resistance among Iranians. Amir Koushkani was in Iran at the time and saw people playing his Rabanna everywhere on their cellphones in public, some "microcasting" it on street corners for groups of listeners. Everyone knew what it signified. Rabbana is no longer simply a piece of inspiring religious chant but also an icon of Iranian identity and now, political dissent.

As events unfolded in the summer of 2009, Shajarian further responded to the crisis by composing a tasnif on the poetry of Fereydoun Moshiri. Entitled *"Zaban-e Atesh* (Language of Fire)" but known more popularly by the key line *"Tofangat-ra zamin bogzar* (Put your gun on the ground)," it was hugely popular in Iran after its release in the late summer and became the highlight of the program featured in his fall tour of Europe with the Shahnaz Ensemble.

Zaban-e Atesh/"Language of Fire"[45]

Lay down your gun,
As I hate this very abnormal shedding of blood.
The gun in your hand speaks the language of fire and iron,
But I, before this fiendish tool,
Have nothing but the language of the heart,
The heart full to the brim with love for you,
Who are in love with the enemy.
The language of fire and iron is the game of fury and bloodshed.
It is the language of Genghis Khan.
Come, sit down, talk, hear.
Perhaps the light of humanity will get through to your heart, too.
My brother, if you want me, sit down for a brotherly chat.

Lay down your gun,
So that the human-killer leaves your body
How much do you know about the ethics of humanity?
If God has bestowed the soul, why then do you take it away?
Why, in the twilight of ignorance,
Do you want to roll and wrap up your brethren in dirt and blood,
The God-given soul?
Let's suppose you are right, my brother, in seeking and telling right and correct
things.
But we ought to not seek even righteous things through the fire-spewing gun.
If it once happens that the pangs of conscience bother you,
Then lay down your gun.

OS

*Certain events have happened that are very disappointing and these events
shouldn't have taken place in our country for the noble people of Iran. What
they wanted was an answer to their question and it shouldn't have been coun-
tered in such a horrific way. This is unacceptable, intolerable. The images and
videos that I have seen, and the people who have been beaten and killed on the
streets, moved me so much that, early in July Moshiri's poem suddenly came to
mind and I spent a few a hours and put a melody to it. Then I gave it to Derakhshani and told him that I must say something, I cannot hold back. I cannot tole-
rate the way people are being treated and Moshiri's poem articulated this situation in the best way possible. Anyway, I told Derakhshani that "I have made this
melody for it, see if you like it and if you can arrange something for it." It
turned out that he did like it and he took the responsibility to arrange it, which
we then performed in the studio, mixed, and made available for the public. The
message for the public is to know that you cannot say the right thing with guns
and fire, but you should say it in another way—perhaps to sit down and talk
about the issues. . . . I composed it last year in Mahur but this year I decided
that Dashti is more appropriate.*[46]

RS

Throughout the many media appearances Shajarian made after the crisis, both
interviewers and emailed submissions from the general public that were often
featured as part of these asked his opinion of the situation. While he clearly
provided this in both his actions and words, he also deflected such enquiries by
stating that the situation was rather obvious, the facts were well-known, that he
wished to avoid redundancy, and he had no solutions. In one such instance he
explicated a conclusion that could have been back-dated considerably: "*I don't
think that after what they [the government] have done they can ever guide the
nation—they can only control it, they cannot do anything else.*"[47] His media
profile skyrocketed during his tour of England, Australia, and North America in
April–June of 2010, with interviews, news profiles, and documentaries. On
Australian television:

Now after thirty years since religion came and entered politics and started handling the government, because this had a very very bad result, everyone had come to this belief: we must separate religion from politics.

Question: In contesting the broadcasting of your music and having your daughter sing for mixed audiences, are you try to gently push the authorities around?
No. No. Because they're taking their path and, as they say, these are divine laws and you can't change them. And whatever we say, they do whatever they want to. They do what they want to do and we do whatever we want to do.[48]

One marvels at the directness, reach, and influence of his openly dissident views. Who else can openly criticize the beleaguered Iranian regime—lacking electoral legitimacy and disgraced with one of the worst human rights records in the world—through global media in this manner and still remain in Iran, Shajarian's principal residence? Other musicians are outspoken and dedicated to resistance but don't have near the profile and, very understandably, live outside Iran. Shajarian's response to the crisis brought a massive surge of admiration and appreciation to his already huge social cachet among Iranians. Even people who never listened to traditional music now admire Shajarian and call him Ostad for purely political reasons.

OS
Question: How do you feel about being called *"Ostad-e Sabz"* by so many people?
It's fine but needs some important qualifications. All those who were against the results of the 2009 election, due to the fact that the election results were not counted properly and it seemed as if it was a coup d'etat, forced people to complain. In any case, because [opposition lead Mir-Hossein] Mousavi chose the colour of green for his campaign, everyone who had a complaint also chose green, and they took green cloths with themselves to the streets. Therefore, all those who were against the results, went under the same umbrella and were called "green." Of those who wear green, not all want the same thing. You see, everyone wants Ahmadinejad to be out of power, but one group wants to support Mousavi and go back to the beginning of the revolution and restart from thirty years ago. Other people, like me, think that this is not intelligent because you should not return to thirty years ago. Furthermore, the Islamic regime has been finally rejected. The Mousavi followers, however, want to keep the regime, and have made a green symbol for themselves, and want its constitution but with more equality. This is due to the fact that some say we cannot overthrow the Islamic regime because we don't have the power. So they say it is better to be on the regime's side for now, until the right time arrives, and then overthrow it. A lot of people have this in their minds but they don't really speak about it. They don't speak about it so they don't become even more oppressed.

But I personally was not in agreement with the Islamic regime from the beginning and I am still not in agreement with them. This Islamic regime must go, because it has made a coup d'etat against itself. Religion must also be separated from politics. So my frame of mind is not the same as Karroubi or Mousavi. They see themselves as green and people call me green too, but my mentality is not the same as theirs. I cannot be in agreement with them.

So the supporters of the green movement are in agreement with each other only in that none of them want Ahmadinejad, but they have different views about what they want instead.[49] This regime is a very dangerous regime. I mean, they can very easily call their opponents "enemies of God" and execute them without even a court hearing—they do this with utmost ease. Furthermore, they have robbed the country as well.

It has been thirty years that we have lived in fear, each week wondering what is going to happen next week, what will happen next month. There are so many intellectuals in Iran but they can never agree on issues and produce a result because the tools and the facilities are not there. (2010)

Notes

1. "Persian musicians had been appreciated for a long time in China: Ibn Battuta heard in Peking musicians singing the verses of Sa'adi, who was alive at the time" (During 1989a:217).

2. *Payam e Nasim* was recorded in Boston. According to Gudarzi et al. (2000:223) performances of two of these programs from a 1989 Europe tour—*Sarv e Chaman* in Karlsruhe and *Payam e Nasim* in Lausanne—were released in 1998. I have not been able to obtain these recordings but apparently the poetry is different in the two versions of *Sarv e Chanan*: Hafez for the European performance and Sa'di for the American (Shajarian et al. 2004:334–38).

3. Some clips of the concert are available onYoutube. http://www.youtube.com/watch?v=rOymCpkdPv8; http://www.youtube.com/watch?v=kwvNjKmY36U. See also: http://www.youtube.com/watch?v=Mg2j4dbS42s&feature=related.

4. The *radif* (repeated end word) of this ghazal is *dast raft* ("lost, missed, perished"), which crashes in unrelenting waves of despair and dysfunction with the conclusion of each beyt.

5. This ghazal from which Shajarian extracted three beyts for *Ghasedak* is traditionally regarding as being Rumi's last, written on his deathbed.

6. The line here refers to Farhad's suicidal fall from the mountain upon being told by the manipulative Khosrow (who was lying) that his beloved Shirin was dead.

7. RS: From a political angle, this could also refer to the loss of faith in religion that many Iranians experienced due to the hypocrisy of the mollahs once they assumed power.

8. From the albums *Dorna: Persian Folk Music* by Sima Bina (Caltex Records 2462 [released in 2000]) and *Songs From a Persian Garden* by Mahsa & Marjan Vahdat (Valley Entertainment 15217 [released in 2008]).

9. All translations are taken from the liner notes of the World Village release.

10. Interview on VOA Persian, broadcast June 19, 2010; http://www.youtube.com /watch?v=wHiPVsJIJlY.

11. From the film *The Voice of Iran* (Christian Braad Thomsen, dir., 2003).

12. For more on these traditions, see Simms and Koushkani (2012).

13. See chapter 3 of Simms and Koushkani (2012).

14. Most of these are short, but the gushe Feyli begins with an extensive introductory tahrir typical of his ghazal singing.

15. The word *"ast"* ("it is") was no doubt added to the title to clearly differentiate this album from Nazeri's earlier setting entitled *Zemestan*, which is the actual title of the poem.

16. Translation by Mahvash Shahegh Hariri. http://iranpoliticsclub.net/poetry/ winter/index.htm.

17. A disparaging term for cheap entertainment.

18. This tendency has a long history in Western music, hearkening back to Palestrina, Beethoven, and Wagner, all of whom cast long, rather intimidating shadows (cf. Bloom 1973). While impossible to trace in prerecording West Asian cultures, it surely applies to the great poets such as Sa'di, Rumi, and Hafez. Many forgers sought fame for their verse by emulating the style of these masters and using the *takhallus* of the latter. In the early recording era, Cemil Bey's 1905 discs functioned in this capacity (During 1987a: 34). It is also instructive to note that, albeit less frequently, individual attractors can also spawn and inspire great creative diversity, a prime example being Jimi Hendrix. Many of the bona fide guitar heroes of the 1970s were deeply inspired by Hendrix but had very different musical voices. They all had something of their own to say and their debt to Hendrix was often not immediately obvious in their playing.

19. Concert program notes written by Shajarian for his North American tour, May and June 2010.

20. The following anecdote is revealing of Shajarian's character with regard to this dilemma. As 2,500 people were emptying the hall after a concert in Toronto in June 2010, a man mounted the stage, slipped past security, found and approached Shajarian backstage. A dedicated fan, he was very physically demonstrative with Shajarian in expressing his enthusiasm. As security zeroed in to remove the intruder, Shajarian signalled that it was fine, fulfilled the man's wish for a picture of them together, and spoke with him for a few minutes (personal communication, Mahmood Schricker, 2010).

21. See Simms and Koushkani (2012) for a discussion of this genre.

22. See chapter 2 of Simms and Koushkani (2012) for a discussion of the central role of truth-telling in various domains of Iranian history and culture.

23. http://www.shajarian.net/2008_03_01_archive.html.

24. Notes to the DVD *Hamnava ba Bam/Compassion for Bam*.

25. *Daftar-e-Honar* 2002: 2073.

26. See Simms and Koushkani (2012) for a discussion of the central role of *adab*, literary humanism, in Iranian culture.

27. World Network/WDR, LC–6759 (released in 1987) and Ocora C–559097 (1989).

28. Featuring only the A-side of the cassette, thus excluding *Homayoun* from the original release.

29. According to a Toronto concert promoter, the biggest non-Iranian proportion of an audience for a concert of Persian music in Toronto to date was for Kalhor, Alizadeh, and Reza Nurbakhsh in 2010, which was marketed toward the audience of Yo Yo Ma's *Silk Road Project*, of which Kalhor is a frequent member. Kalhor's fluent English also

helped in the promotion of preconcert radio interviews. Like Yehudi Menuhin's promotion of Ravi Shankar and Ali Akbar Khan, Ma's profile from the classical world made an effective pivot for Kalhor, both cases showing the crucial role of high-profile Western classical artists in facilitating exposure and the unsurprising fact that Asian instrumental music is more accessible to neophyte Western listeners than vocal music.

30. Interview on VOA Persian, broadcast June 19, 2010; http://www.youtube.com/watch?v=wHiPVsJIJlY.

31. Interview on VOA Persian, broadcast June 19, 2010; http://www.youtube.com/watch?v=wHiPVsJIJlY.

32. The identity of this artist is unclear; possibly a misprint of Zamfir (?).

33. http://portal.unesco.org/en/ev.phpURL_ID=26454&URL_DO=DO_TOPIC&URL_SECTION=201.html.

34. http://www.newworldencyclopedia.org/entry/UNESCO#Prizes.2C_awards_and_medals.

35. Furthermore, Nazeri's legacy is actively cultivated in the United States by his English-speaking son Hafez, who lives in New York.

36. Timbral modulation "affected *taswir al-ma'na* [word painting] for, unlike the addition of ornaments or melodic invention, coloristic shifts could be accomplished without disrupting the articulation of the text. Indeed, vocal colors could be closely linked to the sound and meaning of the text where melodic invention was viewed as devoid of meaning or textual connection. For Egyptian listeners this distinction . . . linked Umm Kulthum's singing to that of the *mashayikh*" (Danielson 1997: 93; see 93ff for a typology of these colors).

37. I have elided the last point from this quote: "and a religious person." Due to the role of religion and the clergy in the politics of Iran, Shajarian distances himself from the religious identity that Um Kulthum actively cultivated.

38. Translation from Avery 2007:247.

39. Concert program notes for North American concert tour, May and June 2010.

40. Or "dust and dirt," literally "small chip of wood, mote, thorn; figuratively, a mean fellow" and "motes, chips, brushwood," respectively according to Haim (1961).

41. "Great maestro Shajarian's interview with BBC persian about the Coup d'Etat in Iran (*sic*)" http://www.youtube.com/watch?v=e_v-rxQS1Ms.

42. shajarian VOA interview (15 shahrivare 88)_part4. http://www.youtube.com/watch?v=52RtJUhOHqc&feature=related.

43. http://niacblog.wordpress.com/2009/07/31/iran-radio-%E2%80%9Cshajarian%E2%80%99s-music-will-never-be-played-on-radio-again%E2%80%9D/.

44. shajarian VOA interview (15 shahrivare 88)_part3. http://www.youtube.com/watch?v=0kPM7EW_C7U&feature=related.

45. Translation taken from: http://latimesblogs.latimes.com/babylonbeyond/2009/09/iran-famous-singer-shajarian-decries-language-of-fire.html.

46. shajarian VOA interview (15 shahrivare 88)_part3. http://www.youtube.com/watch?v=0kPM7EW_C7U&feature=related. NB that Shajarian associates Dashti with suffering, pain, and alienation.

47. shajarian VOA interview (15 shahrivare 88)_part3. http://www.youtube.com/watch?v=0kPM7EW_C7U&feature=related.

48. From Australian television: www.youtube.com/watch?v=bnoGhSCA-kQ.

49. In this respect, the situation is almost identical to the resistance to the Shah's regime before his downfall and the revolution of 1979.

Chapter 4
Presently

This chapter takes a bird's-eye view of the evolution of Shajarian's style of avaz over forty-five years, beginning with statements made by Shajarian at various times regarding his own assessment of his work. We then review his achievement and legacy as an artist and public figure before concluding with a discussion about the present state and possible future of avaz.

Ouevre of Recordings and Evolution of Style

OS

Question: Which of your works do you like? Of course I mean after *Bidad*, which everyone welcomed and regarded as wonderful.

The cassette [Nava] Morakab khani *was successful*; Astan e Janan *was successful;* Dastan *was very successful, and my last program* Yad e Ayam, *although the time since its production is very short, was very successful (Shajarian 1993:44).*

The years between 1980 and 2000 are the best years of my singing career from the perspective of construction, variety, and accents, and it is recommended to study those years. Also the Bayat Tork I sang with Behdad Bababi's setar on Majid Derakhshani's CD[1] is another good example. (2008)

There are noticeable differences in your works from your *Rast Panjgah* with Lotfi (in 1975) to *Bidad Homayoun*. What is the reason behind this?

Well, these are due to the experiences that one gains: how one looks at the people, how one deals with one's inspiration, how one gets influenced by society. Poetry becomes my tool to respond to people's desires. Since I cannot be a poet myself, I pick the poetry of Hafez, Sa'di, Mowlana, and Khayyam and speak with their words, because they speak the language of the people and that is why they have survived all these years and still live among people.

[Later in the same interview]
Please tell me about your direction from 1977 until 1991, what changed in your singing and what was carried over?
As I told you before, you add to your experiences from one week to another. When you are working exclusively in one field and a new road opens up, you gain experience. You are basically walking on a path in the hopes of achieving a summit or your target. When you are focused on that phenomenon that you have chosen and work on it and gain knowledge, they all get piled up together. That is, everything that you hear, everything that you see all get piled up like money that you put in the bank. (2009)

RS

Shajarian was selected from among thousands of nominations to be included on the National Public Radio's (a large American network) series *50 Great Voices*, "an exploration of 50 great voices in recorded history . . . awe-inspiring voices from around the world and across time"[2] that profiled a different singer each week throughout 2010. A seasoned veteran of the radio, the medium has always been central to Shajarian's career, from the beginning of his career on Radio Mashhad through the hundreds of programs that made him a national star in Iran in the 1960s and 1970s. But with an estimated twenty million listeners, the NPR program was probably the widest exposure he ever had for a single broadcast of his music. Concerned that the producers may be unfamiliar with avaz and his own catalog of works when selecting music for his program, which was broadcast on September 27, 2010, he provided them with a set of CDs of material specifically selected for their reference. The contents of these CDs, the tracks listed below in their order of appearance, provide an interesting insight into what Shajarian regards as his strongest and most representative works. The selections are largely of avaz, span his career (though emphasizing work before the 2000s), include all of his most famous and emblematic works (with the exception of *Sepideh*), and highlight various contexts within which he worked. In short, it is a cogent survey of the breadth and highlights of his career. The three tasnifs include one of his own composition (*Del e Majnun*), the ritualistic *Morghe Sahar*, an example from his preservational work with Davami, and his recent hit *Zaban-e Atesh*, which marked his new role as "*Ostad-e Sabz*." Significant career milestones include his national radio debut (*Barg e Sabz #216*), his only film score to date (*Delshodegan*), and his iconic *Rabbana*. Asterisks denote "Performance Examples" in this study.[3]

> *Bidad* (avaz portion)
> *Yad e Ayam* (avaz portion)
> Tasnif: *Dele Majnun*
> *Entezar* (side A; avaz selection [18:23–23:27] featuring his low register)
> *Asman e Eshq* (side A; avaz up to Mokhalef)

Dar Khiyal (avaz of Bayat-e Tork)
Gonbad e Mina (avaz in Dashti)
*Barg-e Sabz #216 (1967 debut singing Afshari)
Delshodegan (unclear which of the two short avaz tracks)
*Golhā-ye Tāzeh #37
Tasnif: *Morghe Sahar*
Moammaye Hasti
*Nava (Morakab Khane)
Payam e Nasim
*Rabbana
Old tasnifs (from *Shab e Vasl*): *Shenidam Māhi* and *Ze Dast Mahbub*
*Dastan
Tasnif: *Zaban-e Atesh*

AK

The evolution of Shajarian's avaz over his career seems to fit into three stages. In the first of these stages, it was music—melodic invention, mode, virtuosity, vocal technique—that played the primary role in his avaz. In some of this earlier work he was trying to fullfil his masters' wishes, trying to convince them that he knew the gushe. He was somewhat restricted and pushed the poem into the music; he couldn't really touch the music. So all of his tahrirs were exactly what he learned from Boroumand or other people. After the revolution, poetry moves to the forefront in the expression of the message and he starts to explore the potential of word painting—*Bidad* and *Astan e Janan* are prime examples. Shajarian brought meaning to tahrirs, using them to support the poem in a way that was unprecedented. The third stage overlaps with *Nava (Morakab khani)*, where the focus on the poetry is coupled with a more innovative compositional approach to avaz, and continued in *Dastan, Yad e Ayam,* and *Zemstan Ast. Nava* was a real pivotal album. With more autonomy and more understanding of what music should do, he actually changed the music, which I believe was the original idea of avaz—you have to change the music. That's one of the reasons this music is flexible. It's like a raw material and you have to put it in a form that will present the ideal of the poem. The music then becomes more enjoyable for the performer, it's more creative. In some of his most recent work, he seems to be less concerned with clarity in articulating the text and with creating novel tahrirs; the latter aspect of his work reached truly amazing heights in the 1980s and 1990s.

RS

It is admittedly cliché to separate an artist's works into distinctive periods—especially the default number of three such periods—but this seems appropriate in Shajarian's case and is indeed clearly implied in his own assessments of his work. As noted throught this study, he was quite conscious of the shift in his style and conception of avaz (in terms of the relationship between music and poetry on the one hand, and the overall function of avaz in society on the other) that occurred after he met Dadbeh in the early years of the revolution. His quote in the section immediately above acknowledges that this "mature period" of 1980 to 2000 is qualitatively distinct from his work in the past decade. That said and the following explication notwithstanding, there is a remarkable degree of consistency in Shajarian's singing throughout his large corpus of recordings with regard to both style and quality. The changes in style were on the whole gradual and cumulative and arose from the same impulse: refinement and improvement in pursuit of the perfection of his art.

As one would expect, Shajarian's range seems to extend higher, and his tone seems brighter and more vigorous in the earlier recordings through the 1960s and 1970s. His early tahrirs are very fast, long, and use a lot of *tekye*, often on each note; they are characterized by a flashy, athletic quality. As illustrated in his performance of *Golhā-ye Tazeh* # 37, they also feature a relatively small variety of centonic units, include more consecutive unvaried repetition of units, and are generally uniform and balanced in overall contour.[4] It is the sound of a gifted, ambitious young singer entering a competitive arena and displaying his technique, skill, and strength. This priority to dazzle and excite—which Shajarian surely succeeds at accomplishing—is also evident in the contemporaneous recordings of his slightly older colleagues (and competition), Golpayegani and Iraj. For those interested, other works from his early period are examined in my dissertation (Simms 1996).

We noted in detail the qualities marking his "mature period" landmark performances in chapter 2. Evoking, glossing, and spinning the meaning of the text through word painting now guided the deployment of his prodigious arsenal of technique. Shajarian began to explore his lower register in the early 1980s with *Nava (Morakab khani)*, a feature that appeared with increasing frequency and duration through the following decades. The understated, relaxed, and somewhat meditative quality of this style is generally less characteristic of the twentieth-century avaz tradition. It further develops and evokes Banan's trademark low-register singing, which usually also contained a paradoxically passionate quality, as well as Dadbeh's beautifully resonant detachment and calm. We obtained unreleased recordings of Shajarian accompanied by ney-player Musavi (also a student of Dadbeh) made at a private *majles* in 1981 that feature long, austere performances in Segah and Homayun of poems by Hafez, Rumi, and Baba Taher that are almost entirely sung in this low register. Shajarian may also be drawing on his early experience with sacred recitation in these instances; indeed the approach seems strikingly similar to certain styles of Qur'anic recitation. While he still sings comfortably in his high register, later performances work more gradually towards it and usually do not remain there as long, whereas some early recordings are sung almost entirely in his upper range.

Shajarian plays much more with dynamics in his later work: shaping long tahrirs, crescendo and diminuendo on long-held tones, and employing more pianissimo in general. This emphasis on pianissimo is interesting, perhaps indicating a greater degree of introspection while offering greater scope for dramatic contrast. His later tahrirs are generally slower than earlier ones but use a wider variety of centonic units in more complex configurations. Consciously influenced by instrumental tahrirs, they are much less predictable in their overall shape and do not fit as neatly into the centonic analysis and standard tahrir typology compared to his early recordings. He also uses a wider range of articulation in these tahrirs; the definitive *tekye* seems to be used less and is contrasted with varying degrees of detaching pitches without *tekye*. His later work shows an overall subtlety, interest in contrast, and attention to detail when compared to his earlier recordings, which seem more sensational and spectacular. While he was always aware and capable of clear enunciation of the text—as attested by his debut national recording in 1967 (*Barg-e Sabz* #216)—this becomes a consistent priority throughout his mature period. His new attention to these parameters is put in service of delivering the text with a heightened dramatic and narrative quality, the latter, of course, expressing his personal interpretation and spinning of the poem.

Shajarian's mature style is also characterized by the frequent and innovative use of *morakab khāni*, likewise for enhancing and manipulating the text but also for the freedom it opened up for creating novel musical forms and adventurous modal walkabouts. He exploited the endless possibilies of this through to his recordings in the early 2000s. His singular skill in this domain shifted away from his earlier explicit athleticism to impress knowledgeable listeners through a more profound, intellectual, and mature level of mastery. In terms of repertoire, he performs Dashtestani more frequently in this period, often coupled with the poetry of Baba Taher, in an explicit salute to Ostad Dadbeh. Above these technical qualities, Shajarian's art in his mature period is marked by a new mandate for the *khanande*: through Dadbeh's influence he is now a reflector and resonator of the feelings of Iranian society at large. With great reknown and great art comes great social responsibility.

There is a venerable tradition of Persian singers performing well into old age—a few past one-hundred years—making one wonder seriously about what powers may be hidden in the music itself when immersed in it over a lifetime, specifically Khatam 'Asgari's claim that "this music prolongs life" (During 1996:360). When discussing the matter of "stylistic periods" of individual musicians, Dr. Hossein Omumi Sr. rightly stressed the logical variable that, in the course of a long career, singers must adjust their style to suit the natural physiological changes that occur with aging, and draw more securely upon their own experience (personal communication, 1996). This is a larger matter of maturing and knowing oneself, and knowing how to accommodate the change, a key criterion of mastery that many otherwise great musicians may lack. I believe that the period of 1980 through the early 1990s featured the optimal balance of physical strength along with mature insight for Shajarian. His versatile voice has aged exceptionally well and at seventy-one years old he is still able to soar confidently in his high register, if for judiciously shorter periods, while his lower (and personally preferred) register has taken on a richer resonance. When I asked him in 2010 if there were any special things he did to care for his voice or if he did any particular warmup before performing he looked somewhat puzzled and answered that no, he had no regimen and simply sang a bit before going on stage. It seems that the natural gift of his voice extends beyond normal capabilities on many fronts.

The exploration of neopoetry in *Zemestan Ast* represents the most interesting development in his post-2000 period, one that holds both considerable challenges and potential for the stylistic evolution of avaz. His albums in the early 2000s with the *Masters of Persian Music* lineup also featured increasing experimentation with large-scale form in the placement of tasnifs, which are frequently interspersed with sections of avaz as opposed to framing the latter. Shajarian often performed short duet sections with his son Homayoun that featured an antiphonal or overlapping echo effect (e.g., "Ham Avaz i Shushtari" on *Faryad* [CD II, track 4] and the end of *Zemestan Ast*).[5] While there were precedents in his earlier work, he more frequently sang avaz over an ostinato groove in the past decade than previously. Other than these points, the main musical development of the past decade for Shajarian was not so much in his singing style as it was in the unexplored potential presented by his new generation of instruments.

Legacy in 2010

> Despite the fading of tradition as a concept, one aspect remains inviolate and transcendent: national feeling, that which is "Iranian." The artist is the one person who internalizes this world and reflects its image for the public. He is the nation's praise-singer, as he was the king's in the ancient monarchies. He sings for the people with or without the support of the government. His voice goes beyond the national borders for a few Western music-lovers, to sustain the diaspora or to represent the cultural force of the nation on the world stage. (During 2002:862)

While During is referring here to Persian artists in general, his description remains quite accurate if he were referring specifically to Shajarian, who stands as the most significant torchbearer of the tradition of avaz in the late-twentieth century to the present.

For Iranian musicians and connoisseurs, Shajarian represents authoritative musical knowledge of a venerable Ostad. His immense range, technique, knowledge, flexibility of voice and style is truly remarkable. From Qur'an recitation to *Zemestan,* to his vast grasp of avaz tradition, radif, poetry, the evocation of mode, mood and word, along with mastery of tasnif, even folk stylings (Dashtestani, Khorasani), no one else comes remotely near his abilities and achievement. He is like a funnel for the immensely broad tradition of Iranian singing in its widest sense. Like his favourite poet Hafez, Shajarian is regarded as a consolidator and "perfecter" of his inheritance.[6] Both of these men parallel Schole's view of Homer (assumed here, however contentiously, to be an individual) "as being the greatest of many generations of Greek epic singers, a master of his art who in the nature of things could not surpass his tradition, but who created the best performances of which the tradition was capable" (2006:23).

But Shajarian also serves as model for judiciously and tastefully renovating tradition while respecting its boundaries, an elegant balance of tradition and individual creativity in both his singing and design of musical instruments, and balance of tradition and modernity in his public presentation of concerts and recordings, and his insistence on the music having a social relevance in the present moment among a mass audience. Like his instrumental mentors Ebadi and Jalil Shahnaz, Shajaraian has demonstrated how to keep Persian music fresh, how to treat and exploit its intrinsic flexibility in order to say something meaningful and beautiful. In these ways he represents somewhat of a compromise between the previous phase transitions in Persian music of the legacies of Farahani and Vaziri, leaning decidedly toward the former in content (indeed his "perfection" is precisely the style emanating from the Farahani line) but taking cues from the latter for accommodating Persian music to its irreversible modern context—which for Shajarian meant mastering its mass mediation. In doing so he established a practice and aesthetic that became the standard for all musicians in his wake. On yet another front, his career trajectory was pioneering, blazing a trail that opened up global professional opportunities for Persian musicians at large. Concomitantly, he played a major role in legitimizing the denigrated role of the musician in Iranian society, efficaciously eroding longstanding taboos.

Shajarian's legacy of recordings is the most comprehensive statement by a single artist, a veritable encyclopedia of the art of avaz, in the late-twentieth/early-twenty-first century: multiple performances in all dastgahs featuring great flexibility of form and novel modal combinations (*morakab khāni*). Many of these recordings are masterpieces. The canonical status of Shajarian's recordings is only enhanced by his conception of them as embodying "his radif," which, despite the great anticipation this holds for musicians, he refuses to record as a dry theoretical demonstration but rather presents in his albums simultaneously integrated as instruction and art. This is a clear call for musicians to reenvision the Qajar radif as something more dynamic than the atrophying tendencies it sometimes showed in recent decades—a literalist, exoteric crutch that approached the debilitation of "frozen music" that characterizes some of the neighbouring modal traditions. It also guarantees that musicians will continue to listen closely and learn from his recordings.

For general listeners in Iran and the diaspora (including the musicians and connoisseurs just discussed, who also listen to him for their pleasure), Shajarian is a symbol of deep Iranian cultural identity as a master of avaz and, more generally, *adab*. In performing avaz he performs *adab*, by which in turn he performs "Iranian-ness," all aiming at a distinctly highbrow level. Despite this setting of a high bar, Shajarian played a major role in rebooting popular interest in avaz, particularly after the revolution. His music is a primary vehicle for the activation and continuation of the tradition of avaz as it was always intended to be: a celebration, for both audience and performers, of the very moment it exists in performance, a reflection on beauty, pain, the mystery of life and ourselves.

Shajarian's deployment of avaz plays with a form of time travel that strategically conflates past and present, channelling the past to haunt and inform the present. The self-similarity, fractal scaling of individual artistic expression and society at large, of past and present, are brought into sharp focus. In the archetypal tradition of Iranian narrative performance, Shajarian plays an important role as a massmediated teller: making old archetypes and narratives (i.e., poetry and the radif) relevant to contemporary Iranians and thereby telling the story of contemporary Iran. As an Iranian blogger observed, "If one day researchers had to write about our social history during the last 25 years, one indication of the condition of people who lived during this time would be Shajarian's body of work. He has always sung about and for the people" (Alavi 2005: 238). In a longstanding process of social feedback, he listens, gathers and assesses the collective sentiments of Iranians around the world and reflects it back to them. Following this archetypal bardic function, he also includes his own points of view. A recurring message in his music from the 1980s onward acknowledges and laments present difficulties, but calls for patience and wisdom as a means to coping with, and ultimately rising above, the chaos and pain contemporary Iranians continue to endure. The mask of poetry and music allows him to speak with authority and impunity, to transcend his individuality and speak from the common core that we all share, that Hafez and Sa'di shared, and that is embedded in the anonymous, supraindividual source of the Persian musical tradition.

The celebration and time-shifting narration facilitated by avaz begins, as it always has and must, with the live performance itself, be it in the studio with musicians and technicians, or the concert hall with an appreciative audience. It extends, however, in a way that is uniquely contemporary: listeners enjoy the technological recreation of the experience at their whim and convenience for moments, both special and trivial, in the privacy of their homes and on the move in their cars and with their iPods. They continuously reperform his music by listening to it in infinite, ever-changing occasions of their personal lives, adding yet another layer of temporal complexity, superimposition, and feedback. For millions, his music is an important component of the "soundtrack of their lives"; with the visceral, suprarational intensity that only music can provoke, it is associated with specific personal experiences, memories, moods, and habits. His fans represent the whole gamut of social classes and age groups, in this respect his music functions as a rare point of convergence. Shajarian was particularly successful at drawing young people toward Persian music in the 1980s and 1990s. True, as Shajarian himself acknowledges below, rock and rap speaks more directly and forcefully to Iran's youth majority, as they must. But many twenty-somethings still show up for his concerts in Iran and North America. His recording and touring in 2009 and 2010 with the *Shahnaz Ensemble* showed his concerted effort in mentoring young musicians.

As with the subculture of Persian musicians, many of his fans see Shajarian as promoting an elegant and successful balance of traditional and modern values. The Iranian popular press has helped cultivate his image among his fans of being associated with things traditionally and uniquely Iranian, of things highly valued by Iranians as intellectually and aesthetically prestigious—Persian poetry, calligraphy, gardening, and musical instrument making—again, a veritable embodiment of refined *adab*. Reflecting the deeper levels of *adab* pertaining to "deeds," he added an admirable personal integrity and solidarity with modern Iranians, remaining in Iran after the revolution when many left and he easily could have, and donating his time and money towards various charities. He has clearly stated that "his music could not survive entirely in exile, and that he needs to *'return to Iran to reconnect with the essence of what I sing'*" (Ditmars 2009:66). His famous postelection crisis remark of "dust and trash" was an unequivocal, powerful show of popular solidarity.

Shajarian is viewed as a sophisticated and well-travelled progressive, softening Iran's rigid stance on art and politics, advocating moderation and openness while respecting tradition. He has assumed a public position of peaceful resistance, of shrewdly exploiting loopholes in the complex web of official government regulation, whether deploying a well chosen poem by Hafez in his avaz or interviewing on international airwaves outside Iran (to Iranians and the world), chipping away at the hypocrisy and injustice of the perishing republic. Shajarian has become increasingly open in his confrontation with the regime, recently challenging the proscription of women singing in public—a so-called "abandoned/prohibited question," a divine a priori truth according to official policy—via his daughter Mojgan singing solo in his concerts. His recent affiliation with the *Shahnaz Ensemble*, with its prominent inclusion of young women, brings unprecedented profile to issues of female musicians playing in public. If, as Behnam submits, the ideal aim of Iranian culture with regard to globalization "is to become competent to live in the contemporary world, and live with contemporary peoples, while maintaining cultural identity" (2004: 14), then amidst the dreadful failure of Iranian politicians on this front, Shajarian is showing a clear path forward within his field of traditional Iranian arts.

In a word, Shajarian shows leadership during these precarious times in Iran: grassroots, inspiring, unofficial but bona fide. In a dynamic not seen since the *Mashrute* and 'Aref's role of leadership and engagement of Persian music toward the democraticization of Iran in the early decades of the twentieth century, Shajarian was popularly proclaimed *"Ostad-e Sabz"* following the election crisis of 2009. In reviewing the ancient foundations of contemporary Iranian identity, Del Giudice asserts that the *Shahnameh* "is haunted by the idea that those most ethically fitted to rule are precisely the ones most reluctant to rule, preferring instead to devote themselves to humankind's chief concerns: the nature of wisdom, the fate of the human soul, and the incomprehensibility of God's purpose" (2008:63). Shajarian disavowed any explicit affiliation with politics right after the revolution but quickly emerged with an approach that resonated with this archetypal dynamic: he sought not to rule but rather to lead, wielding the forces of *adab* and his personal integrity. According to Dabashi's analysis of the nature of power in Shi'a Islam (2007:190), Shajarian can lead and be influential precisely because he doesn't rule.

Shajarian showed two quite different faces of his power over the decades. In the 1980s it was, on the one hand, the power of merely being present, active, and continuing to sing and record in the harsh desert that constituted postrevolutionary musicking. On the other hand, his ingeniously shrewd critique—which was at once stealthy and yet patently transparent—demonstrated immense personal power in terms of intellect, courage, capability, and clout within the tightly controlled infra-structure of music publishing. His current display of power is of a more conventional variety, though rather unprecedented in contemporary Iran: defiant, confrontational, explicit and reaching a mass audience both inside Iran and around the world, Shaja-rian is a dissident expressing what the vast majority of Iranians may only think or discuss in paranoid secrecy. In reviewing his musicianship we have noted that Shaja-rian is a master of musical timing. He appears to also be master of timing on the larger temporal scale of decades: lying low and speaking obliquely yet effectively through his music when necessary, and stepping up and speaking out explicitly now that he is able to, through the very direct means of interviews.

What is the tongue in the mouth, wise one? It is the key to the door of
    the treasure house of the skilled.
When it is held, how can it be known whether one is a seller of jewels
    or a peddler or junk?
Although in the opinion of the wise silence is decorum, at the right
    time it is better to speak.
Two things are contrary to intelligence: to hold the tongue when it is
    time to speak and to speak when one should be silent.
—Sa'di[7]

And yet the example set by Shajarian speaks beyond his own life to a larger power and truth: the power of the individual, the local, the butterfly effect, and sensitivity to initial conditions. Small things matter, so we must take responsibility within our own circle of influence, however humble that may be. Without megalomaniac delusions or insisting on making such an impact as Shajarian and other famous activists have, individuals and small groups of individuals influence the big picture. Margaret Mead's famous dictum[8] is corroborated by both history and chaos theory. Emergence is driven by individuals.

While the poetry of Sa'di, Rumi, and Hafez that Shajarian sings has long been admired and loved around the world, he is the first truly global representative of Persian music. Moreover, he represents a balanced, positive—indeed inspiring—face of Iranian culture to a world community in which Iran is a self-imposed pariah state. Among other things, the UNESCO awards in particular show international acknowledgement and indeed empowerment for Shajarian to continue on the course of engaging his talent and intelligence toward peaceful proaction, normalization, and connection of Iran with the world. *Adab* and Persian music function as an attractively accessible bridge appealing to human sensibilities of inspiration and beauty.

Beyond the wildest imaginings of the previous generation of Iranian Ostads, Shajarian is a contemporary musical legend. And increasingly, even among Iranians who don't like Persian music, in the Iranian version of "Life the Movie" (à la Gabler 1998) whereby celebrities perform in a "real-life" collective drama outside their professional vocations: a public hero. It's impossible to historically extrapolate with any accuracy in our unprecedentedly fast-moving world (and fanciful to compare our chaotic, inchoate perception of the past decades with previous periods of history), but it is perhaps not too extravagant an exaggeration to venture that Shajarian's achievements transposed to a previous era would likely have placed him in the legendary, quasimythological category of a Barbad, Zyrab, and such lofty company. But perhaps again, this is no longer possible in our Age of Information, where overly abundant and exacting documentation will henceforth keep in check the creative, embellishing muse of future generations' mythic imagination. Perhaps, alas, legends can never again be what they used to be. Not knowing things about great people is always more interesting and creative than actually knowing.

Avaz and Persian Music: Now and the Future

Environmental Changes and Challenges

While the constant political instability in Iran throughout the twentieth century was palpable to all, profound degradation of the environment accompanying rapid industrialization and urban growth crept up more stealthily on public consciousness throughout the second half of the century, as it did around the globe. Persian music is performed throughout Iran but it has always been a distinctly urban genre (previously of the court) and its activity has unquestionably centered on Tehran throughout the twentieth century and will continue to do so through the foreseeable future. Renowned during Safavid times for its trees, rivers, gardens and natural beauty, Tehran's population was around fifteen thousand when Agha Mohammad Khan declared it the capital of the Qajar dynasty in 1795.[9] The population grew to 210,000 by 1921, and then by leaps and bounds—690,000 (in 1941), 1.5 million (1956), 4.5 million (1976), and 6 million (1986)—to the most recent census (2006) of 8.4 million in the urban area, 13.4 million in the metropolitan. Its urban area in 2000 was one hundred times larger than it was in 1921 (Pourahmad et al. 2007: 254; Statistical Center of Iran [2006 census]). These huge changes in Tehran's urban environment have had an incalculable impact on lifestyle, collective psychology, and culture.

The first public concert in Iran—a truly historic event given the lowly position of music throughout the previous four or five centuries—was held in a garden outside Tehran in 1906 and reportedly lasted twenty-four hours (Zonis
1973:144); likewise many early photographs of musicians performing or posing
were taken in gardens (ibid.:188, 197).

> Many musicians feel that instrumental timbre and intervals or elementary
> modal motifs reflect the nature of Iran:
>
>> Kīānī: This music is made in a luminous land, inundated with sun-
>> light, under a sky filled with brilliant stars. This must be reflected in
>> the timbre of the instrument as well as in the sounds of the language,
>> the voice, the song, and in painting, rugs, ceramics, and so on.
>
> Traditional culture includes not only what is produced but also the relation-
> ship of the subject to his or her milieu. It is fundamentally synthetic and to-
> talizing, integrating nature and culture—unlike modernity, which separates
> and opposes nature and culture. Each element refers to the whole . . . One
> day Kīānī told the master Davāmī that he was afraid traditional music might
> disappear; but Davāmī began to laugh and answered, "No, this music is nat-
> ural; as long as nature is there and God is there, this music will also be
> there." Nature is the space in which people live and sing. It is this whole that
> constitutes the traditional framework. (During 2002:856)

Alas, according to Davami's criteria, it would appear that Persian music must
survive now solely from the grace of God in Tehran. While both air and noise
pollution were on the rise in the 1960s, Nettl felt that in the mid 1970s that the
growth of Tehran had affected Persian music little, and rather that music benefitted from the city's role as the center of the nation both in terms of government
patronage, media access, and proximity to the largest market in the country
(1978:169, 171). But performances needed to be shortened and thoroughly
planned to accomodate the faster pace of city life. In jostling for space with the
great plurality of styles flourishing in cosmopolitan Tehran during the 1960s and
1970s, Nettl observed that Persian music kept "a posture of aloofness" and was
"decidedly selective" in what it absorbed stylistically (1978: 171). The tipping
point, however, was just around the corner in the form of the upheaval of the revolution, the Iran-Iraq War (with Tehran under siege from Iraqi scud missile attacks), and the exponential growth of Tehran and its concomitant environmental
degradation.

Tehran is now one of the most polluted cities in the world (Pourahmad et al.
2007: 256; BBC 2007), particularly with regard to its air quality, 94% of which is
caused by automobiles, according to the government's own statistics (Curtis and
Hooglund 2008:88). It was estimated that between 2005 and 2006 smog killed
nearly ten thousand people—including 3,600 in one month—through heart attacks and respiratory illnesses, leading a senior Iranian official to say that living

in Tehran was like "collective suicide" (BBC 2007). Schools are regularly closed for several days at a time when the toxicity in the air reaches critical levels (Curtis and Hooglund 2008: 88). Of course, humans are not alone in reaping the deleterious effects of the toxic environment. Recent studies confirm that birds have been fleeing Tehran in increasing numbers due to air pollution and unregulated development (read: destruction) of the urban avian habitat (Guardian 2009). Pigeons and nightingales—the very symbol of Persian music and partial source of Shajarian's musical acquisition—have fled in large numbers and, surprisingly, so have the black crows, supposedly the toughest "pollution-resistant" species.

> Experts fear the departure of the crow—long decried in Iranian culture as a symbol of bad news and gossip—could be the death knell for wildlife in Tehran, where many plants have already lost their smell and colour as a result of the polluted atmosphere. . . . Mohammad Bagher Sadough, the head of the city's environment agency, said the crow exodus was a sign of a disturbed ecosystem. Eventually the remaining bird species will also leave, turning the city into an urban desert of high-rise buildings and traffic jams. . . . "The continued existence of crows, particularly with the departure of other birds, had given us hope that wildlife could survive in the city. With their migration that hope is fading and our concern over the destructiveness of urban environments has deepened." (ibid.)

Iran also has one of the world's highest rates of traffic accidents, with much of this accruing in Tehran. "Around 22,000 people are killed each year with 400,000 crashes in 2002 alone. Poor roads, unsafe cars and a blatant disregard for traffic laws by drivers are blamed for the high toll" (BBC 2004). The number of registered motor vehicles increased nineteen-fold between 1986 and 2004, seriously exacerbating both the pollution and chaotic traffic (Curtis and Hooglund 2008:185). The accomplished setar player Masud Shoari noted how these new contexts impact contemporary Persian musicians:

> Our era differs significantly from that of the Qajar period when there was more leisure time and therefore fewer problems occupying one's mind. Today there are a variety of problems and issues that did not exist hundred years ago; therefore, new methods of teaching are even required. For example, one hour after the students leave the classroom and enter the urban environment, they fail to remember whatever they were taught because they are exposed to so many polluted sounds. In the old days all we heard after coming out of classroom was the sound of nightingales and the sound of the wind moving through trees. (Shoari 2006: 29)

Understandably, like the birds, many musicians have simply chosen to leave Tehran for outlying areas of the city, the country, and beyond (During 2005: 378).

As if lethal air, noise, and aggressive traffic were not apocalyptic enough, Tehran is also built upon a major forty-seven-mile-long fault line and about one hundred smaller fractures; "there is daily seismic activity in Tehran and on average three to four identifiable tremors of up to three on the Richter scale—every day" (CNN 2003). There have been several devastating earthquakes in Iran throughout the past decades and indeed throughout the twentieth century. Spectacularly overextended and unprepared, Tehran awaits "The Big One." The ground is soft and brittle, building codes are ignored, and to cope with the continuously growing population, the city builds relentlessly upward. Cheap Soviet-style blocks mushroomed after the Iran-Iraq war to cope with the flood of refugees from around the country, as well as a steady stream from Iraq and Afghanistan. The last big quake to hit Tehran was 1830; it is estimated that a similar event would kill hundreds of thousands of people—perhaps up to one million—and damage or destroy about 80 percent of the buildings. Two independent studies predict the potential for a quake of between seven and eight on the Richter scale (CNN 2003). It is both remarkable and surprising that, with all the seismically stable places in the world, so many Iranians (among them a good number of Tehranians) after the revolution chose to seek refuge in Los Angeles, which is now home of the largest expatriate community.

Toxic, crowded, noisy, aggressive, and precarious. Birdless and adorned with flowers that are neither fragrant nor colorful.[10] Contemporary Tehran is not particularly conducive to the quiet, meditative mysticism cultivated and embodied in Persian music, let alone functioning as its undisputed center. We saw above how Shajarian gauges the effectiveness of his live performance through the feedback of silence with his audience. For Shajarian, a skilled and knowledgeable gardener, this very incongruence highlights the new function of Persian music in the past few decades as a therapeutic detoxification and escape from a pathological environment. Persian music now functions as an aural oasis of serenity and cultural continuity, a lush garden of repose within the mind amidst the madness induced by frenetic, unrelenting change.[11] As noted above, Nettl felt that stylistically Persian music in the late 1960s had responded little to the growth of Tehran, but perhaps this therapeutic, shielding function of the music was already recognized and operative even at this relatively simpler time. Could Iranian proclivities for the exaggerated echo and reverb used in recordings of the time express a yearning for quiet, open space? Of control and manipulation of the environment that was now only possible through technology and soundproofed recording studios?

OS

Question: What are your views on the change of the environment in Iran, the shift from gardens and a slower life style to the craziness of today, how does that affect your music?

This is something that I have always witnessed and mentioned. Technology has changed the image of the whole world and has to some extent altered the foundations of authenticity and tradition. Although technology can distort the founda-

tions of authentic values, they nevertheless always return to their original posi-
tion. It is possible that technology can distort the "appearance" of the needs of
the today's society in the world but it cannot really change it in an overall way.
So if someone travelled in a horsecart one day, she is now traveling in a Con-
corde airplane, so she arrives at her destination faster. But she can never forget
her classical music because that music provides her with relaxation. Because
each one of us, when we work, we eventually need to relax. This is where music
regains its value and does not go astray.

It is true that throughout the whole world classical music has comparatively
less listeners. At the same time the youth, according to their needs and motiva-
tions and energy, need exciting and upbeat music. However, this form of music
does not have a long life, in the same way that the youth's energy does not last.
One day that young individual will lose his youth and energy, and will seek lei-
sure and that is when the upbeat music that he listened to twenty years ago will
annoy him. This is when he seeks a music that has stronger foundations, and is
more classical and more comforting. That young individual will eventually get
there. I mean, anybody starts from that point in their youth and will eventually
get here.

This view is opposed to some Iranian musicians who specialize only in one
branch of music and always defend their area of expertise and do not care about
whether or not the whole of society gains anything from their specializations.
They write prescriptions for each other that everyone must pay attention to what
they know. Now this is an absolute error. We have to recognize the real problems
of society. We have to understand what kind of music children like, what teenag-
ers like, what people in their thirties, forties, and fifties want, and then write pre-
scriptions for them. But in general we don't even have the right to write prescrip-
tions for anybody and, for example, force teenagers to listen to a particular kind
of music. People should choose for themselves but in general we must understand
the problems of society and realize that each age group has a different taste in
music. They all need a music that can respond to their own needs, both the needs
of their thoughts and the needs of their bodies.

I never approve of parents who play my music at their homes and force their
children to listen to it. I always tell them that you should not provoke children—
that child needs another kind of music. You should give them their own music, not
force my music to them. The same way that loud and high-energy music is irritat-
ing for people over sixty, our music is very heavy and irritating for a child—it
can even cause depression. Those teenagers have to choose this music for them-
selves must have the need for it. I don't like to force them to listen to any of my
works.

I am not just concerned about the music of Iran but I always have the music
of the whole world in my mind. The different varieties of music that have taken
shape have all been due to the desires of the society, otherwise they wouldn't
have been created. So at one time a particular pop artist or different schools of

jazz, pop or rap music were popular. Those people who claim that these kinds of music are poor and should be thrown away all belong to a particular mindset or culture. Nevertheless, these musics have been created because of the needs and desires of some part of a society, in some part of the world. Then these kinds of music have been popularized through media and they all have become well-known to the whole world. Now, if this music has any solid foundation and if it has any correlation with the needs of people, then it will continue to exist. But if it does not have these attributes, then it will become like the spring flowers that grow in springtime, and will be gone after a period of time. But we don't have the right to fight against those kinds of music. The only thing we can do to defend that which we believe in, I mean our work, is to take its quality to a higher level and then present it to people. Therefore we create choice for our listeners and let them decide for themselves. (2008)

Stylistic Stasis?

RS

An honestly objective view of Persian music through the past one hundred years clearly shows a rather constant flow of stylistic change, though viewed globally during the same period, it is of a comparatively modest magnitude and slow pace. An overall continuity pervades amidst flowering variation. Experimental moments occasionally arise but vanish like fleeting bumps in the road. Millions of people genuinely love this music in one or several of its myriad microstylistic manifestations. However, some musicians and listeners of various age groups feel that the pervasive continuity, the stylistic attractor, is a now closed equation, a stale, predictable loop that has run its course and lost its genuine relevance. They feel that it lost its existential authenticity as a fresh, vital musical platform in sync with the present moment of historical unfolding. For these stakeholders the lionizing of past tradition—now a thoroughly idealized past—via the *Markaz*, the Mahoor Institute's historical recordings, and the transcription subindustry works from the same impulse as the government's promotion of Islamic history, culture, tradition, and values, enforcing a false obedience and slavish, inauthentic conformity. Does this musical stance reinforce a notion of authority and repression? Is Persian music "stuck" as a stagnating nationalist monument along with the more conventional fixtures of national construction: the census, map, and museum? Is it in denial of the present and stuck in time? Is this not precisely the point in view of exponential social change: to hearken back, for those interested, to the centering spirituality that was always integral to the music and stands in stark contrast to global hyperactivity and hyperconsumption, the fidgety, empty "busyness" symptomatic of widespread angst? Is Persian music simply another genre, now stylistically branded for the market, among the pluralistic spectrum of globalized musical culture in a thousand station, "narrowcasting" mediascape? Does the inconsistent value and conception of

Persian music really constitute a pressing problem at present for Iranians? Is there any point in even asking for an answer or reason to account for such an intrinsically multidimensional, complex situation, to divide the whole that constitutes contemporary Persian musical culture into partial questions or points of view?

While debate does indeed swirl around these questions of Persian music in general, we have also noted that Shajarian's brilliant achievement as a singer, his establishment of a powerfully expressive style that is indelibly his own and yet deeply rooted in tradition, has been so hugely influential as to create another layer of canonical style within the contemporary continuation of the tradition. His style is a powerful attractor that has in many ways steamrolled the spectrum of individualistic variety that characterized the public performance of avaz before his ascendance, moving beyond being a benchmark for other singers to being *the* benchmark. Viewed in this way, it is a remarkable achievement but also initiates a crisis of craft over art among contemporary professional singers, an arresting "anxiety of influence" (Bloom 1973).

Of course, it is not Shajarian's fault that he was gifted and worked hard, and that subsequent singers (with perhaps the exception of Shahram Nazeri) have been unable to offer compelling alternatives. Shajarian consciously chose and assiduously studied his influences, but moved on to make his personal statement, his mark, and the ball has been in the court of younger singers for a few decades now. If this tendency persists, it seems highly likely that Homayoun Shajarian will succeed in continuing the legacy of his father with few challengers, as no one has received anywhere near the intense direct grooming and transmission that Homayoun has had, to say nothing of his genetic advantages for maintaining the continuity of the style. No doubt there are many great amateur singers of avaz who sing in small private circles, outside of which they will never be known (Youtube notwithstanding), and who preserve the wide range of individuality and stylistic variety that characterized the recordings of the pre-Shajarian era. The discussion here pertains to singers in the public, professional sphere, which is naturally the most influential but not necessarily the exclusive or most important sphere of activity from an aesthetic or "traditional" point of view.

Poet Reza Baraheni believes that *aruz* and beyt-based avaz has gone as far as it can stylistically—largely thanks to Shajarian—and that the next stage, the way forward is naturally to pursue neopoetry with asymmetrical, nonlinear phrase lengths and lyrical rhythms (personal communication, 2010). Following Partch's line of thinking of avaz as "Corporeal" music, if you change the poetry you will change the music, a point forcefully driven home by Shajarian's rendition of *Zemestan Ast*. While Shajarian has expressed interest in pursuing this further, it remains to be seen if this is among his priorities for developing in the immediate future.

From another angle, it may be that we are witnessing the establishment of a de facto "Shajarian *maktab*," a concrete contemporary illustration of the general process described in chapter 1 of our companion volume (Simms and Koushkani 2012) of feedback between the tradition, the gifted individual, and group consensus. Unlike

previous schools, this one is largely transmitted via recordings—a feature that is
entirely in accord with the founding Ostad's methods.

OS
Some people have the point of view that Persian music is lacking popularity in
recent years, and compared to the first few years of the revolution, there is less of
a tendency towards this kind of music. Of course, I am in agreement with this
opinion. The most important issue that has resulted in this lack of appreciation is
that this music is monotonous, and also its chaotic market has grabbed it by the
throat. This monotonous nature is not unimportant in the outcome of selling a
fewer number of cassettes. Furthermore, the younger singers who are working
these days imitate the works that are already out and sing those same songs. Due
to this, people do not see any variety in the works released. It is natural that lis-
tening to repetitive works is tiresome for the listeners. Also, the radio and the
television do not pay enough attention in their choice of music. Not everyone
wants to listen to Shajarian—I use my own name as an example so there is no
misunderstanding. Even I cannot stand my own voice all the time. The music that
is being played on the radio and the television doesn't take into account its lis-
teners. There is no appreciation as to which age group this music is being played
for, or what situation. Early in the morning the radio plays Afshari, which is not
attractive for the listener. (Qaneeifard 2003:77–78)
    The essence of Persian avaz is creativity and innovation. Avaz is composition
in an instant. The singer who performs avaz, composes in the moment. One can
sing Mahur but each time perform it in a way that is different from the time be-
fore. I am against the idea that someone's avaz of Mahur is similar to another
singer. Perhaps, in regards to a tasnif one can accept this idea. No authentic art-
ist [singer] can repeat his or her avaz exactly the same each time. Avaz is closer
to the essence of art. Avaz has a broader form. The artist performs avaz in rela-
tion to the meaning of the poetry. When the poem changes, the avaz changes too.
    I am very much against imitation in art and put a lot of emphasis on creativ-
ity and innovation. Because I think imitation opposes the jewel of art; in fact,
imitation squanders art. Perhaps some people may find this an extremist idea but
I believe that only a work of art that has innovation will survive. Imitated art has
an expiry date and will be forgotten after a while. Only those remain in the realm
of art who present their own unique art. Those who imitate, at best, try to perform
exactly what has been done before.
    But there is no problem: we just have to separate it from the authentic works
of art. This problem goes back to our definition of art: art is man's reaction to his
own environment. Not all people react to the same environment in the same way.
The artist is the same. Each artist has his own taste, the work of each artist, has
its own fragrance. Hafez calls this fragrance the latifeye nahani, *"secret attrac-*
tion." Each artist has her own unique sensitivity and expresses this sensitivity
through her own way, like reading poetry. Each individual reads poetry in his

own way. Are the feelings of sadness or happiness and other feelings of humans all equal? A unique feeling requires a unique expression. This fragrance or lati-feyeh nahani *cannot be imitated; imitation is only for technique [and learning]. For example, one can imitate and try to sing like another person, but one can't imitate another's sensitivity or feeling* (hess). Latifeyeh nahani *in art cannot to be imitated. (Qaneeifard 2003:43)*

Question: In many traditions certain individual musicians develop a personal style that is highly influential and widely imitated by other musicians. It is the same with you and the way you sing, now all the other singers are imitating your style. Do you see this as a negative or a positive outcome?

This is based on the noble and authentic [nezhadehgi va esalat] *outcomes inherent in any activity that one occupies oneself with, be it music, singing or anything else. Because authenticity has roots, it has roots in the earth and in the blood, it has roots in the being of people. The closer you are to being authentic, the more influential you become especially if you are in relation with your authenticities. People gravitate towards these artists because they have adopted many of the authentic principles of their traditions in their styles and presented it in a very effective way—not many can present authenticity in a good manner. When you put all your energy to present an authentic principle in its best way possible and at the same time have a unique character yourself, and have a different message, this authentic principle becomes eternal. (2009)*

People like [renowned contemporary poet Ahmad] Shamloo have criticized traditional music in that it is just a repetition of the same material and that the radif is only three or four hours of music and nothing more. Is there anyway one can expand traditional music?

With all my respect to my dear Ahmad Shamloo I must disagree with him. He has only looked at our music as a group of fixed melodies. This is like saying that our literature is bound to only Hafez or that our literature is only Shamloo's poetry and nothing else. But this is not the case, because if we look at music as a language we realize that it is infinite. You can make an infinite number of different pieces. But yes, the radif is an example of the way you can construct sentences of our music, but this is not the whole thing. When you listen to Jalil Shahnaz, you realize that none of the radif sentence constructions are there in his playing, but it is the authentic music of Iran and it gives you so much pleasure. It is Abu Ata or Hejaz, but how wonderful is he playing it? None of his motifs are in the radif. So this is a language, a language that you can speak when you know its grammar. These are called motifs, and motifs together make a sentence and then we can make music with these sentences, just like writing a book. You can make hundreds and thousands of hours of music like this, when you look at it as a language. But when you look at it as a system that has been passed on from the past, then yes it is only three to four hours of motifs and music. Music is beyond language in that it can even be more diverse than this vocabulary.

So what kind of an environment should the music be in, in order to reach its potential?

Our music has all the potential in the world, and it can respond to all the needs of the humankind. But when the authorities stress that there should not be music, there should not be teachers, you must close down universities, then naturally there is no ground for the musicians to grow from to make a new composition, give a new performance and basically show their abilities in society. But the capacity is evident in the essence of our music, just like it is in our language or any language, to be able to say new things with its own preexisting phrases. Therefore, the environment is very important to be able to nurture the potential of the music. The reason why our music hasn't become an international phenomenon is because it has never been presented in the right places; indeed until only seventy or eighty years ago no one was allowed to play music or any instrument. They would have thrown him out of the community or pour liquid lead into his ear and these sorts of things. But you have seen how greatly it has evolved in the last century and has found its own place. Thankfully today, with the advent of technology, no one can stop anyone from their activities and music is really finding its place.[12]

Another issue that is instrumental to this [critique], resulting in works of lesser originality and encouraging imitation, is the lack of protection of artist's rights. The absence of this law takes away the assertion of capital in the artistic world, and all the moral and financial rights of investors are ignored. Therefore, some terms must be instituted so that secure investment becomes possible. Furthermore, the law of copyright and protection of artists is not practiced. Of course, it is not enough to just have a law if even this is not practiced. Unfortunately, the hands of the art thieves are open and, in any case, one cannot lay down a law against imitation. I mean if someone imitates another, one cannot stop them through a certain law. . . . If you want to use a big band or if you want to use the best musicians to obtain the best quality, this will result in higher expenses. The way the market is, a lot of these expenses would not be returned, and for this reason, investing in music has declined. The first step towards this is to protect the moral [ma'navi] rights of the artist. . . .

I have even taken this up in court. Many years ago when some profit-oriented groups distributed and copied my works illegally, I took them to court but nothing was settled. The only conclusion I came to was that instead of the government paying subsidies, they should have firmer and more precise regulations for the moral and financial rights of the artists. In this way, the artists would achieve what they want to achieve and there would be no need for the government's assistance, because the people have enough appreciation of authentic works that they would support it. This fact alone would result in the artists working in better circumstances and taking care of their own needs. . . .

Not recognizing the moral rights of the artist is the most important point because by changing a piece of art, they have committed the biggest crime towards the artist, and the artist no longer sees himself as the creator of that work. There is no concern regarding the radio and the television. If they do not play high-quality music and if the best musicians do not work together, the music has instead found its place in society because it responds to the spiritual, emotional, and sentimental needs of the people. I am optimistic that the ground for working will become wider and our music will get more exposure. (Qaneeifard 2003:78–80)

[Radio and television broadcasters in Iran] should, first of all, officially recognize music and fight against whatever is stopping its progression. Then, at the next level, if they agree to do this, they should find the best musicians and, to find the best musicians, they need to spend and make big investments. Music can be used for different reasons, sometimes it is used for nohe *[antiphonal religious hymns] and at other times it is used differently. Every kind of music should exist freely, for every hour and every day and in different circumstances and surroundings. It shouldn't be confined only to a certain mind set—be it* nohe, rowze, *or* maddahi. *Some people only want music to spread their own ways of thinking and have no interest in understanding its essence. They want to use music for their own benefit and advertise with it. So they would even take my tasnif and put their own interpretation on it.*

I performed a song by the name of "Gar be to oftadam nazar" *["If my glance fell on you"] more than twenty years ago, and just recently saw that the television has taken that song and, based on their own taste, have put images to it. This is a big insult. They have no right to do such things. One thing that the radio and television does not recognize is the divine rights of the artist. Furthermore, I performed a piece in the time of war, and they play it, but if some parts of the song disagree with their taste, they take them out. I am talking about the song* "Mihan ey Mihan" *["Motherland, Oh Motherland"]. Unfortunately, they do not listen no matter what I do. The rights of the artist have no meaning for them and that is why I no longer listen to radio or watch television.*

Before the revolution there were two programs by the name of Golhā *and* Golhā-ye Tāzeh *that were officially recognized. Not everyone could participate in those programs, they only selected the best artists and Ostads. They had a fixed hour of every day solely for their own program and on those recognized hours, they only played Persian music and talked about Persian music and it was not like other programs that played only a tasnif in the middle. In the last twenty years some people came to make another program like* Golhā *but they were all closed down after a few weeks. The way the radio and the television uses music is only to fill in gaps between programs and for places when they have nothing interesting to show. I would also like to know why they do not show the images of the instruments. Do the images of tar and tombak deceive the viewer? Is it that revolting to show someone playing the violin or tar? When they insult the artists and the musicians to this level then there is no reason to work with them. For example, when they play avaz or a song or any other music on the television, they*

show images of bees and waterfalls, trees and mountains. They must also show
the musicians. (Qaneeifard 2003:143–45)

Present Stasis, Future Prospects: Now What?[13]

RS

While the narrative of Iranian history includes various long periods of cultural
and political stagnation, time moves faster now in the twenty-first century and the
revolution is over thirty years old. Given Iran's demographics, the vast majority
of Iranians were born after the revolution, a relatively distant event that is somewhat of an abstraction for most of them. Not surprisingly, there is a marked de-
cline in "revolutionary romanticism" among youth (Jahanbegloo 2004: xxii), if not a
flat out disconnection and rejection. Decades after Shajarian so powerfully appropriated Hafez's words in *Bidad*, there is still no one whom contemporary Iranians
may ask *ke dāwr-e ruzgārān-rā, che shod?*—"what has happened to the wheel of the
times?"

   At present Iran is on top of the United States government's precarious hit list
and subject to the ritual sabre rattling (fittingly nuclear for our times), chest
thumping, and *rajaz* that precedes any violent conflict. Iran duly plays its scripted
role, upping the ante of brinksmanship in this latest chapter of the continuing historical drama of the East-West showdown, the hackneyed clash of civilizations
narrative. This historical performance has had the amazingly long run of over a
millennium, featuring a vast revolving door of cast members playing the en-
trenched *dramatis personae*. Western media continue to cultivate and spin the
reification of Iran as the old Oriental Despot archetype (which, sadly, is not entirely untrue). Knee-jerk responses of *kāfar* and *jihad* are predicatably spun back
by the Islamic Republic, along with a more sophisticated rereading of America's
role in post-World War II global order that resonates beyond the fringe of con-
spiracy theorists. Meanwhile the revolution succeeded stupendously in creating a
generation of Iranians that harbors a great mistrust of religion and a sincere interest in Western popular culture. As Wheatcroft has detailed through the history of
this epic encounter, words and gestures matter a great deal here (2004). Among
the major sponsors, this present episode of the drama has been "brought to you
by" the realpolitik of fossil fuel dependency, which has eerily greased the wheels
of the West Asian theatre for the past century. With wells literally running dry, it
looks like the curtain may be dropping soon on this front. But the powers that be
will surely wring out this anachronistic fuel source, the concomitant absurdity of
its consumption paradigm, and the brutal logic of its geopolitical operating system to the last drop.

   The Islamic Revolution, the Iraqi Invasions (a.k.a. Gulf Wars), the War on
Terror, and fundamentalist religion are some of dedicated players that course
through our present historical episode. The real star of the show is power, in all of

its mineral and human manifestations, while the dramatic tension centers on how it will be channeled. Which side, which level of consciousness wins in this timeless battle of light and darkness? The promise for centuries has been "Light, of course (i.e., *our* side), but not now—tomorrow." Yet tomorrow never comes. And so it goes: Iran, the West, and the Rest continue to limp along in circles of habit, denial, and ruthlessness.

Music is a conduit and tool for healing and hope amidst the bleakness. When considering the long view of Iran's history, the present regime has had its run and will collapse. As a *khānande*, Shajarian's job has been to reflect the sentiments of the people, to appropriately address the occasion, and to provoke questions. He has clearly said that he has no answers other than courageously stating the obvious: that the Islamic Revolution failed to serve Iranians, its premises and operating systems are corrupted and only function through ruthless coercion and brute force. History testifies that the spontaneous power of the human spirit will prevail over such a desperate grid. Iranians must act collectively and chart the way forward in their epic quest for freedom. May they do so by nonviolent means. In the midst of this struggle the power of music operates on many fronts: as a coping mechanism for relief, comfort, and healing; it connects and entrains people, helping them to acknowledge their common lot and identity; it is a vehicle for truth, public will, and social transformation; it serves as a form of peaceful resistance, a mode expressive power that chips away at oppression; and it is a means of spiritual development and realization, a shift of consciousness.

Presently seventy percent of Iranians are under the age of thirty. According to Rastovac (2009), many of these young people are attracted to the underground music scene and assimilate an eclectic array of popular music genres in a conscious attempt at decentering their national identity in favor of cultivating a global (*jahāni*) one. Sadighi and Mahdavi (2009) feel, quite to the contrary, that these attempts are ineffective forms of resistance precisely because they are not Iranian enough to do the job under the current conditions. What price are people willing to pay to "go global"? Some will say it is worth sacrificing ethnic markers and values that make a traditional music special in order to reach a consciousness that is more communitarian and bonding, pointing forward to less violence and oppression. Shajarian clearly supports the plurality of musical styles preferred by young Iranians and trusts that interest in Persian *asil* music will naturally kick in as they age. Indeed, their natural sense of identity is distorted and sabotaged through the hyperpoliticization surrounding music and everything else in their lives. Under these conditions it is perfectly natural that they look eagerly outside: human nature is such that the more they are squeezed and pushed, the more they will turn to the outside. My personal experience working with young émigré students in a Canadian university corroborates Shajarian's view: left to their own devices, by the time they hit their mid or late-twenties, they begin reexamining and revaluing their roots, including an interest in *asil* music.

Great artists are both products of their time and transcend their time; in the long run, people tend to remember the great artists and downplay, even forget the petty potentates. In the continuous feedback of history, art frequently trumps and transcends temporal power. We don't pay much attention to Shah Shuja but we remember and love the poetry of Hafez. Johann Sebastian Bach surely made a more memorable and valuable contribution to humanity than Frederick the Great (the latter's fugue subject that triggered Bach's *Musical Offering* notwithstanding). Similarly, while Shajarian will always be located and associated historically with postrevolutionary Iran, the significance of much of his music will transcend those vicissitudes and continue to move listeners on emotional, aesthetic, and spiritual levels long after the synchronic political conditions so vital to its creation become irrelevant. Decades from now people will listen to his recordings in moments of solitude and connect to a deep listening experience; they will marvel and be thankful for the experience of hearing this incredible singing amidst the existential mystery of life.

The future of avaz and Persian music is of course unpredictable but we can be reasonably certain that Shajarian's recordings will function as an important link to whatever comes next, thereby forming a solid bridge of continuity to his mentors and the Qajar legacy of the Farahani family that they inherited. Shajarian will likely be viewed as a gifted and venerable guardian of his inheritance, fulfilling his task as an artist to both transcend and include it. It is also safe to assume that the great Iranian traditions of narrative performance, including some form of sung poetry, will continue to reiterate, reinvent, and reanimate the archetypal tales, the powerful role of the tellers, and the transformative act of telling. However the exterior forms might change in their future manifestations, whatever darkness and stormy weather may prevail, the impetus to continue performing both narrative rituals and performing *adab*—"the refinement of thought, word, and deed"—is probably unstoppable. We'll always need fresh spin to continue propelling the human journey forward. Like Rumi's *Masnavi*, the "Persian Qur'an," the story of avaz is engaging and beautiful, endlessly provoking a deepening of our consciousness, enriching our lives. Like Rumi's masterpiece it also remains unfinished, awaiting the next generation of gifted, creative individuals to continue the tale and its telling. But my account of Ostad Shajarian and the art of avaz ends here.

AK

Personally, the work we have presented in this study reinforces my view that avaz is the most important component of the art of Persian music in relation to all of its many facets. However, as a performing musician who has listened to the comments of many audience members I know many people look at avaz as subordinate to tasnifs, rengs, pishdaramads and so on, as if avaz is an intermission, a waiting period for the next rhythmic piece. They associate avaz with religious genres like *rowze khāne* and the religious narratives, which can easily be conflated with government policies of training such singers to propagate the narratives and the fundamentalist ideology that has been unfortunately attached to them. They don't realize that if they pay attention, they can understand much better what

Rumi was saying. Without a dictionary they can understand the depth of what he was talking about.

Avaz has the potential to be flexible in reacting to poetry, to present differ-ent meanings and even give a new meaning to a poem. It can transfer the ad-vanced thinking encoded in a poem. If I have a good grasp of Persian, I can get something from reading a poem but an avaz singer like Shajarian can teach me how to read this poem and dig deeper into it: for example, staying on a certain word for a bit longer that you would normally gloss over—it is important and can signify a deeper meaning. Mr. Shajarian is inviting you to stay here and think about it, and staying in that moment, with that word, may help you see another dimension of the poem. There is an endless variety and depth in avaz. Avaz is a set of very important tools—not only for music but for sending us important cultural messages from the past, from people we can trust. We have to pay atten-tion to this art and see all of the advanced tools it wields. Avaz is the most impor-tant part of our music that in fact generates a lot of excitement. It brings so many things together—music, cultural messages, and poetry—the latter being very advanced in Iran. The art of avaz needs attention and Shajarian is one of the sa-viours for keeping it alive.

We have to learn to think about these tools and the best way to use them instead of imitating each other. Because of its flexibility avaz provides the oppor-tunity to create new melodies and rhythms; all elements are movable. In thinking and reacting to the poem we make something much deeper than the original poem or bring out all the meaning latent in the layers of *iham* in the poem. Through hard work and concentration we need to bring together intuition and cognition in this art. Paying attention to this opens up so many great possibili-ties.

The Legend of Arash is a famous epic story in Iranian culture that you can find in the Avesta, Shahnameh, and various later sources. It's a long narrative with many different versions but in a nutshell it's about the ancient Iranian and Aniranian armies making peace and agreeing that the border between their terri-tories would be set by the Iranians letting an arrow fly, and wherever it landed would mark the border. With the help of divine intervention the Iranians design a special bow and choose Arash to fire it. When he does, it travels all day and lands at an incredibly far distance, making Arash a hero. As with all mythology, this story is not just about land, which is just the surface level of its *iham*: it's about our potential capabilities as individuals. It can be about art. Some people send their arrows about five meters distance and without a point. Other people like Mr. Shajarian have a very good bow and arrow and send it very far—all the way to UNESCO and beyond! Or look at Rumi, his arrow has been travelling for centuries around the world and he's now one of the top writers in the United States, and non-Iranian scholars of various disciplines from all over the world drop quotes of Rumi in their presentations and interviews. Even these people trust Rumi's work. This is his arrow.

When we are "sending something" in art and in life, we have to think. I try to bear this in mind in my own work. And it's not about me, it's about the message. We are all messengers, all carriers. Some singers of avaz don't get this. "I don't really understand the message but I like the idea of it and it seems that other people like it." They are trying to present something they don't grasp and end up mindlessly imitating or are reduced to mumbling. So they become like puppets—no meaning. They don't know the message. It's very proper for the messenger to know what the message is, as far as she is able to, otherwise it won't go anywhere or will be an empty shell. This is the moment when art is born. Ostad Shajarian understands the message very well and has the knowledge and ability to give it the delivery it deserves.

OS

Thankfully I have had many students and still do . . . I have around seventy-four students and they are all very good . . . I am not worried about the future of avaz. Maybe I was worried three years ago because they were singing mostly tasnifs. You see, if avaz starts to fade, ghazal also fades and the real value of the ghazal can only be manifested in avaz. Because of the complexity of rhythm in tasnif, sometimes the real meaning of the poetry gets lost. But in avaz, once they learn how to find the music implied in each word and learn how to present it, it is at that moment that the real value of poetry shines. Music then assists the poetry and can convey the meaning of the poetry in its absolute best: this is avaz. If avaz disappears, our ghazals will fade as well.[14]

Question: How do you see the future of avaz? Considering all the modern innovations and new ways of living, do you think avaz can respond to the needs of today?

Yes, you know why? Because poets like Hafez and Sa'di have existed and avaz is their language. As long as these poets have their place in society, avaz too will have its place. (2009)

What kind of concluding statement would you like to make for this study?

The people of Iran are very dedicated to their poetry, and their poetry has its own music, that is the asil, *authentic music. These two are together and inseparable, and as long as this language and this poetry exist, this music will exist. The younger generation has a very deep interest in the music that is combined with these poems. This music will remain alive because it is the language of the hearts of its people, it is the language of the complaints of its people, and people want to achieve freedom and democracy through this music. (2010)*

Gol hamin panj ruz o shash bāshad
V 'in golestān hamisha khwash bāshad.

Roses last but a few days, yet this rose garden
Of mine will stay perpetually in bloom.

—Sa'di (*Golestan*)

Notes

1. While Derakhshani was the composer, arranger and group leader, the CD, *Dar Khiyal*, is actually published under Shajarian's name (though not by Delawaz). He chose the avaz from this CD to represent himself on Mahoor's *100 Years of Avaz* collection.

2. http://www.npr.org/templates/story/story.php?storyId=114013402.

3. Sincere thanks to Cindy Carpien for kindly providing this information.

4. This specific performance and the centonic analysis are both discussed in Simms and Koushkani 2012.

5. This technique was also practiced by Alim Qasimov in duet with his daughter Ferghana around the same time.

6. Cf., the notion of the so-called "summational artist" such as Bach, Mozart, Oscar Peterson or Um Kulthum.

7. Prologue from *Golestan* (trans. Thackston 2008: 6). Performance example 4 (*Nava*) evokes this very idea from a ghazal of Sa'di.

8. "Never doubt that a small group of thoughtful, committed, citizens can change the world. Indeed, it is the only thing that ever has."

9. http://www.lonelyplanet.com/iran/tehran/history.

10. These real-life images bring to mind the ghazal by Hafez that Shajarian set in his most famous recording *Bidad* (1984, discussed in Chapter 2), which surveys a dystopia, repeatedly asking "What happened?"

11. Ambient New Age music is particularly popular in hyperurbanized Japan, where it serves a similar function.

12. Interview on VOA Persian, broadcast June 19, 2010; http://www.youtube.com/watch?v=wHiPVsJIJlY.

13. Shortly after completing writing this book, the call for freedom erupted and spread like wildfire throughout the Arab world, challenging what was unthinkable months earlier, when the iron fist of repression seemed impermeable. Many commentators cite the response of the Iranian people to the June 2009 election crisis as the source and inspiration of the remarkable phase transition of Tunisia in early 2011, which spontaneously launched the so-called "Arab Spring." Quickly hitting Egypt, the rumblings continued through Libya, Yemen, Syria, and other countries in a manner reminiscent of the domino effect that led to the dissolution of the Soviet Union only two decades ago, albeit more violent. Equally significant, the failure of Egypt to make a decisive shift to a new democratic order in the following months and the unsavory elements that might fill the power vacuum are also likened to Iran in 1979. While we must applaud and support these courageous grass-root calls for change, it is clear that expelling corrupt leaders is less than half the battle toward bona fide democratic reform.

14. Interview on VOA Persian, broadcast June 19, 2010; http://www.youtube.com/watch?v=wHiPVsJIJlY.

Appendix
Recording Releases

Delawaz Releases

"Finglish" transliterations, English title translations, and all other information are given as they appear on the recordings (whenever provided) and the English Delawaz website (delawaz.com/en). There is no catalog numbering. Following the conventions of Delawaz and Persian literature on Shajarian, the recordings are listed chronologically by date of release. All recordings are CD releases (most are also available on cassette), except those with an asterisk, which denotes a cassette-only release. Some streamed tracks are available at www.delawaz.com (on the Persian site only; the English site has some information in English but no streamed tracks). CD orders are available through the website. Up through the 1990s, the CDs are transfers of cassettes that were usually conceived as two thirty-minute continuous tracks. Tracks are often released under different album titles in varied combinations, indicated by cross-referencing numbers in parentheses. An alphabetical listing of titles follows for easier reference.

	Title	Dastgah	Accompanist or Group Leader	Date Performed/released
1	*Golbang/ The Rose's Cry (2 volumes)	Vol. 1: Esfahan, Mahur (Rak); Vol. 2:Mahur, Dashti	1: Payvar, Houshang Zarif; 2: Ebadi, Bahari	1977/1978
2	*Peygham e Ahl-e Raz/ Message of the Secret People (2 volumes)	1: *Raze Del:* Dashti 2: *Entezar e Del:* Afshari Segah	Payvar	1979 (Tehran)/1980 1979
3	Chahargah	Chahargah	Farhang Sharif	? /1983
4	Bidad (Homayoun)/ Injustice	Bidad Homayun	Meshkatian Bikchekhani	1982/1985 Dec. 1984/1985

5	Astan e Janan/ The Domain of Souls	Bayate Tork, Bayate Kurd	Meshkatian	1982 (Tehran)/ 1986
6	Serr e Eshgh/ The Mystery of Love	Mahur	Meshkatian	1982/1986
7	Nava Morakeb Khani	Nava	Meshkatian	1982/1986
8	Dastan/The Tale	Chahargah	Meshkatian	1987/1988
9	Payam e Nasim/ Message of Breeze Alternate version?	Abu Ata	Pirniakan	1990 (Boston)/1991 (1989 Lausanne concert released in 1998?)
10	Del e Majnun/ Insane Heart	Bayate Tork, Afshari	Pirniakan	1990 (USA)/1991
11	*Khalvat Gozide/ Deliberate Seclusion	Shur No avaz on b	Payvar	1980/1991
12	Entezar e Del/ The Waiting Heart & Khalvat Gozide/ Deliberate Seclusion	Afshari (2/2a) & Shur (11a)	Payvar	1979 & 1980/?
13	Delshodegan/ The Lovers	Short avaz in Shushtari, Bayate Tork	Alizadeh	1991/1992
14	Āsman e Eshgh/ The Sky of Love	Segah	Pirniakan	1991/1992
15	Yad e Ayam/ Memory of the Old Days	Shur	Pirniakan	1992 (USA)/1995
16	Cheshme-ye Nush/ Heavenly Fountain	Rast Panjgah, Morakebkhani	Lotfi	1995 (France)/1995

17	*Jan e Oshagh/* Soul of Lover & Gonbad eMina/ The Azure Dome	Esfahan & Dashti	Meshkatian	1985/1995
18	**Jan e Oshagh/* Soul of Love	Esfahan (17a) Shur	Javad Ma'ruff Pirniakan	1985/1995 1988 (Tehran)/1995
19	**Gonbad Mina/* The Azure Dome	Dashti (17b) Segah (tasnif) Mahur/ Chahargah (34)	Meshkatian Payvar Pirniakan	1985/1995 1980/1995 1994 (Tehran [Iran-Japan Institute]/1995
20	*Homayunmasnavie*	Homayun	Mansur Sārami	1984/1995
21	*Saz e Ghesseh Gu & Konsert Bozorg-dasht Hafez/* The Speaking Lute & Tribute Concert for Hafez	Segah (2/2b) Shur (18b)	Payvar Pirniakan	1980 1988 (Tehran)/1996
22	**Ghasedak/* Dandelions	Mahur	Meshkatian	1994 (Europe)/1996? (release denied)
23	*Eshgh Danad/* Love Knows	Abu Ata	Lotfi	1981/1997
24	*Rosvayie Del/* Love Stricken	Segah	Pirniakan	1996 (Dubai?)/ 1997
25	*Shab e Vasl/* Night of Union	Mahur	Tala'i	1997/1997
26	*Moammaye Hasty/* Enigma of Life	Shur	Lotfi	1997 (Köln)/1997
27	*Rast Panjgah*	Rast Panjgah	Lotfi	1975 (Shiraz)/1998
28	*Chere bi Chehre/* Face to Face	Nava	Lotfi	1977 (Shiraz)/1998

29	*Shab, Sukut, Kavir/* *Night, Silence, Desert*	Khorasani maqams	Kalhor	music 1994, Shajarian dubs vocals in 1997/ released 1998
30	*Sarv e Chaman/* *The Strutting Cypress*	Mahur	Pirniakan	1989 (Karlsruhe)/ 1998
	(Alternate version?)		?	1990 (USA)/1991?
31	*Aram e Jan/* *Quiet of the Soul*	Afshari	Pirniakan	1998 (live)/1999
32	*Be Yad e Pedar/* *Remembrance (for my father)* (2 volumes)	Qur'an recitation	n/a	Performed: Vol.1: 1978, 1979 Vol.2 : 1979–1982 released 1999
33	*Ahang e Vafa/* *Tune & Faith* (with Homayun Shajarian)	Mahur	Mohammad Firuzi	1999/2000?
34	*Bahariyeh/* (Re-issue of 20b)	Mahur-Chahargah	Pirniakan	1994 (Tehran [Iran-Japan Institute]/2000?
35	*Raz e Del/* *Secret of the Heart* (re-issue of 2, v.1)	Dashti	Payvar	1979 (Tehran)/2000?
36	**Entezar e Del/* *The Waiting Heart* (re-issue of 2, v.2)	Afshari Segah	Payvar	1979/2000?
37	*Bouye Baran/* *Scent of Rain*	Chahargah Afshari	Yousefzamani; Harir Sharif-zade Shahram Mirjalali	1970s?/2000?
38	*Peyvand e Mehr/* *Bond of Affection*	Shur, Abu Ata	Farhang Sharif	May 1984/2000?
39	*Zemestan Ast/* *It's Winter*	"Dad & Bi-dad," Homayun	Alizadeh	2001 (California)/ 2002?

40	*Bi To Besar Nemi-shavad/ Without You*	Nava, Bayate Kurd	Alizadeh	2002 (live)/2002
41	*Faryad/The Cry*	Rast Panjgah	Alizadeh	2002 (Los Angeles) /2003
42	*Ghoghaye Esh-ghbazan/The Tu-mult of Lovers*	Shur, Afshari	Derakhshani	?/2007
43	*Soroud e Mehr/ Song of Kindess* (with Homayun S.)	Bayate Tork, Afshari	Alizadeh	2007 (Tehran)/2007
44	*Saz e Khamoush/ Instrument of Si-lence* (with Homayun S.)	Dashti	Alizadeh	2007 (Tehran)/2007
45	*Ah! Baran/ Ah! Rain*	Dashti	Mazda Ansari; Farhang Sharif	?/2009
46	*Rendan e Mast/ Drunken Rends*	Homayun	Derakhshani	2009 (Tehran)/ 2009

Alphabetical Ordering of Delawaz Releases

Title	Table #	Title	Table #
Ah! Baran	45	Homayunmasnavie	20
Ahang e Vafa	33	*Jan e Eshgh	18
Aram e Jan	31	Jan e Eshgh	17
		&	
		Gonbad eMina	
Āsmān-e Eshgh	14	*Khalvat Gozide	11
Astan e Janan	5	Moammaye Hasty	26
Bahariyeh	34	Nava Morakebkhani	7
Be yad e Pedar	32	Payam e Nasim	9
Bi To Besar Nemisha-	40	Peygham e Ahl e Raz	2
vad			
Bidad (Homayun)	4	Peyvande Mehr	38
Bouye Baran	37	Rast Panjgah	27
Chahargah ba Far-	3	Raz e Del	35
hang Sharif			
Chere bi Chehre	28	Rendan e Mast	46
Cheshme-ye Nush	16	Rosvayie Del	24
Dastan	8	Sarv e Chaman	30
Del e Majnun	10	Saz e Ghesse Gu	21
		& Konsert Bozorgdasht	
		Hafez	
Delshodegan	13	Saz e Khamoush	44
*Entezar e Del	36		
Entezar e Del	12	Serr e Eshgh	6
&			
Khalvat Gozide			
Eshgh Danad	23	Shab, Sukut, Kavir	29
Faryad	41	Shab e Vasl	25
Ghoghaye Eshghbazan	42	Soroud e Mehr	43
Golbang	1	Yad Ayam	15
*Gonbad Mina	19	Zemestan Ast	39

Selected Releases on Other Labels

While most of Shajarian's music is released on Delawaz, some early work came out on Lotfi's *Chavosh* label (and was later re-issued by Lotfi's Sheyda Institute) and other companies. Other occasional releases followed outside of Delawaz. The following list is by no means complete but includes the most prominent of these that contain performances of avaz (there are several compilations of tasnifs, which are not included here). Some Delawaz productions were also licensed to other labels, indicated here with asterisks, the numbers in parentheses indicating the original recording on the Delawaz chart above. All transliterations are given as they appear on the albums.

Chavosh 1: Be Yad e 'Aref/ *In Remembrance of 'Aref*	Bayate Tork	Lotfi	1977/
Chavosh 2: Shab Na- *vard/Rolling Night*	Dashti	Lotfi	1970s/
Chavosh 6: Sepideh/ *Dawn*	Mahur	Lotfi	1979/
Chavosh 9:Jan-e Jan/ *Soul of the Soul*	Segah	Lotfi	1976 (Tus)/
Deylaman (prod. by K. Roshanravan for the Institute for the Intellectual Development of Children and Young Adults, no cat. #)	Chahargah, Segah, Shur, Deylaman	Rahmatullah Badi'i	1977/
Jām Tohi/Empty Chalice (Ravian honar-e Shargh Institute)	Mahur (reissue of *Golhāye Tāze* #77)	Habibollah Badi'i	1975/ 2007
Dud e 'Ud/ *Smoke of the 'Ud* (Taraneh Entrprises, TAR61)	Nava	Meshkatian (Tehran SO; Bahari & Tala'i)	1987/ 1988
Dar Souge Banan/ *Mourning Banan's Loss* (with Dadbeh)	Homayun (Dadbeh: Dhastestani)	Musavi	1985? (majles) /1988

Iran: Mohammed Reza Shadja-rian; Musique classique per-sane (Ocora C-559097 [HM 83])	Afshari	Meshkatian	1989/ 1990
Mohammed Reza Shajarian and Ensemble 'Aref (World Network/WDR, LC-6759)	Chahargah	Meshkatian	1987/ 1991
Dar Khiyal/ *In the Imagination* (Soroush Records, SIS 143)	Segah Bayate Tork	Derakhshani	1995/ 1996
*Mohammad Reza Shadjarian. *Vol I:Bidad, Homayoun* (Al Sur, ALCD 191)	Bidad Homayun (reissue of 4)	Meshkatian	1982/84 /1996
*Mohammad Reza Shadjarian. *Vol II:Dashti* (Al Sur, ALCD 192)	Dashti (reissue of 2/1)	Meshkatian	1979/ 1996
*Mohammad Reza Shadjarian. *Vol III:Mahur* (Al Sur, ALCD 193)	Mahur (reissue of 6)	Meshkatian	1982/ 1996
The Abu Ata Concert (Kereshmeh, KCD-107)	Abu Ata (reissue of 23)	Lotfi	1981/ 1997
Roba'iyat-e Khayyam/ *Khayyam's Quatrains* (Mahoor Institute, M.CD-027)	Mahur	F. Shahbazan (composer)	1976/?
Night Silence Desert (Traditional Crossroads, CD 80702-4299-2)	Folk maqams (reissue of 29)	Kalhor	1997/ 2000
Without You (World Village Music, 468011)	Nava, Kurd (reissue of 40)	Alizadeh	2002/ 2002
Faryad (World Village Music, 468023)	Rast Panjgah (reissue of 41)	Alizadeh	2002/ 2005
Bidad (Injustice) (World Village Music, 468011)	Bidad (reissue of 4a)	Meshkatian	1982/ 2005

Golbang-e Shajarian 1:	Esfahan	Payvar	1977
Bote Chin/Chinese Idol	Mahur	Zarif	/2005
(Mahoor Institute, M.CD-192)	(reissue of 1/1)		
Golbang-e Shajarian 1:	Mahur	Ebadi	1977/
Dowlat-e 'Eshgh/State of Love	Dashti	Bahari	2005
(Mahoor Institute, M.CD-193)	(reissue of 1/2)		

Glossary

'Aref Qazvini: (1882–1934) Singer and composer of politically charged, nationalist tasnifs in the *Mashrute* period.

aruz: System of classical prosody in Persian poetry.

asil ("authentic, rooted"): A common epithet used to denote traditional Persian art music.

attractor: In chaos theory and fractal geometry, a point around which other points in a dynamic system organize themselves or to which they are drawn (water pouring into a drain is a commonly used simplification).

beyt: A couplet of poetry.

chaharmezrab ("four strokes"): A fast instrumental piece, usually in compound meter and characterized by an ostinato plectrum pattern; may be composed or improvised.

daramad ("coming in"): The first and most important gushe of a dastgah that establishes the fundamental modality of the latter.

dastgah ("apparatus"): A classical mode or modal system represented by an ordered series of gushes; there are seven dastgahs (Shur, Mahur, Homayun, Chahargah, Segah, Rast Panjgah, and Nava) and five "secondary" dastgahs (Abu Ata, Dashti, Afshari, Bayate Tork, Esfahan). *Dastgahi* is a Persian adjective referring to this system. See appendix 1.

Farahani family: A "dynasty" of musicians, primarily tar and setar players, associated with the Qajar court and credited with establishing and transmitting the radif. Important members include Ali Abkar (1810–1855), his sons Mirza Abdollah (1843–1918) and Aqa Hossein Qoli (1853–1915), and their respective sons Ahmad Ebadi (1906–1992) and Ali Akbar Khan Shahnazi (1897–1985).

feedback: When a system or equation feeds back into itself in a cyclical, ever transforming, and nonlinear manner (e.g., microphones picking up the signal of amplifers, pointing a video camera at a monitor). See reiterated/restored behaviour.

forud ("descent"): A melodic device of varying lengths that brings about a return to the modality and tessitura of the main mode of the dastgah. Ostad Shajarian often uses these to modulate to another dastgah.

ghazal ("gazelle"): A short form of Persian classical poetry, usually of mystical-erotic content, consisting of monorhymed couplets, commonly used for avaz texts.

gushe ("corner"): A submode, subsection, and melodic formula of a dastgah; characterized by a particular and narrow ambitus, a functional hierarchy of modal degrees, specific thematic material, and occasionally chromatic alterations of the main mode (creating the effect of a modulation); gushes have

211

proper name designations and vary in length from a few seconds to several minutes.

hāl ("state"): A temporary state of grace, transcendence, and ecstacy; used by musicians to denote inspiration and depth in perfomance.

iham: The multilayered, ambiguous, polysemous quality exploited in Persian poetry.

jawab ("answer"): Instrumental interludes that frame sections of *avaz* singing.

khānande: A singer of avaz.

majles: A small, private musical gathering, usually held in a private home.

maktab: A "school" or style of singing or playing, usually associated with a particular city.

Mashrute/Constitutional Revolution: (1905–1911) A popular revolt by Persian citizens against the corruption of the Qajars, resulting in the democratic infrastructure of the Constitution of 1906 and the creation of a parliament (*majles*).

Masnavi: The great poem of Jalal ad-Din Rumi (thirteenth century); avaz settings of texts from Rumi's *Masnavi* (also transliterated as *Mathnawi*), characterized by a particular rhythmic treatment.

misra: A hemistich of poetry.

Mohammad Reza Pahlavi: (1919–1980) Was installed as Shah in 1941 after his father Reza Shah was forced to abdicate. Continuing the modernization agenda of his father, he cultivated a close relationship with the United States as a supplier of oil and "policeman" of West Asia. He was deposed by the Iranian people in the revolution of 1979.

morakab khāni: Modulating from one *dastgah* to another in the same performance.

motreb: An urban minstrel in traditional Iranian culture, used with decidedly derogatory connotations of "low-life," cheap musicking.

oj: The melodic apogee of a dastgah, as it occurs in a particular gushe.

Ostad: Prestigious/honourific title given to master artists in the Muslim world.

Pahlavi dynasty: (1925–1979) So-called dynasty established by Reza Shah, consisting of him and his son Mohammad Reza.

phase transition: The change of a system from one state to a markedly different one (e.g., water freezes at 0 degrees Celsius and boils at 100 degrees).

pishdaramad ("before the daramad"): A composition that initiates the performance of a dastgah, characterized by a moderate triple meter and based on important gushes of the dastgah.

Qajar dynasty: (1794-1925) Dynasty of Turkish origin that established Tehran as the capital of Iran in 1795, grew increasingly bankrupt and ineffectual through the nineteenth century and was *de facto* rendered obsolete with the Constitutional Revolution until it was dissolved in 1925.

radif ("series, row"): 1) The entire aggregate of gushes, organized into twelve dastgahs in the late nineteenth century, that constitutes the repertoire of Persian classical music. It is traditionally memorized exactly as transmitted to students by their teacher, and then becomes the basis for improvisation and composition. According to various sources it consists of 200 to 300 gushes comprising four to six hours of music. 2) In poetry, a refrain of one to three words used to end *beyts* throughout a ghazal.

rajaz: A declamatory style of recitation used in public discourse, especially in addressing troops or the enemy before battle or in storytelling. Rajaz is also a prosodic meter and a gushe in the radif.

reiterated or restored behaviour: A term used in Performance Studies to describe the repetition of actions, rituals, routines in art and daily life that are consciously or unconsciously "rehearsed."

reng: A dance piece in moderate or fast compound meter, often concluding the performance of a dastgah.

sabk: The style or methods of a particular artist.

samā': In Sufi orders, the use of music, both ritualized and spontaneous, for spiritual development.

self-organization: The dynamic wherein complex and chaotic systems spontaneously display order on a higher level (such as urban sprawl, the economy, a traffic jam).

self-similarity/scaling: The recurrence of a similar pattern on various levels of organization in a complex system or fractal (e.g., a cauliflower or a cloud where various component parts resemble the whole).

shāhgushe ("king gushe"): The most essential and definitive gushes of a dastgah.

tahrir: Extended melismata that employ *tekye* ornaments.

takhallus: A poet's name or pen name appearing in the final *beyt* of a poem as a "signature."

tasnif: A composed, metrical, and frequently strophic setting of a classical poem.

tekye ("lean"): Glottal flip appogiatura; definitive ornament of avaz.

Bibliography

Abazari, Youseff Ali, et al. 2008. "Secularization in Iranian Society." *Media, Culture and Society in Iran: Living with Globalization and the Islamic State*, ed. Mehdi Semati, 238–54. London: Routledge.

Abdollahi, Mehnāz. 2003. "Sāl Shomār-e Mohammad Reza Shajarian (Chronology of Mohammad Reza Shajarian)." *Daftar-e-Honar.* 10/15:2068–71.

Alavi, Nasrin. 2005. *We Are Iran: The Persian Blogs.* Vancouver: Rainforest Books.

Arberry, A.J. 1962. *Fifty Poems of Hafez* (second edition). Cambridge: University of Cambridge Press.

Ardalan, Nader and Laleh Bakhtiar. 1973. *The Sense of Unity: The Sufi Tradition in Persian Architecture.* Chicago: University of Chicago Press.

Avery, Peter, trans. 2007. *The Collected Lyrics of Hafiz of Shiraz.* Cambridge, MA: Archetype.

Bahktiar, Laleh. 1976. *Sufi: Expressions of the Mystical Quest.* New York: Thames and Hudson.

BBC. 2004. "Iran's roads take heavy toll." June 25, http://news.bbc.co.uk/2/hi/middle_east/3839509.stm.

———. 2005. "Not long left for cassette tapes." June 17, http://news.bbc.co.uk/2/hi/technology/4099904.stm.

———. 2007. "Iran smog kills 3,600 in month." January 9, http://news.bbc.co.uk/2/hi/middle_east/6245463.stm.

BBC Persian. 2007. "*Matn-e kamal pāsokh-e Shajarian be porsesh-haye shoma* (The Complete script of Shajarian's responses to your questions)." April 25, www.artmusic.ir/news/show.asp?CC=24&Id=12405.

———. 2009. "*Pazhovak-e ruzegar* (Echo of the Times)." [video documentary], http://www.irannewsnow.com/2010/05/video-bbc-persian-documentary-on-iranian-maestro-shajarian/.

———. 2010. "*Rabbana-ye Shajarian o vākonesh-hāye moāfeq o mohkālef* (Shajarian's Rabbana and opinions for and against)." August 17, www.bbc.co.uk/persian/arts/2010/08/100809_l44_rabana_shajarian.shtml.

Behnam, Jamshid. 2004. "Iranian Society, Modernity and Globalization." In *Iran: Between Tradition and Modernity*, ed. Rahim Jahanbegloo, 3–14. Lanham, MD: Lexington Books.

Bloom, Harold. 1973. *The Anxiety of Influence: A Theory of Poetry.* New York. Oxford University Press.

Bohlman, Phillip. *World Music: A Very Short Introduction.* Oxford: Oxford University Press, 2002.

Briggs, John and David Peat. 1989. *Turbulent Mirror.* New York: Harper and Row.

———. 1999. *Seven Life Lessons of Chaos: Spiritual Wisdom from the Science of Change.* New York: HarperCollins.

Brogo, David. 2005. *Sync or Swarm: Improvising Music in a Complex Age.* New York: Continuum.

Campbell, Joseph. 1988. *The Power of the Myth.* New York: Doubleday.

Caton, Margaret. 1988. "Banan, Golam-Hosayn." In *Encyclopaedia Iranica*, Online Edition, December 15, http://iranica.com/articles/banan-golam-hosayn

Chehabi, Houshang. 1999. "From Revolutionary Tasnif to Patriotic Surud: Music and Nation-Building in Pre-World War II Iran." *Iran* 37:143–54.

Chelkowski, Peter and Hamid Dabashi. 1999. *Staging a Revolution: The Art of Persuasion in the Islamic Republic of Iran.* New York: New York University Press.

CNN. 2003. "Expert: Tehran doomed if 'big one' hits." December 29, http://www.cnn.com/2003/WORLD/meast/12/29/quake.iran.doomsday.reut/.

Correale, Daniela M. 1980. *The Ghazals of Hafez: A Concordance and Vocabulary.* Rome: Cultural Institute of the Islamic Republic of Iran.

Curtis, Glenn E. and Eric Hooglund. 2008. *Iran: A Country Guide.* Washington, DC: Federal Research Division of the Library of Congress.

Daftar-e-Honar. 2003. 10:15, March 21. (Issue dedicated to Shajarian).

Danielson, Virginia. 1997. *The Voice of Egypt: Umm Kulthūm, Arabic Song, and Egyptian Society in the Twentieth Century.* Chicago: University of Chicago Press.

Dabashi, Hamid. 2005. "Ta'ziyeh as Theatre of Protest." *The Drama Review* 49/4:91–99.

———. 2007. *Iran: A People Interrupted.* New York: Norton.

De Bano, Wendy. 2009. "Singing against Silence: Celebrating Women and Music at the Fourth Annual Jasmine Festival." In *Music and the Play of Power in the Middle East, North Africa and Central Asia,* ed. Laudan Nooshin, 229–44. Surrey: Ashgate.

Del Giudice, Margerite. 2008. "Ancient Soul of Iran: the Glories of Persia Inspire the Modern Tradition." *National Geographic* (August) 214/2:34–67.

Ditmars, Hadani. 2009. "Persian Melodies: Vancouver has become the hub of classical Persian music where East meets West." *The Walrus* Jan/Feb 2009:62–66.

During, Jean. 1984. *La musique iranienne: Tradition et evolution.* Paris: Editions Recherche sur la civilisation.

———. 1984a. "La Musique traditionelle Iranienne en 1983." *Asian Music* 15/2:11–31.

———. 1988. "Conservation et transmission dans les traditions musicales du Moyen-Orient : Les donées nouvelles." *Cahiers de Musiques Traditionelles* 1 :100–111.

———. 1988a. *Musique et extase: L'audition mystique dans la tradition soufi.* Paris: Albin Michel.

———. 1989. *Musique et mystique dans les traditions iraniennes.* Paris: Institute Francais de Recherche en Iran.

———. 1989a. "Les Musiques d'Iran et du Moyen-Orient Face a l'Acculturation Occidentale." In *Entre l'Iran et l'Occient: Adaptation et assimilation des idées et techniques occidentals en Iran,* ed. Yann Richard, 193–223. Paris: Editions de la Maison des sciences de l'homme.

———. 1992. "L'oreille islamique: Dix annees capitales de la vie musicale en Iran 1980-1990. " *Asian Music* 13/2:135–64.

———. 1992a. "What is Sufi Music?" In *The Legacy of Mediaeval Persian Sufism,* ed. Leonard Lewisohn, 277–87. London: Khaniqahi Nimatullahi Publications.

———.1994. *Quelque chose se passe: Le sens de la tradition dans l'Orient musical.* Lagrasse: Verdier.

———. 1994a. "Question de goût: L'enjeu de la modernité dans les arts et les musiques de l'Islam." *Cahiers de musiques traditionnelles* 7: 27–49.

———. 1996. "La Voix de Esprits et Face Cachee de la Musique: Le Parcourse du Maitre Hatam 'Asghari." In *Le Voyage Initiatique en Terre d'Islam: Ascensions célestes et itinéraries spirituels,* ed. Mohammad Ail Amir-Moezzi, 335–73. Paris: Peeters.

————. 1996a. "'Ebādī, Ahmad." In *Encyclopaedia Iranica*, Online Edition, December 15, http://iranica.com/articles/ebadi-ahmad.

————. 2001. "Sufi Music and Rites in the Era of Mass Reproduction Techniques and Culture." In *Sufism, Music and Society: in Turkey and the Middle East*, eds. Anders Hammarland, Tord Olsson and Elizabeth Özdalga, 149–68. Istanbul: Swedish Research Institute.

————. 2002. "Tradition and History: The Case of Iran." In *The Garland Encyclopedia of World Music Volume 6: The Middle East*, eds. Virginia Danielson, Scott Marcus and Dwight Reynolds, 853–64. New York: Routledge.

————. 2005. "Third millenium Tehran: Music!" *Iranian Studies* 38/3:373–398.

————. 2006. *The Radif of Mirza Abdollah: A canonic repertoire of Persian music.* Tehran: Mahoor.

————. 2009. "New Challenges for the Musical Tradition in Contemporary Iran." In *Proceedings of International Musicological Symposium "Space of Mugham,"* 124–29. Baku: Şərq-Qərb.

————. 2010. *Musiques d'Iran: La tradition en question.* Paris: Geuthner.

During, Jean, Zia Mirabdolbaghi and Dariouche Safvat. 1991. *The Art of Persian Music.* Washington: Mage.

Erguner, Kudsi. 2005. *Journeys of a Sufi Musician.* London: Saqi.

Farhat, Hormoz. 1991. *The Dastgah Concept in Persian Classical Music.* Cambridge: Cambridge University Press.

Firuzi, Mohammad Ali (ed). 2003 [1382]. *Ghazaliāt Sa'di.* Tehran: Qoqnoos.

Flaes, Rob. *Brass Unbound: Secret Children of the Colonial Brass Band.* Amsterdam: Royal Tropical Institute, 2000.

Gabler, Neal. 1998. *Life the Movie: How Entertainment Conquered Reality.* New York: Knopf.

Gudarzi, Mohsen, Mohammad Javad Kashi and Mohsen Ali Asghar Ramezanpour. 2000. *Raz-e Mānā: Didgāh-hā, Zendegi va Āsar-e Ostad-e Avaz Iran Mohammad Reza Shajarian* (The Eternal Secret: Viewpoints, Life and Impressions of the Master of Iranian Avaz, Mohammad Reza Shajarian). Tehran: Nashr Ketab Fara.

Habibi Nezhād, Zabihollah (ed). 2004. *Latife-ye Nahāni: Gozide-ye Goftoguhā va Goftarhā-ye Mohammad Reza Shajarian* (Secret Attractions: Selected Conversations and Statements of Mohammad Reza Shajarian). Tehran: Mahoor.

Haim, Soleyman. 1963. *The Shorter Persian-English Dictionary.* Tehran: Beroukhim.

Jahanbegloo, Rahim (ed). 2004. *Iran: Between Tradition and Modernity.* Lanham, MD: Lexington Books.

Kasmai, Sorour and Henri Lecomte. 1991. "Le Pelerinage aux Sources: Mohamed Reza Shajarian au Tadjikistan." *Cahiers de Musiques traditionelles* 4:247–53.

Khiabany, Gholam. 2008. "The Iranian Press, State, and Civil Society." In *Media, Culture and Society in Iran: Living with globalization and the Islamic state*, ed. Mehdi Semati, 17–36. London: Routledge.

Lewis, Franklin. 2008. *Rumi: Past and Present, East and West.* Oxford: Oneworld.

Lohman, Laura. 2010. Umm Kulthūm: Artistic agency and the shaping of an Arab legend, 1967–2007. Middletown, CT: Wesleyan University Press.

Manateqe Azad. 2001. "Biography of Mohammad Reza Shajarian, Renowned Iranian Singer." *Manateqe Azad: Economic, Social, Cultural (Monthly)* June 2001, No.119:20–22. (http://netiran.com/Htdocs/Clippings?Art/010628XXAR01.html. Accessed July 2, 2002).

Manuel, Peter. 1993. *Cassette Culture: Popular Music and Technology in North India*. Chicago: University of Chicago Press.

Ma'roufi, Musa. 1963. *Les systems de la musique traditionnelle de l'Iran (Radif)*. Tehran: Secretariat d'Etat aux Beaux-Arts.

Miller, Lloyd. 1999. *Music and Song in Persia: The Art of Avaz*. Salt Lake City: University of Utah Press.

Musavi, Mohammad. 2003. Liner notes to CD *A Century of Avaz, vol.1*. Mahoor M.CD-133.

Nederveen Pietrse, Jan. 2004. *Globalization and Culture: Global Melange*. Lanham, MD: Rowman & Littlefield.

Nelson, Kristina. 1985. *The Art of Reciting the Qu'ran*. Austin: University of Texas Press.

Nettl, Bruno. 1978. "Persian Classical Music in Tehran: The Processes of Change." In Bruno Nettl, ed., *Eight Urban Musical Cultures*. Urbana, IL: University of Illinois Press, pp.146–85.

———. 1983. *The Study of Ethnomusicology: Twenty-nine Issues and Concepts*. Urbana, IL: University of Illinois Press.

Nooshin, Laudan. 1996. "The Processes of Creation and Recreation in Persian Classical Music." PhD diss., University of London.

———. 1998. "The Song of the Nightingale: Processes of Improvisation in dastgāh Segāh (Iranian Classical Music)." *British Journal of Ethnomusicology* 7:69–116.

———. 2001. "Shajariān, Mohammad Rezā." In *Grove Music Online. Oxford Music Online*, http://www.oxfordmusiconline.com.ezproxy.library.yorku.ca/subscriber/article/grove/music/48512.

———. 2005. "Subversion and Countersubversion: Power, Control, and Meaning in the New Iranian Pop Music." In *Music, Power and Politics*, ed. Annie J. Randall, 231–72. New York: Routledge.

——— (ed). 2009. *Music and the Play of Power in the Middle East, North Africa and Central Asia*. Surrey: Ashgate.

Partch, Harry. 1974. *Genesis of a Music (2nd ed)*. New York: Da Capo Press.

Pourahmad, A., et al. 2007. "The Impact of Urban Sprawl up on Air Pollution." *International Journal of Enviromental Research* 1(3): 252–57

Qaneeifard, Erphane. 2003. *Sorush-e Mardom: andishe-ha va 'eqlid-e Mohammad Reza Shajarian darbare avaz va honar-e musiqi* (The Inspiration of Society: the collection of Shajarian's opinion about the Iranian Classical-Music [sic.])" Tehran: Dadar.

Rastovac, Heather. 2009. "Contending with Censorship: The Underground Music Scene in Urban Iran." *intersections* 10/2: 59–82.

Reckord, Thomas. 1987. "Chant in Popular Iranian Shi'ism." PhD diss., University of California at Los Angeles.

Sadighi, Ramin and Sohrab Mahdavi. 2009. "The Song Does Not Remain the Same," *Mid East Report Online*. March 12, http://www.merip.org/mero/mero031209.html.

Sarkoohi, Faraj. 1989. "*Goftogu ba Hossein Alizadeh* (Interview with Hossein Alizadeh)." *Adineh* 39:33-39; 40:29–33.

Saunders, Doug. 2010. *Arrival City: How the Largest Migration in History is Reshaping our World*. Toronto: Pantheon.

Scholes, Robert, James Phelan & Robert Kellog. 2006. *The Nature of Narrative*. Oxford: Oxford University Press.

Semati, Mehdi (ed). 2008. *Media, Culture and Society in Iran: Living with Globalization and the Islamic State*. London: Routledge.

Shajarian, Mohammad Reza. 1993/1372. *"Hamishe va Hamchenān 'Khāk rāh-e mardom mehrbān va 'aziz hamutan hastam'"* (Always and Accordingly "I am the Dust on the Path of the Kind and Dear Compatriots"). *Fazelat* [Sal-e dovvom, Mehr 1372] 16:40–47.

Shajarian, Mohammad Reza, Kazem Motlaq, Mehdi Abedini & Hamid Javaharian. 2004. *Hezar Golkhāneye Avaz* (A Thousand Orchards of Avaz). Qom: Faragoft.

Shoari, Masud. 2006. *"Goftogu bā Masud Shoari* (Interview with Masud Shoari)." *Farhang va Ahang*, September, 2006 issue.

Simms, Rob. 1996. *Avaz* in the Recordings of Mohammed Reza Shajarian. PhD diss., University of Toronto.

———. forthcoming 2012. (Complete Transcriptions of Ostad Shajarian's Avaz on Landmark Albums). Tehran: Delawaz Culture and Art Institute.

Simms, Rob and Amir Koushkani. 2012. *The Art of Avaz and Mohammad Reza Shajarian: Foundations and Contexts*. Lanham, MD: Lexington Books.

Sreberny-Mohammadi, Annabelle. 1990. "Small Media for a Big Revolution: Iran," *International Journal of Politics, Culture, and Society* 3/3:341–71.

Tehran Times. 2009. "Shajarian withdraws from Bam Art Garden project." May 26, http://www.tehrantimes.com/index_View.asp?code=195515.

Tehranian, Majid. 2008. "Epilogue: Wither Iran?" In *Media, Culture and Society in Iran: Living with Globalization and the Islamic State,* ed. Mehdi Semati, Mehdi, 257–69. London: Routledge.

———. 2004. "Power and Purity: Iranian Political Culture, Communication and Identity." In *Iran: Between Tradition and Modernity,* ed. Rahim Jahanbegloo, 185–206. Lanham, MD: Lexington Books.

Thackston, W.M., trans. 2008. *The Gulistan of Sa'di: Bilingual English and Persian Edition with Vocabulary*. Bethesda, MD: Ibex.

Weatherford, Jack. 2010. *Indian Givers: How the Indians of the Americas Transformed the World,* 2nd edition. New York: Random House.

Wheatcroft, Andrew. 2004. *Infidels: A History of the Conflict Between Christendom and Islam.* London: Penguin.

Wilber, Ken. 2000. *A Theory of Everything.* Boston: Shambhala.

Williams, Alan, trans. 2006. *Spiritual Verses: the First Book of the Masnavi-ye Manavi by Jalāl al-Dīn Rūmī*. London: Penguin.

Wolf, Eric. 1982. *Europe and the People without History.* Berkeley: University of California Press.

Wright, Owen. 2009. *Touraj Kiaras and Persian Classical Music: An Analytical Perspective.* Surrey: Ashgate.

Youssefzadeh, Ameneh. 2000. "The Situation of Music in Iran since the Revolution: The Role of Official Organizations," *British Journal of Ethnomusicology* 9/2:35–61.

Zonis, Ella. 1973. *Classical Persian Music: An Introduction.* Cambridge, MA: Harvard University Press.

Sound Recordings

Alizadeh, Hossein and Hamāvāyān Ensemble. 1998. *Rāze-e No* (The New Secret). Tehran: Mahoor Institute of Culture and Art, M. CD–38.

Musavi, Mohammad, ed. 2003. *A Century of Avaz: An Anthology.* Tehran: Mahoor Institute of Culture and Art, M.CD. 133, 134 and 135.

Rajai, Farhang, ed. 1994. *Ganj-e Sukhteh: Pizhuhushi dar musiqi 'ahd Qajar* ("Burnt Treasure: An Inquiry into the Music of the Qajar Period") [5 cassettes and text]. Tehran: Aheya' Kitab.

Film/DVD

ca. 1991. *Persian Music & Poetry: Mohammad Reza Shajarian in Concert.* Delawaz.VHS tape. (Dastgahs Abu Ata, Dashti [i.e., *Payam e Nasim*]; Bayate Zand, Afshari [*Del e Majnun*])

2003. *The Voice of Iran: Mohammad Reza Shajarian—The Copenhagen Concert 2002.* Director, Christian Braad Thomsen. (Concert and interview)

2006. *Hamnava ba Bam* ["Compassion for Bam"]. Delawaz. (Tehran concert and background documentary)

2007. *Konsert e Mohammad Reza Shajarian va Gruye Ava.* Delawaz. (Iranian concert featuring dastgahs Mahur, Afshari)

Index

Abdolrasuli, Morteza, 9

accompaniment, 15–16, 23, 42, 63, 100, 102, 119, 122, 139

adab, 26, 32, 134, 136, 141, 146, 171n26, 179, 181, 183, 196,

aesthetics, x, 7, 19, 31n4, 43, 44, 81, 99, 122, 138, 139, 140, 155, 162, 164, 179, 181, 189, 196

Ahang e Vafa (album), 102

Ahmadinejad, Mahmoud, 116, 165, 166, 169, 170

Akhavan Sales, Mehdi, 117, 119, 120–22, 130

Aliyev, Habil, 143

Ali-Zadeh, Franghiz, 161

Alizadeh, Hossein, 3, 17, 22–24, 26, 28, 95, 97, 101, 116, 119, 121–22, 126, 136, 144, 171n29

Andelebi, Jamshid, 74, 97–98

'Aref (ensemble), 74

'Aref Qazvini, 5, 22, 26, 28, 132, 148, 181

aruz, 81, 121, 189

asil music, 4, 24, 81, 102, 103, 195, 198; instruments, 101

Astan e Janan (album), 8, 16, 19, 34, 129, 173, 175; description of, 55–56; lyrics of, 56–59; word painting in, 59–62

Attar, 7, 28, 96, 99, 101

authenticity, 29, 146, 186, 188, 191

avaz, acquisition of, 156; and environmental changes, 183–87; and issues of artistic vitality, 188–94; and oral composition, 82, 130, 147, 149, 190; art of, 7, 148, 196–98; as narrative performance, 74, 81, 126, 129; as rhetoric, 82, 83; function of, 25; future prospects of, 194–98; innovations in, 16, 27, 101, 104, 106, 111, 121, 143, 178, 180; style of, 28, 34, 38, 102, 104, 146; neopoetry and, 119–20, 122; classical poetry and,

121, 149, 150. *See also* accompaniment

Baba Taher, 8, 10, 55, 99, 101, 129, 176, 177

Badi, Habibollah, 122

Bahari, Asghar, 16, 164

bam sorahi (instrument), 158

Banan, Gholamhossein, 16, 17, 28, 32n21, 136, 156, 176

Barbad, 98, 104, 154, 183

Barg-e Sabz radio programs, 175, 177

Bashir, Munir, 142

Be Yad e Pedar (album), 15, 103

Bidad (album), 15, 26, 55, 56, 99, 129, 137, 163, 173, 175, 194, 200n10; description of, 35–36, 42–45; lyrics of, 36–38, word painting in, 38–42; musical analysis of, 45–46

Bi Hamzaban (musical piece), 149, 150

Bikchekhani, Gholamhossein, 42

Bina, Sima, 56, 112, 114, 170n8

Bi To Besar Nemishavad (album), 116

Boroumand, Nur Ali, 45, 96, 175

Bouchnak, Lotfi, 144

Bouye Baran (album), 119

cassette, format and culture of, 6, 11, 19–22, 25, 44, 95, 100, 139

celebrity, 134, 183

censorship, 4, 6, 13, 19, 25, 26, 44

centonization, 83, 176, 177, 200n4

Chavosh Institute and movement, 3, 11, 26

Dadbeh, Gholamreza, 1, 7–11, 28, 55, 63, 110, 175, 176, 177

Dad o Bidad (musical piece), 119, 122, 126, 129, 130

Dar Khiyal (album), 102, 175, 200n1

Darvishi, Mohammad Reza, 16, 30, 121

Darvish Khan, 100, 148, 149

Dastan, (album), 98, 173, 175; alternate performances of, 82–89; description

of, 74–75; lyrics of, 75–77; word
painting in, 80–82
Davami, Abdollah, 5, 126, 129, 174,
184
Delawaz Cultural Co., 9, 10, 13, 15,
31n8, 43, 63, 64, 74, 82, 90n6,
91n16, 98, 99, 101, 102, 112, 116,
117, 119, 122, 138, 148–49, 156,
200n1
Delshodegan (album), 23, 101, 174, 175
Derakhshani, Majid, 102, 118, 119, 148,
157, 159, 161, 168, 173, 200n1,
Dud-e 'Ud (album), 16, 24,
During, Jean, 95

Ebadi, Ahmad, 10, 21, 23, 32, 136, 179
Ebtehaj, Hushang, 12, 13, 28, 101
election crisis (of 2009), 116, 119, 136,
141, 146, 164–70, 181, 200n13,
Entezar e Del (album), 13
Erguner, Kudsi, 142, 143
Eshq Danad (album), 13, 55, 103

Fakhri, Saba, 144
Farahani family, 23, 32, 80, 133, 179,
196
Faryad (album), 117, 137, 138, 141;
lyrics of, 117
Ferdowsi, 135
folk music (Iranian), 4, 10, 20, 24, 28,
29, 30, 32n19, 56, 62, 101, 102,
103, 160, 170n8, 178

Ghoghaye Eshghbazan (album), 119
globalization, of Persian music, 93–97,
136, 138, 155, 179
Golbang (album), 10, 16
Gol-e Sad Barg (album), 25
Golhā radio programs, 21, 23, 28
Golpayegani, Akbar, 176
Gonbad e Mina (album), 16, 24, 100,
103, 175
Green Party *(Jonbesh-e Sabz)*, 165, 169,
174, 181

Hafez, 7, 13, 15, 16, 28, 35, 36, 38, 42–
44, 45, 53–56, 62, 90n4, 91n17, 96,
101, 103, 112, 135, 137, 138, 148,
149, 160, 163, 165, 170n2, 171n18,

173, 176, 178, 180, 181, 182, 190,
191, 194, 196, 198, 200n10; ghazals
of, 34, 36–38, 45–47, 56–9, 104–06,
117, 150
Homayoun (from album *Bidad*), 15, 35,
42, 129, 137, 173; lyrics of, 46–48;
word painting in, 52–55
Homayoun Masnavie (album), 15,
91n13, 103
Hamnava ba Bam (DVD), 117, 171n24

iham, ix, x, 2, 14, 53, 62, 64, 91n16,
111, 112, 129, 135, 139, 197
imitation, 103, 190–92
improvisation, 35, 82, 133
instrumental music, 23, 133, 139, 142,
150, 172
Iraj (singer), 17, 176
Iran-Iraq War, 1, 3, 13, 25, 34, 36, 43,
45, 53, 97, 98, 184, 186, 193
Islam, 9, 10, 14, 31n3
Islamic Republic of Iran, 4–7, 10, 11, 14,
16, 28, 33, 97, 135, 141, 165, 166,
169, 170, 194
Islamic Revolution, 1–4, 30, 31n5, 45,
53, 54, 132, 195

Jan e Oshagh (album), 16, 103
jawab, 23, 83. *See also* accompaniment
and *saz o avaz*

Karroubi, Mehdi, 170
Kasa'i, Hassan, 9, 24
kereshme (instrument), 159
Khalvat Gozide (album), 13, 34, 103,
111, 135
Khansari, Adib, 5, 28
Khatami, Mohammad, 6, 98, 116, 121
Khayyam, Omar, 96, 173
Khorasan, 24, 101, 102, 103, 112, 114,
178

Lotfi, Mohammad Reza, 3, 11, 12, 13,
26, 28, 63, 95, 97, 99, 103, 120,
137, 144, 148, 173

Mahoor Institute, 22, 30, 188, 200n1
majles, 34, 35, 63, 176
maktab, 189

repertoire, 19, 23, 24, 103, 104, 133, 155, 156, 177, 212
Reza Shah (Reza Khan Pahlavi), 2, 5, 118
rhetoric, ix, 48, 82, 83, 91n25, 111, 120, 124, 130, 165
Roshanravan, Kāmbiz, 16
Rosvayie Del (album), 99
rowze khāni, 18, 135, 193, 196,
Rudaki (*Vahdat*) Hall, 12, 13, 42, 103, 135
Rumi, Jalal al-Din (*Mowlana*), 25, 26, 28, 73, 81, 96, 99, 100, 135, 138, 144, 148, 149, 170n5, 171n18, 173, 176, 182, 196, 197

sabu (instrument), 157, 158
Sa'di, 7, 15, 28, 71, 72, 80, 81, 82, 91n19, 96, 99, 137, 149, 170n2, 171, 173, 180, 182, 198, 200n7; ghazals of, 64–66, 73, 75–77, 100, 182, 199
Sa'idi, Davud, 9
saghar (instrument), 159
samā' polemic, 2, 4, 6, 7, 23, 25
Sarv e Chaman (album), 148, 150, 170n2; lyrics of, 150
saz o avaz, 64, 110, 122,
scholarship, of Persian music in Iran, 29–30
Seda. See NIRT
shahbang (instrument), 157, 158, 162
shahnavaz (instrument), 158
Shahnaz Ensemble, 118, 119, 134, 157, 167, 180, 181
Shahnaz, Jalil, 118, 140, 179, 191
Shahnazi, Ali Akbar, 32, 52
shah sorahi (double-bass), 158, 162
Shajarian, Mohammad Reza, ambitions of, 7, 17, 103–04; and calligraphy, 163; and gardening, 163; and Green Movement, 164–70; and poetry, 28, 35, 36, 38, 43, 44, 46, 55, 62, 64, 73, 81, 112, 113, 117, 120–22, 200n10; and revolution, 1, 3, 26–27, 28, 30, 44, 196; and Um Kulthum, 145–47; and World Music, 142–43; awards of, 116, 141–42; charitable work of, 98–99, 117–18, 147, 181; compositions of, 82, 130, 147, 148–

53; contributions and legacy of, 179–83, 195, 197–98; in concert, 31n14, 32n18, 42, 74, 98, 99, 100–111, 112, 114, 117, 119, 126, 129–30, 177–78, 180; influence of Dadbeh upon, 7–11, 110; interests in non-Iranian music, 140; global profile of, 93, 95, 97–104, 116, 136–40, 141, 147; musical instrument designs and constructions of, 118, 154–62, 179; on his ouevre of recordings, 173–75; professional activities of, 11–17, 97–104, 116–119, 134, 135, 164, on radif, 32n19,103, 110; public recognition of, 19, 26, 99, 104, 131–33, 134, 135, 147, 174–76, 179, 180, 189; recordings of, 19, 21–22, 33–35, 42, 43, 45, 90n6, 99, 101, 103, 106, 135, 173, 179, 201–09; stylistic innovations of, 22–25, 26, 27, 45, 48, 52–55, 63, 71, 80, 91n13, 100, 101, 102, 110, 120–21, 133, 186, 189; stylistic periods of, 175–78; tours of, 96, 97, 98. *See also* album titles; tasnif
Shajarian, Homayoun, x, 98, 100, 101, 102, 131, 178, 189
Shamloo, Ahmad, 191
Shankar, Ravi, 142, 145, 172
Sharif, Farhang, 15, 119
Shi'ism, 31n2, 44, 90n9
Shoari, Masud, 185
sorahi 157, 158, 159, 160, 161, 162
sorud, 5, 11, 12, 17, 147. *See also* tasnif
Sorud e Mehr (album), 10
Sufi music, 25, 143

Taherzade, Hossein, 136
Taj Esfahan, 5, 9
Tala'i, Dariush, 16, 94, 98, 99
tasnif, 5, 7, 16, 26, 28, 35, 42, 45, 52, 56, 81, 84, 91n3, 100, 101, 102, 110, 111, 112, 114, 118, 120, 147, 148–53, 167, 174, 174, 175, 178, 190, 193, 196, 198
tondar, (instrument), 157, 159, 160
Tudeh party, 12, 13

About the Authors

Rob Simms is a multi-instrumentalist and author of *The Repertoire of Iraqi Maqam* and co-author (with Amir Koushkani) of *The Art of Avaz and Mohammad Reza Shajarian: Foundations and Contexts*. He is associate professor of music at York University in Toronto.

Amir Koushkani is a soloist and collaborative performer, composer, arranger, and instructor of the traditional Persian stringed instruments tar and setar. He is a PhD candidate in ethnomusicology at York University, Toronto.